Hinduism
&
Hindu Way of Life

by

K. C. Gupta

Published by:

F-2/16, Ansari road, Daryaganj, New Delhi-110002
☎ 23240026, 23240027 • *Fax:* 011-23240028
Email: info@vspublishers.com • *Website:* www.vspublishers.com
Online Brandstore: *amazon.in/vspublishers*

Regional Office : Hyderabad
5-1-707/1, Brij Bhawan (Beside Central Bank of India Lane)
Bank Street, Koti, Hyderabad - 500 095
☎ 040-24737290
E-mail: vspublishershyd@gmail.com

Branch Office : Mumbai
Jaywant Industrial Estate, 1st Floor–108, Tardeo Road
Opposite Sobo Central Mall, Mumbai – 400 034
☎ 022-23510736
E-mail: vspublishersmum@gmail.com

BUY OUR BOOKS FROM: AMAZON FLIPKART

ISBN 978-93-579421-7-1
Edition 2020

DISCLAIMER

While every attempt has been made to provide accurate and timely information in this book, neither the author nor the publisher assumes any responsibility for errors, unintended omissions or commissions detected therein. The author and publisher makes no representation or warranty with respect to the comprehensiveness or completeness of the contents provided.

All matters included have been simplified under professional guidance for general information only, without any warranty for applicability on an individual. Any mention of an organization or a website in the book, by way of citation or as a source of additional information, doesn't imply the endorsement of the content either by the author or the publisher. It is possible that websites cited may have changed or removed between the time of editing and publishing the book.

Results from using the expert opinion in this book will be totally dependent on individual circumstances and factors beyond the control of the author and the publisher.

It makes sense to elicit advice from well informed sources before implementing the ideas given in the book. The reader assumes full responsibility for the consequences arising out from reading this book.

For proper guidance, it is advisable to read the book under the watchful eyes of parents/guardian. The buyer of this book assumes all responsibility for the use of given materials and information.

Preface

V&S Publishers has always been in the forefront of presenting reading materials in a meaningful and concise manner. Numerous books are available in the market, which form part of Hinduism. Some books are quite long and go into vast depth whereas others are too short and fail to give a clear picture. The present book on Hinduism reflects on the essential elements of Hindu religion and Hindu way of life. The book is a concise compendium for understanding & knowing about Hinduism especially for younger generation.

In some ways Hinduism is the oldest living religion in the world. Yet Hinduism resists easy definition partly because of the vast array of practices and beliefs found within it. It is also closely associated conceptually and historically with other Indian religions such as Jainism, Buddhism and Sikhism.

Unlike most other religions, Hinduism has no single founder, no single scripture, and no commonly agreed set of teachings. There have been many key figures teaching different philosophies and writing numerous holy books on Hinduism. For these reasons, writers often refer to Hinduism as 'a way of life' rather than a single religion.

Beliefs in Hinduism:

- Hinduism embraces great philosophical ideas of over thousand of years . For this reason, it's referred to as a "way of life" as opposed to a single, organized religion.
- Hindus recognize that there is one Supreme God but worship Him in the form of many gods and goddesses depending upon one's spiritual inclination
- Hindus believe in the doctrine of "Samsara" (continuous cycle of life, death, and reincarnation) and Karma (universal law of cause and effect).
- One of the key philosophy of Hinduism is "atman," or Soul. This philosophy holds that all living creatures have a soul which is identical to Supreme Soul. The goal of human birth is to achieve "moksha," or salvation, which ends the repeated cycles of births and deaths and Soul meets the Universal Soul. All Hindu scriptures exhort to strive for salvation because only man can achive liberation and no other life form like animals, birds and even devtas. Devtas have to take human birth to get salvation as per Hinduism.
- One fundamental principle of this religion is the idea that Karma which include – Thoughts, Words and Deeds , past and present determine the quality of current life and also the subsequent births. Hinduism emphasizes purity of Karmas–thoughts, words and deeds to reduce karmic accounts.Hindus strive to perform all actions according to Dharma, which is a code of living based on Hindu scriptures and which emphasizes good conduct and morality.
- The Om and Swastika are two unique symbols of Hinduism.
- Hindus believe in co-existence and revere all living creatures; consider as cow a sacred animal and worship Peepal tree
- Hinduism is closely related to other Indian religions, including Buddhism, Sikhism and Jainism and society is well integrated while following religion of choice.

Hindu Texts:
Hindus value many sacred writings such as vedas, Ramayana, Mahabharata, Gita, Puranas etc. The primary Hindu texts are known as the Vedas. This collection of sacred verses and hymns was written in Sanskrit and contain revelations received by ancient *Rishis*, and sages directly through meditation over a very long period of time.

The four Vedas are: 1. Rig Veda 2. Samaveda 3. Yajurveda 4. Atharvaveda

Hindu Sects:
Hinduism has many sects and is divided primarily into the following:

(i) Shaiva (followers of Shiva)

(ii) Vaishnava (followers of Vishnu)

(iii) Shakti (followers of Devi)

Hindu Deities:
Hindus worship a variety of gods and goddesses depending upon their individual beliefs. Some prominent deities include:

- Brahma: the god responsible for creation of the world and all living things
- Vishnu: the god that preserves and protects the universe
- Shiva: the god that destroys the universe in order to recreate it
- Durga: the goddess that fights to restore dharma

Rama – God of Highest Virtues:

- Krishna: the great Karamyogi and restorer of Dharma
- Lakshmi: the goddess of wealth and purity
- Saraswati: the goddess of learning

All Hindus have the images of chosen gods and goddesses in their home for worship. Generally there are temples in residential areas for worship and to hold religious ceremonies. Many have images of gods at their desks. In other words, Hindus love to be in the company of gods all the time.

Hindu Festivals:

Hindus observe numerous sacred days, holidays and festivals. Some of them are following.

- Diwali: The festival of lights and celebration
- Dusshera: Festival to celebration victory over evil deeds
- Holi: The festival of colours
- Janamashtami: Celebrated to commemorate Lord Krishna's
- Raksha Bandhan: Festival to celebrate of affection between brother and sister
- Mahashivaratri: The great festival of Lord Shiva

Hindu Teerathsthanas:
Hindus have innumerable places of pilgrimage like Char Dhams, Jyotirlingas, Shaktipeethas etc.

All hindus strive to visit these places as many as possible during his life time to get the blessings of the gods.

We sincerely hope that book will meet the expectation of average readers and help him to get a good idea of this great religion in a structured way whose philosophy is attracting millions of followers from across the world.

Contents

Chapter 1 : What is Hinduism

Hindu religion, or Hinduism, is considered to be the oldest religion in the world. The ancestors of Hindu religion were known as Aryans. They initially called it *Arya Dharma* – the religion of the Aryas. Later, *Arya Dharma* became popular as *Sanatana Dharma.* Unlike other religions, there is no single prophet in Hinduism. Indians have always been curious to find out about the nature of God, life after death, and relation of the individual soul (*jiva*) with the universal soul. Indian *Rishis* have communicated with God for thousands of years through meditation to find an answer to the puzzle of Existence. The answers they got from the Supreme are recorded in the Vedas. The *Rishis* heard the truth directly from God during their extra- conscious state of Samadhi. The sum total of the contents of the Vedas and other Hindu scriptures based on Vedas constitutes 'Hinduism'.

Hinduism has accommodated a variety of thoughts and continues to absorb the values of the present day without sacrificing the basics of the Vedas. For this reason, all categories of people–saints, *Rishis*, thinkers, ritualistics, householders, even the unbelievers, have enriched the Hindu religion and its philosophy of life.

It will not be out of place to mention that it is the great spirituality of India and not its political structure which has enabled the country to survive in spite of many aggressions from outside. Many old civilizations like the ones found in Greece, Iran, Egypt, and Mexico have lost their glory in the cauldron of time but not India; rather India is regaining its prosperity and at the same time, continues to retain its values. It is also to the credit of Hinduism that India has never invaded any country but always believed in peaceful co-existence with rest of the world. India is, therefore, seen as a great hope in a world torn with conflicts. Hindu religion is highly tolerant, in the sense that it accommodates the other religions with equal reverence; hence it has kept the people of India united, in spite of so much of diversity in terms of language, race, geography, etc.

The Holy Texts

Vedas

Hinduism is what is written in the Vedas and in the scriptures based on the Vedas. The Vedas are the oldest texts of Hinduism. 'Chintana' (meditation) of thousands of *Rishis* over thousands of years, to know the Truth of Existence, is contained in the Vedas. Vedas are called *Shrutis* (*Sunana*) as they record the communication and dialogues between the *Rishis* and God. The truth written in the Vedas is considered Eternal and cannot be contested. In earlier times, the *Rishis* stored these experiences in their memories, and their disciples also memorized them. This method of transferring the wisdom of the Vedas continued for centuries. Subsequently, the Vedas were systematically compiled in the present form by *Rishi* Vyasa. Because of his great contribution in editing the Vedas, *Rishi* Vyasa is popularly known as Ved Vyasa. His birthday in celebrated even today as Guru Purnima.

The four Vedas in the present form as compiled by Ved Vyasa are:

(I) **Rig Veda:** This is the oldest of the four Vedas. It is in fact, considered to be the oldest religious scripture of the world. According to some scholars, the Rig Veda was written in 5000 BC. The mantras of this Veda contain the greatest truth about 'Existence'.

(II) **Sama Veda:** This Veda is said to have been composed around 1300–1000 BC. It is known for its poetic recitation of mantras. It is considered as the Veda of holy songs. Singing of Sama Veda hymns brings stability and peace to mind.

(III) **Yajur Veda:** This Veda contains rituals and rites for various occasions and ceremonies. It talks about the requirement of ceremonies in religion and also covers sacrificial rites; some of which are still observed by Hindus. Its probable date of writing is 1500 BC.

(IV) **Atharva Veda:** This Veda has a collection of hymns of diverse subjects which include Creation, diseases, herbs for treatment, family, meditation, etc. Probable date of writing of this Veda is also 1500 BC.

According to the Vedas, everything and every being is divine. God is one and he is present in the entire Creation——from small insects to animals, in human beings, and in all plants and non-living things. The purpose of life is to seek God and liberate the soul from *Samsara*, the cycles of birth and death.

The last portion of the Vedas is called Upanishad. The Upanishads are also called Vedanta—end of Veda. Upanishads contain the philosophical teachings of the Vedas. There are nearly 108 Upanishads, but the following 10 are the Principal Upanishads. We shall briefly describe these here.

(I) **Aitareya:** This Upanishad is one of the earliest Upanishads of Rig Veda. It gets its name from Sage Aitareya, who taught its teachings very widely. This Upanishad explains that everything in the Universe is guided by and is based on Consciousness i.e. the *Brahman.*

(II) **Chandogya:** This Upanishad is one of the oldest Upanishads of Sama Veda. It is a very popular Upanishad as it explains a number of truths; e.g. the importance of chanting AUM, the doctrine of reincarnation, and the identification of the individual Self with Brahman.

(III) **Kena:** This Upanishad is also among the early Upanishads of Sama Veda. Its central teaching is that the knowledge of Ishwara (God) would lead to the path of self-realisation (union with God).

(IV) **Katha:** This Upanishad belongs to Krishna Yajur Veda. It tells great philosophical truths through a dialogue between Lord of Death, Yama, and Nachiketa, son of King Vajashrava. This Upanishad addresses the answer to a universal puzzle—What happens to beings after death?

(V) **Taittiriya:** This Upanishad is part of Krishna Yajur Veda. It emphasizes that the ultimate goal of life is to realize 'Brahman' because He is the only Truth and source of permanent bliss.

Aryans performing Havan

(VI) **Brihad Aranyaka:** This Upanishad belongs to Shukla Yajur Veda. Its central message is that the Soul is identical in all beings around us.

(VII) **Ishavasya:** This Upanishad also belongs to Shukla Yajur Veda. Its central idea is that Ishwara (God) permeates the entire world and we should dedicate each and every action to Him to attain liberation-free from repeated cycles or births and death.

(VIII) **Mandukya:** This Upanishad belongs to Atharva Veda and derives its name from *Rishi* Mandukya. It contains the meaning of AUM. It is said that proper study and understanding of this Upanishad leads to self-realisation (union with God).

(IX) **Mundaka:** This Upanishad belongs to Atharva Veda. The study and understanding of this Upanishad also leads to self-realisation (union with God).

(X) **Prashna:** This Upanishad belongs to Atharva Veda. 'Prashna' means question. It imparts the knowledge of Brahma in the form of questions and answers between Sage Pippalada and a group of other *Rishis.*

Puranas

Puranas are a later creation and are believed to have been written by Ved Vyasa. Puranas contain the teachings of Vedas in the form of stories and parables so that ordinary people can also benefit from the ancient wisdom. The philosophy contained in the Vedas and Upanishads are beyond the comprehension of ordinary people. It was a DIVINE act of *Rishi* Vyasa to write the Puranas. The common man in India continues to observe the teachings of the Vedas in his daily life because of his exposure to Puranas through texts, discourses, and nowadays through television, the internet, etc. It is believed that there were 64 Puranas, however, as on date **18 Maha Puranas** and some Upa Puranas are available.

The 18 Maha Puranas have been divided in three categories namely:

(I) **Vaishnava Puranas:** These glorify Lord Vishnu and include Vishnu Purana, Naradiya Purana, Vamana Purana, Matsya Purana, Garuda Purana, and Srimad Bhagavata Purana.

(II) **Brahma Puranas:** They glorify Lord Brahma and include Brahma Purana, Bhavishya Purana, Agni Purana, Brahma Vaivarta Purana, Brahmananda Purana, and Padma Purana.

(III) **Shaiva Puranas:** These glorify Lord Shiva and include Shiva Purana, Linga Purana, Kurma Purana, Markandeya Purana, Skanda Purana, and Varaha Purana.

It is believed that Puranas were written in their final form between 300 AD and 1000 AD.

Epics- Mahabharata and Ramayana

Ramayana and Mahabharata are two very popular epics of India. Every Indian is familiar with their content. Both the epics describe not only interesting stories but also contain highly spiritual content of immense value. These two epics have played a very important part in the philosophical views of Hindus. They have been, therefore, given the status of Vedas.

Ramayana

It is the story of Lord Rama and demon Ravana, the king of Lanka. Lord Rama was an incarnation of Lord Vishnu and took birth to eliminate demons. Rama went to exile for 14 years with his brother Lakshman and wife Sita to fulfil the commitment of his father, King Dasratha. While in the forest, demon king Ravana of Lanka abducted Sita. Rama waged a war against Lanka with the help of Hanumana and his 'vanar sena' (army of monkeys), killed Ravana and other demons, and freed Sita.

Throughout the text of the Ramayana, the message is to be an ideal brother like Bharat, an ideal human being, an ideal king like Rama, and an ideal wife like Sita. Ramayana also teaches that good always triumphs over evil.

Mahabharata

It is the story of the battle between Kauravas, sons of Dhritarashtra and Gandhari, and the Pandavas, sons of Pandu and Kunti, over the kingdom of Hastinapur. The Pandavas were virtuous and always observed Dharma. After the death of Pandu, Dhritarashtra was ruling Hastinapur. The Pandavas were elder and deserved a part of the kingdom, if not full. Duryodhana, the son of Dhritarashtra, was power hungry and refused to give land to Pandavas equivalent to the tip of a needle, in spite of pursuance by elders and by Lord Krishna himself. War became inevitable for the Pandavas in order to get their due share in the Hastinapur Kingdom. Both sides fought fiercely in the battle field of Kurukshetra. There was total annihilation in this bloodiest battle of the world. The Pandavas destroyed the Kauravas and secured victory.

Mahabharata exhorts mankind to follow Dharma in daily pursuits because Dharma alone can bring lasting prosperity and peace.

Shrimad Bhagvad Gita

Shrimad Bhagvad Gita, popularly called Gita, is a part of the Mahabharata. It contains spiritual teachings in the form of dialogues between Lord Krishna, a divine incarnation, and Arjuna when the latter showed his inability to take part in the battle at Kurukshetra. Arjuna became sad on seeing his elders like Bheeshma, Guru Dronacharya, all Kaurava cousins, friends, and relatives on the opposite side and whom he was supposed to kill. Lord Krishna was the charioteer of Arjuna. Without Arjuna, the war could not be won by the Pandavas. Shri Krishna then revealed to Arjuna the highest truth of life, which is contained in 'Srimad Bhagvad Gita'. The revelations of the Gita removed Arjuna's illusions and attachment to his kins and motivated him to fight as that was his divine duty at that moment. An enlightened Arjuna then demolished the Kauravas and secured victory for the Pandavas and restored Dharma.

The Gita contains the sum and substance of the Upanishads and Vedas. Its philosophy of the four paths of Bhakti Marga, Karma Marg, Janan Marga and Raj Marga for the realisation of God or the liberation from 'samsara'—cycles of birth and death—is meant to suit the variety of human temperament. People of all faiths and religions including from Western countries follow its teachings for spiritual upliftment. One remarkable feature of the Gita is that its teachings are independent of any religion.

The contents of all the Hindu scriptures have been dealt with in greater detail in chapter 3 of the book.

Darshanas – Hindu Religious Philosophy

The teachings of the Vedas and Upanishads are fundamental to Hindu philosophy. Various *Rishis* have given their interpretation on the philosophy of Vedas. Accordingly, six systems of Hindu philosophy have emerged, called 'Darshanas'. Darshanas explain the philosophy contained in the Vedas. The various Darshanas are briefly explained here. All Darshanas lead to the achievement of salvation which is the ultimate aim of human birth.

Sankhya Darshan

This school was founded by Saga Kapila. It postulates two eternal and ultimate realities, namely Purusha and Prakriti. Purusha is the centre of consciousness and Prakirti is the source of all material existence. One can attain freedom from miseries and sufferings, and ultimately liberation, when one realizes the distinction between Purusha and Prakirti through knowledge.

Purva Mimamsa

This school, founded by Sage Jaimini, is based on the 'Karam Kand' (rituals) of the Vedas. It gives philosophical justification of rituals of the Vedas. It supports Vedic rituals and advocates that one can achieve salvation by observing and respecting these rituals.

Uttara Mimamsa or Vedanta

This school was founded by *Rishi* Vyasa and is based on the philosophy of the Upanishads. When Purva Mimansha was merged with the Upanishads, it was called Uttara Mimamsa. It explains that individual 'jiva' (soul) is identical with the Universal Soul or "Paramatma" and that the individual aspirant can attain salvation through the knowledge and understanding of this Eternal Truth.

Yoga Darshanas

This school was founded by Mahrishi Patanjali around 2nd century BC. It advocates an eight-fold path of physical and mental discipline through various techniques to achieve 'Self' realisation (union with God).

Nyaya Darshan

This school was founded by *Rishi* Gautama around 300 BC. As per this philosophy, the atom is the cause of cosmic manifestation. The knowledge of the senses, inference, analogy, and verbal testimony, leads to Moksha.

Vaisheshika Darshan

This school was founded by *Rishi* Kanada around 6 BC. According to this school, the cause of manifestation is a combination of atoms. All physical things are a result of the combination of atoms of earth, water, fire, and air and this atom is made active through the divine will of God. Moksha can be achieved by understanding the atomic nature of the Universe.

Some thinkers like Shankaracharya and Ramnujacharya have given commentaries on the philosophical aspects of Darshanas. The details have been omitted to retain simplicity of the text.

Doctrine of Karma

Hinduism believes in the doctrine of Karma. When a man desires something, he performs some action to fulfil his desire. Desires are never satiated in us; hence we are continuously performing actions and deeds. According to this theory, all actions or deeds bring results. Good deeds bring joy and happiness and bad deeds bring suffering and pain. The fruits of actions, good or bad, are stored for each individual and are called "Sanchit Karma". These have to be experienced by the "jiva" in various births; there is absolutely no escape.

In daily life, all of us witness the events being shaped by the theory of Karma. When a child is born as handicapped, say blind, it is because of results of bad deeds done in earlier life. Similarly, we find ascetics, holy people, monks, and nuns suffering from severe diseases because of Karmic effects of past life though now they are leading a spiritual life. Sufferings of animals and poor people around remind us to be mindful about our deeds to avoid a similar fate. It is said that a person may have to take repeated births of small durations because of his bad deeds. The agony of such a person can be very well understood. There is, therefore, a very important lesson; we should watch our deeds and follow the teachings of the scriptures. It is also clarified here that Karma (action) is all inclusive—thoughts, words, and deeds, not merely actions.

It also follows automatically that, since we reap the harvest of our own karmas, we should accept the good and bad experiences of life as our own creation and deal with unfavourable experiences with wisdom and courage without blaming others. It also implies that we should reduce our desires so that we do not have to unnecessarily perform avoidable Karmas. In fact, Buddha's central teaching is that desires alone cause sufferings and elimination of desires should be done by following the middle path i.e. Right Living, Right Earning, Right Conduct, Right Thinking, etc. The middle path of Buddha also leads us to "Nirvana".

It may, however, be clarified that Karmic forces are just one of the many forces which control a man's life. The silver lining is that man has quite a bit of freedom of actions in life. He should exercise this freedom by acting in a manner which brings him nearer to God. Such spiritual practices help to reduce the effects of past misdeeds and, therefore, mitigate the sufferings.

It may also appear that when a man is responsible for his deeds—he undergoes pleasures and pains as per his deeds—then what is the role played by God in life? Hinduism explains that God never behaves in a biased or partial manner. He showers mercy on everybody equally and unconditionally. It is for the individual to take benefits of that offer, e.g., a cloud gives rain over so many fields but a farmer who has prepared the field properly by way of ploughing, by way of manoeuvres, by providing good quality seeds, gets richer harvest compared to the farmer who has not bothered to prepare the fields. In the same way, those people who follow the scriptures, lead a spiritual life, and conduct themselves properly, will definitely reap the benefit of God's blessings and complete this journey of life with lesser sufferings and greater bliss.

God in Hinduism

Hinduism has been evolving continuously for thousands of years. Gradually Indo Aryans and *Rishis* came to the conclusion that there is only One and Only one cause of everything, One and Only one God, who is called 'Brahman'.

According to Hinduism, God existed before Creation. He, of His own, created the universe. He is called the Nirguna Brahman, 'the Supreme Spirit'. The Universe comes out of Him, rests in Him, and merges in Him and this phenomenon has been going on eternally.

Nirguna Brahman is neither male nor female. Vedas use the word "Tat", That, to address Him. Further, Nirguna Brahman is Infinite, Eternal, and Immutable yet He is the basis of the ever-changing forms of nature. Nirguna Brahman is the One and the Indivisible and is free from all qualities. Nirguna Brahman is also called Satchitanand, meaning Sat, "Absolute Truth", Chit, "Pure Consciousness", and Anand, Infinite Bliss; He is "Antaryami" and he is the "Self." Nirguna Brahman cannot be fully described in words.

Since it is difficult to imagine and worship a formless Nirguna Brahman, Hinduism has given the name Sagun Brahman or Ishwara to facilitate worshipping, meditation, and concentration on God. Ishwara is worshipped by Hindus in the form of Brahma the Creator, Vishnu the Preserver, and Shiva the Destroyer. These three functions are being carried out by Him uninterrupted. Further, Ishwara is worshipped by Hindus as father, as mother, as friend, or as sweetheart depending upon the spiritual inclination of the devotee, e.g., Hindus worship Ishwara in the form of Goddess Lakshmi, giver of wealth; in the form of Goddess Saraswati, bestower of knowledge and learning. Shri Rama Krishna Paramhansa worshipped God as divine mother.

"Tavem Mata cha Pita Tavem;	त्वमेव माता च पिता त्वमेव ।
Tavem Bandhu cha Sakha Tavem;	त्वमेव बन्धु च सखा त्वमेव ।
Tavem Vidhya cha Dravidam Tavem;	त्वमेव विद्या च द्रविणम् त्वमेव ।
Tavem Sarvum, Mum Dev Dev.	त्वमेव सर्वम् मम् देवदेवा ॥

This is the manner in which God is remembered /respected by Hindus.

Divine Incarnations

According to Hinduism, when religion (Dharma) suffers and irreligion (Adharma) gains prominence on earth, all life forms suffer. People pray to God for relief and succour. God then comes down to earth as divine incarnation or 'Avtara' to restore Dharma. Lord Krishna in the verse IV.7 of Bhagvad Gita says

"Yada yada hi dharmasya galani bhavti Bharat
Abhutthanam adharmasya, tda atmanam sirjamayham."

यदा यदा हि धर्मस्य ग्लानिर्भवति भारत ।
अभ्युत्थानमधर्मस्य तदात्मानं सृजाम्यहम् ॥

"Whenever there is a decline of righteousness, O Arjuna, and rise of unrighteousness, then I manifest Myself."

And in verse IV.8 Lord further says

"Paritranai sadhunam vinashaya cha duskirtam
Dharama-samsthapan arthaya sambhawami yuge yuge."

परित्राणाय साधूनां विनाशाय च दुष्कृताम् ।
धर्मसंस्थापनार्थाय सम्भवामि युगे युगे ॥

"For the protection of good, for the destruction of evil and for the establishment of Dharma, I am born from age to age".

God takes a human form on earth, lives like a human but performs divine actions. He punishes the wicked and mighty, protects the righteous one, takes care of his devotees and spiritual followers and thus restores religious and spiritual order in the planet. It is said that God has taken several incarnations from time to time for such divine purposes.

Shri Rama and Shri Krishna have been two popular divine incarnations of Vishnu. They are de facto Supreme Lord for Hindus. They are worshipped by Hindus across the country for their divine deeds for the welfare of beings and devotees.

Shri Rama took birth as son of King Dasharatha and Queen Kaushalaya of Ayodhya. He showed his divine form (Virat Swaroop) to his mother when she asked to open the mouth. He killed many demons who were disturbing the *Rishis* in the forest. He attacked and killed mighty Ravana, the king of Lanka, and freed Sita, his divine consort, from Ravana. His kingdom in Ayodhya was considered the ideal one called "Ramrajya" where everybody including holy people, women, animals, and even the poor enjoyed peace and prosperity.

Shri Krishna was the most magical, illustrious incarnation who played a decisive role in the welfare of mankind. He killed Kansa, the cruel king of Mathura and relieved the people from his tyranny. Shri Krishna was a great lover and used to have divine romance with the cow-herding women of Vrindavan. The tales of his romance with his divine lover "Radha" is sung in the form of bhajans across India. He saved the honour of Draupadi, the Pandavas' wife, in the Kaurava assembly when even mighty Bheeshma and Arjuna showed their helplessness. Shri Krishna was the friend and adviser to Pandvas and guided them to kill the great warriors like Bheeshma, Dronacharya, Karna, and Duryodhna in the great battle of Kurukshetra. When war at Kurukshetra was about to start, Arjuna showed his unwillingness to fight seeing the Kaurava elders and cousins on the other side. It was a very difficult situation. Without Arjuna the war would not have been won by Pandavas. Shri Krishna taught Arjuna, in the battlefield itself, the true meaning and purpose of life and the duty of the kshatriya in that situation; he showed Arjuna the universe through his "Virat Swaroop." Arjuna was enlightened and was convinced that it was his divine duty to fight at that moment. The dialogues between Krishna and Arjuna in the battlefield are a deep philosophy of life and are documented in the world's most sacred book, the Shrimad Bhagvad Gita. The teachings of the Gita are eternal, independent of any religion and are followed worldwide even today for spiritual upliftment.

Mahatma Buddha, the great reformer, son of King Suddhodana and Queen Maha Maya of Kapilavatthu, is also considered the incarnation of Lord Vishnu. Buddha did tapasya and meditation for years and got enlightenment. Subsequently, Buddha spread his message (Dharma) for 45 years in India and abroad by travelling extensively. His doctrine paved the way for a new religion called "Buddhism".

Realisation of God – Four Paths

According to Hinduism, the purpose of human birth is a God-given opportunity to attain liberation from cycles of birth and death 'samsara'. Hindu scriptures provide different paths for people with different temperament for realisation of God. Those who are emotional and have inclination for bhakti/devotion can choose Bhakti Marg; those having craving for learning can go in for Jnana Yoga; those who believe in action can follow Karma Yoga, and those who prefer meditation, can go in for Raj Yoga. These paths are described briefly below.

Bhakti Yoga

All of us respect God. This respect is to be converted into intense love for God by the aspirant of Bhakti Yoga. The devotee is asked to remember God constantly by ritualistic worship, attending kirtans/satsang, reciting bhajans, chanting God's name through Japa (mental/silent), reciting the prayers, etc. The devotee is encouraged to develop a relationship with God as that of friend (Sakha), or that of lover, or that of mother depending upon his mental inclination, e.g., Shri Rama Krishna Param Hansa had the attitude of mother for God. These techniques help the devotee to come closer to God and ultimately results in Realisation of God. Meera Bai is a real example of achieving Realisation of God through Bhakti Yoga.

Jnana Yoga

Man is not something other than God. He is divine by himself. To know our divine identity or divine Self is the ultimate goal of 'Jnana Yoga'. Jnana Yoga means to realise God through knowledge. The devotee takes the help of an enlightened teacher (guru) to follow this path. He has to practice purity of thoughts, train concentration of mind, develop faith in his guru, and have faith in the teachings of the scriptures. The first lesson to the student is "Tat tvam asi" which means "You are Divine". The guru then asks the aspirant to meditate on this true inner "Self". The aspirant then contemplates on his divine Self and by "manana" reasoning, he understands the true meaning of "Self". He then identifies himself with the "Universal Self".

Raja Yoga

This Yoga was founded by *Rishi* Patanjali. This Yoga technique provides for graded courses of mental concentration to achieve self-realisation. This is also called Ashtanga Yoga as the technique involves eight steps. The eight steps are:

(I) **Yama:** Inner restrain. The aspirant has to train himself to abstain from stealing, violence, falsehood, and indulging in passions, etc.

(II) **Niyama:** The aspirant has to cultivate good habits like keeping the body and mind clean, austerity, contentment, reading of scriptures, etc.

(III) **Asanas:** Through the techniques of Asanas, the aspirant learns to sit erect for a long time with head, neck, and back in a straight line.

(IV) **Pranayama:** The aspirant learns concentration of mind through breathing techniques from the guru (teacher).

(V) **Pratyahara**: The aspirant learns the art of withdrawing the senses and mind from external objects.

(VI) **Dharna**: The aspirant learns the art of fixing the mind on a chosen object of contemplation for a short duration.

(VII) **Dhyana**: The aspirant learns the concentration of mind on the chosen object of contemplation for a longer time.

(VIII) **Samadhi**: It is a state of most intense concentration on the chosen object of contemplation.

The ultimate aim in Raja Yoga is to train the mind to concentrate in a 'Samadhi'. The mind is then lost in the chosen object of concentration; it is no longer aware of itself and it is now without thoughts and is established in Self. This state of mind is the ultimate aim of Raja Yoga.

Karma Yoga

A Karma Yogi believes in action and deeds. However, for liberation through this path, the aspirant has to leave the fruits of Karma to God. In our daily life, whatever we do, we have a purpose in hand, e.g., to make some profit, to get a good job. We even give donations with a specific benefit in mind. Our every action or deed, including thoughts and words, binds us to 'samsara'—and gives either pleasure or pain as their fruits in the present life or in later births. Accordingly, work has to be done without expectation of fruits so that we are freed from its *karmic* fruit. The art and science of performing unselfish and unattached work is called Karma Yoga, which ultimately leads to liberation. The aspirant of Karma Yoga is trained to do work for the pleasure of God, not for one's own sake, and not for a purpose.

Four Ashrams

In the Vedic period, life was divided in four stages called Ashrams viz. Brahmacharya Ashram; Garhastha Ashram; Vanaprastha Ashram, and Samyasa Ashram. The duties were prescribed for each stage to fulfil the purpose of human birth.

Brahmacharya Ashram

The first 25 years of life were called Brahmacharya Ashram and were meant for physical and mental growth, completion of formal education under a guru (teacher), acquiring of knowledge of scriptures and character building. The student was supposed to observe complete celibacy. The guru used to be highly accomplished and a role model for the student. Girls also used to study with boys. The girls also learned singing, dancing, paintings, sewing, and other fine arts. In other words, the students used to get complete education to lead a life of fulfilment.

Grahastha Asram

Brahmacharya Ashram was followed by Garhastha Ashram, when the Hindu youth would marry, raise a family, pursue a profession, do charities, etc. He would lead a life of a householder but following the teachings of scriptures, i.e., by adhering to Dharma. It was a tough period of life but he would do his duties happily.

Vanaprastha Ashram

At the age of 55 years, a Hindu would enter the next stage of life, Vanaprastha Ashram. He would now give the charge of family to the children and leave the house. He would stay in a secluded place. At this stage, he would minimise his needs, eat fruits and vegetables, read scriptures, abstain from pleasures, and observe celibacy.

Samyasa Ashram

At the age of 75 years, a person would enter in to "Samyasa ashram". Now he would travel totally alone like a sanyasi; scantily covered, arranging food by begging, and fully detached from the world. He would surrender to God so that he is liberated from the samsara–cycles of births and death.

The above Vedic time concept of life has undergone a change in present Hindu society because of the influence of time and mixing of the civilisations of the East and West. In present times, luxurious life has taken the place of restrain and sacrifice. Children are indulging in sexual activities at a young age. Guru–shishya relationship has totally gone. The education system is based on mass education in schools and colleges. Now women are also earning members of families, partly due to high cost of living and partly because of women's liberation movement across the globe. Now a Hindu elder does not observe the formal Vanaprastha and Sanyasa Ashramas. He does not leave the house when he is free from children's upbringing, however, he mentally prepares for a diminishing role in home and society. He slowly turns to God; spends greater time in spiritual activities, kirtans, social service, visiting holy places, charities, etc. The silver lining is that Hindus have retained their spiritual leanings while adjusting to the new reality of a global civilization of the present times.

Four Varnas

In Vedic time, society was divided in four categories (Varnas) viz. Brahmanas, Kshatriyas, Vaishyas, and Shudra depending upon the inherent aptitude or potential of the person to do a job. This social set-up provided balance, harmonious growth, and happiness for everybody. Brahmins were pious, holy, learned people having knowledge of scriptures. They were supposed to guide the kings, ruling class, and society to follow the path of Dharma. Kshatriyas were kings, rulers, persons with aggressive behaviour and having inclination for war and battle which was necessary to defend the people and country. Vaishyas were traders, who would grow food by agriculture, rear animals and generate money and wealth to support the king, brahmins, and society. The fourth category was of 'Shudras' who would do the lower-level jobs like cleaning and other labour-based activity, etc.

This structure of society based on profession continued for thousands of years. In due course of time, it degenerated in to a cast based society not Varna based. It was easy for the son of a tailor to pick up the trade of tailoring; similarly a trader's son would pick up the basics of the trade very easily; it was also common to pass on the kingship to the next generation, and so on. Accordingly generations after generations, families were doing the same profession which ultimately gave rise to the caste system. Birth not the profession decided the "Varna" of the person. Society got divided into superior castes and inferior castes. Sudras doing labour and artisan work became inferior class and were excluded from the mainstream. This disparity in privilege resulted in to inter-caste jealousy, hatred, and conflict and continued for a very long time and in fact exists even today. There have been many saints, reformers and leaders in India who have opposed caste system and to give their due to the so-called backward classes. Shri Chaitanya, Shri Rama Krishna Paramhansa, Raja Ram Mohan Roy, Mahatma Gandhi, Swami Dayananda, and Swami Vivekananda, to name a few, have done a commendable job in uplifting the masses from the curse of caste system.

After Independence, the Govt. of India has taken measures to correct this malaise in the society. The Govt., as a rule of law, has given equal access to higher education and in government jobs irrespective of caste, creed, religion, sex, etc. Disadvantaged sections are now being given reservation in government jobs of higher professions of teachers, doctors, engineers, advocates, and in all India services like IAS, IPS etc. The results are highly encouraging. There is a greater acceptance of lower-caste people in society and they are now joining the mainstream. Inter-caste marriages are also taking place in India especially in big cities.

Moksha/Mukti

According to Hinduism, the soul passes through repeated cycles of birth and death called "Samsara". Birth is normally associated with pain. Hinduism advocates very forcefully and consistently that the purpose of human life is to get liberation from 'Samsara'. All Hindu scriptures like Upanishads, Ramayana, Mahabharata, Gita, Puranas, etc. exhort to live a disciplined life with control of senses and mind, to do right actions (by thoughts, word and deeds), seek God through meditation, knowledge and devotion, etc and attain liberation. A spiritual life leads to Realisation of God, which leads to Moksha/Mukti. The liberated soul then remains in the presence of Paramatma and enjoys permanent bliss.

Though all the scriptures of Hindus are a strong advocate of salvation, at the same time, Hinduism recognizes the intense human desires and aspirations in the form of Kama—pleasure—and Artha—wealth. Kama and artha provide a great motivation in life for sustained efforts. The Mahabharta goes to the extent that without artha-money one cannot get Mukti because through wealth only we do charities, pilgrimage, observe vratas which are helpful in going towards God. Hinduism, however, cautions and puts a rider that both Kama and Artha have to be in conformity with Dharma, otherwise one can falter in life and results can be disastrous.

The Doctrine of Re-incarnation

Quite often we hear that a person knows his past, he remembers his previous parents, place of birth, and also some important event of his previous life. This is called re-incarnation; the desires of the previous birth lead to rebirth of such people.

✡✡✡

Chapter 2 : Hindu Samskaras

Over a period of time, Vedic period society became mature. From the worship of element (Fire, Earth, Water and other Gods) they shifted for a more meaningful life. They evolved "Samskaras" to be observed from the conception of baby to all the four stages of life and ultimately depart to heaven. The 'Samskaras' are mentioned in Vedas and other Hindu scriptures. Veda prescribe 'Samskaras' for the purification of the mind and the soul and to reach a stage of acquiring a disciplined personality. The purpose of samskaras had been many. One of the aims was to ward of bad influence of ghosts, demons or supernatural forces. Another aim had been to gain in wealth, intellect and long and healthy life, etc. Samskaras covered the full span of life from conception to death and even beyond.

Samskaras contain rituals, ceremonies, prayers, etc. The Atharveda provides the manner in which rites, rituals and ceremonies are to be performed and it contains the meanings of sacrifices according to the ceremonies used in the Samskaras.

Samskaras started in the Vedic period. They were fully in vogue in the Grahsutra period. Subsequently, changes have taken place both in rituals and their importance in life. What is described here is a general and simplified version of Samskaras to give an idea of the thought and rituals behind them in ancient times.

There are some variations in the numbers and names of Samskaras in different Hindu Shastras; however, the revered *Rishi* Ved Vyasa has named 16 Samskaras to be observed in life. Each Samskara contains the ceremony and sacrifice to be performed.

Sixteen Samskaras

Garbhadhana Samaskara (Conception)

The purpose of this Samskara was to make the wife conceive for getting a virtuous child in the family.

According to this Samaskara, conception is not a random affair, but a great responsibility. It should be timed properly. The proper time of conception was considered to be when the wife was physically fit to conceive. The prescribed time for conception was from the fourth to the sixteenth night after the monthly course of the wife was over. Only nights were prescribed for conception and the daytime was prohibited. It was believed that a male child shall be conceived on even nights and a girl child shall be conceived on odd nights of copulation. The attributes of children were laid depending upon the dates of conception, e.g. a son conceived on the fourth night would be shortlived and without wealth, a girl conceived on the seventh night would be barren, etc.

It is worth mentioning that Hindu scriptures mention that it is the duty of the husband to satisfy his wife and vice versa, otherwise they are liable for committing a sin. Therefore, sex and childbearing was a sacred aspect of Hindu married life.

Pumsavana Samaskara (Fertilisation)

After the conception of a baby was confirmed, Pumsavana Samaskara was performed. The samaskara was generally performed when there was movement of the embryo in the womb. It comprised pouring the juice of a banayan tree in the nostrils of the pregnant woman. Then after the morning bath, she was asked to sit with a pot of water in her lap; the father would touch her stomach and pray for the protection of the baby.

The Simantonnayana (Parting of Hair) Samaskara

This Samaskara involved the parting of the hair of the pregnant mother. This Samaskara was generally performed in the 4th or 5th month of pregnancy. The purpose of removing the hair was to ward off the evil spirits who were supposed to be continuously haunting the pregnant mother and her child. The wife was asked to sit on a chair and the husband parted the hair of wife upwards. He would cut the hair while having a bunch of unripe Udumbara fruits, Darbha-grass and a stick of the Viratara wood in his hand; there after Brahmins were served meals.

Precautions to be taken by the pregnant woman: It is very interesting to know that many precautions were prescribed to be observed by the pregnant woman for a safe delivery and good progeny. For example, the mother should not sleep too much in the daytime; should spend time worshipping Gods and stay in good company; she should avoid mounting a horse, an elephant, climbing a mountain or highrise buildings; she should not ride a bullock-cart; she should avoid swift walking, should not eat very spicy food, should not quarrel, etc.

Further, the duty of the husband was to fulfil the wishes of the pregnant wife; otherwise it would have adverse effect on the child's health.

It is thus seen that barring the ritualistic part of the Samskara, the other precautions being taken both by the husband and wife were perfectly in consonance with the requirement of good physical and mental health of both mother and child.

The Jatakarma Samskara (Birth Samskara)

There was detailed arrangement for giving birth to the baby. The purpose of 'Jatakarma' Samskara was to protect the child and mother from supernatural forces and praying to Gods to provide long and healthy life and virtues to the newcomer in the world.

A separate room called the 'Shutika Bhavana' used to be prepared. The room was very well ventilated and used to face in the auspicious directions of East or North. A highly spiritual environment was created by worshiping of family Gods, feeding Brahmins and cows, recitation of mantras and auspicious verses, etc. The mother would then be shifted to this room few days prior to the expected date of delivery. Many experienced women would take care of the mother. She, thus, had the assurance that both she and the baby were in safe hands.

When delivery was over and a normal child was born, a fire was lighted in the room to warm the utensils and to smoke the child and mother, presumably to disinfect the area. The fire was kept burning till the purification day—Havana. The time of birth used to be noted very carefully for preparing the horoscope and to know the future of the child. The practice of preparing the horoscope, as we know, continues till today. A gist of ceremonies performed in the Jatakarma Samskara is given below.

The first ceremony to be performed was 'Medhajanana' ceremony. The father would give to the baby ghee and/or honey with a spoon of gold among the chanting of mantras. Both ghee and honey were supposed to stimulate the intellect of the baby.

Next, the father would perform Ayusha ceremony for wishing long and healthy life to the child. The father would murmur near the right ear the names of things having long life such as trees, *Rishis*, sacrifice, ocean, etc. and by association of ideas, it was expected that the baby would have a long and healthy life.

Next, he would exhort the baby to be strong like an axe and face life with courage come what may. At the same time, the father would praise the mother for giving him a son.

Next the naval-cord was severed. The baby was washed and breastfeeding started. Thereafter, the father would keep a pot of water near the head of the mother, praying to the gods to protect both mother and child from evil forces.

The ceremony used to be concluded with donations to the poor and feeding Brahmins and giving them gifts in cash and kind.

We have to be bear in mind that in Vedic times, there was heavy dependence on deities for the general well-being, and in this case for the well-being of mother and child. The blessings of gods used to be sought by reciting the mantras in all ceremonies.

We can also see that separate room for the expecting mother was highly scientific because it gave the mother the much needed privacy and would avoid any infection to both the mother and the the baby.

Jatakarma samskara

Namakarana Samskara (Name Giving)

Giving a name is a social requirement of a civilised society. It greatly facilitates communication with the baby. Hindus recognised the importance of name and converted the naming ritual in to a ceremony. It was a professional exercise among Hindus. Lots of Dos and Don'ts were observed in adopting the name of the newborn baby. For example, Grahyasutra prescribes that a name of two syllabi should be given to earn name and fame in life. The name of the boy should be of even number of syllabi and that girl child should be of odd number of syllabi. *Rishi* Manu has prescribed that the name of a girl child should be easy to pronounce and pleasing to hear. Further, the name was to reflect the social status of the baby. The name of a kshatriya would reflect power, e.g., the name 'Yudhishtira' contains the word 'yudh' meaning war. Different Hindu shastras prescribed a variety of recommendations on names to reflect the total personality of the child. The system saw lot of changes over a period in the giving a name to a baby.

Namkarna ceremony showing a mother, new born baby and priest

Gradually, the fourfold mode of naming came into practice. In this system the first method was to name the baby after the Nakshtra-constellation in which he or she was born. There are 27 constellations in Hindu astrology; each has its own deity. For example, Rohini Nakshatra has Prajapati as its deity. A girl born in Rohini Nakshtra would be given the name Rohini. The names were also given after the deity of the month in which baby was born. Each of the twelve months of the Hindu calendar is associated with a deity; e.g. the deity of Falguna month is Chakri. The third mode of naming was based on the family deity, say Rama, Krishna, Parvati, Lakshmi, etc. As we know, these names were quite popular among Hindus till recent times. The fourth mode was to give a popular name prevalent in society based on the above criteria. A popular pleasing name which reflected the status, caste of the family, and its deity was given. The present trend, however, is to give a distinct name having an impressive meaning.

Ceremony associated with naming — The naming ceremony was performed on the tenth or twelfth day after the birth of the child. It was also called Shudhikaran (Purification). The house used to be washed. The child and the mother would take a bath. The father would take the baby and worship the deities, Agni and Soma, etc. The father would then attract the attention of the baby (through his/her breath) and then would give him/her a name. Subsequently, Brahmins were given food and gifts, etc.

Niskarmana Samaskara (First Outing)

This Samskara was performed when the child was taken out for the first time from the confines of the house. It was an important event in the life of a child as his universe was going to expand from then onwards. The ceremony was observed between the 12th day to 4 months of birth.

The courtyard of the house used to be plastered with cow dung and grains of rice were scattered on the floor. The 'Swastik' sign was also made on the floor. The child was given a ceremonial bath and dressed in new and rich colours. The deities like Sun, Moon, Vasudeva and family deities were worshipped. Brahmins were given food. The child used to be taken out to a temple by the father amidst the recitation of Vedic verses and music. The baby would pay his respect to the Gods and Goddesses and seek their blessings. Later blessings and gifts were given to the baby by other family members.

Annaprasana Samaskara (First External Feeding)

When the child was about six months old, external food was given to him to meet his requirement of increased food and also for slowly freeing the mother from feeding the child. Different types of foods were prescribed. A mixture of curd, ghee and honey was quite common.

The ceremony for Samaskara was the following.

Firstly, food itself used to be prepared with the chanting of Vedic verses. Oblations were offered to the goddess of Speech, Vigour etc with appropriate verses. The Vedic prayers were offered so that all the senses (such as ear, eyes) of the child were gratified. Subsequently, the food was served to the child. In the end, Brahmins were given food and gifts.

It is now widely recognized that food has a direct bearing on the mind. If food is prepared in a 'satvik' (pure) environment, it impacts the mind in a positive manner; therefore, this Samaskara was on a highly scientific line.

Chudakarana Samskara (Tonsure)

Behind this Samskara was the belief that tonsuring (removing the hair) increases the life of the child. Charaka, the Vedic-period physician, mentions that the cutting and dressing of hair and nails gives strength, life, purity and beauty.

The ceremony was generally conducted between 1 year to 3 years of age of the child. The ceremony was performed on an auspicious day when the Sun was in Uttarayana. The ceremony used to be performed at home but it was shifted to temples when temples came into being.

An important aspect of the Chudakarana ceremony was the arrangement of 'Shikha' (choti). Different families had different number of tufts, e.g., only one tuft was kept by the descendents of Vashishtha, five were kept by those of Angiras and none by the families belonging to *Rishi* Bhirgu, etc. Nowadays, Brahmins engaged in spiritual activities and who believe in traditional values still keep 'Shikha' but by and large it is on the decline.

The ceremony of Chudakarna was conducted as follows.

An auspicious day was fixed. Worship of Ganesha and other deities was done. Next food was distributed among Brahmins. The child was given a bath. The mother would then take the child in her lap and sit before the sacred fire. The father would moisten the hair with a mixture of fresh butter or ghee or curd and water with the recitation of Vedic verses. He would put three young kusha with the citation of verses. The father then would take the razor and cut the hair chanting Vedic verses and praying for the prosperity, good progeny, and valour of the child etc. This way the hair of left side, right side, and behind were moistened and hair removed. The removed hair was thrown in to a lump of bull's dung kept nearby. Finally, the dung and hair was hidden in a cowstall or thrown into a pond of water or buried in the vicinity of water. Suitable gifts were given to all concerned. The ceremony is still observed; however the venue has been shifted to the temples.

The Karnavedha Samskara (Piercing the Ears)

Karnavedha (piercing the ear) had been a tradition in India from ancient times, mainly for ornamental purposes. Slowly it became a Samskara and started being performed ceremoniously. The age for this ceremony varied in different times. According to *Rishi* Brihshpti, it should be performed on the 10th, 12th or 16th day after the birth of the child. Further, depending upon the status of the family, the needle could be of gold or of silver or of copper or even of iron.

An auspicious day was chosen. The child was seated facing east. He/she was given some sweets to engage his/her attention. The right ear was pierced with the citation of Vedic verses and then the left ear was pierced. Brahmins were served good food and suitable presents in cash and kind were given to them.

The Vidyaarambha Samskara (Learning of the Alphabet)

This Samskara marked the beginning of formal education of the child. In ancient times, education was confined to only hearing the Vedic verses, mantras and memorizing them. Slowly the alphabets were introduced to store the large volume of knowledge which otherwise was becoming impossible to memorise. The alphabets were invented around 7th century AD and thereafter the Vidyarambha Samskara came into being to introduce the child to the world of written language. For this reason, this Samskara is also called 'Aksararambha Samskara'.

The prescribed age for the Vidyarambha Samskara was five to seven years. The ceremony was performed on any auspicious day, when Sun was in Uttrayan. The child was given a ceremonial bath nicely dressed and decorated. Lord Ganesha, Saraswati, family goddess, etc. were worshipped. Rice was spread on a silver plank and letters written on it with an ordinary pen. Basically prayer and praises for gods and goddesses of learning like Ganesha, Saraswati. were written; the teacher then made the child read thrice what was written. Subsequently, the child would pay respect to the gods and goddesses in a ceremonial manner.

The child then presented clothes and other gifts to the teacher. Brahmins were given food and presents.

The Upanayana Samskara (Initiation)

Now the child had come of age and ready for education and undergo other training required to lead a complete life. The child was inducted into formal training by performing Upanayana Samskara. Upanayana was called a second birth since it elevated the social status of the child. This was also the beginning of Brahmacharya Ashram when the child would undergo comprehensive education in which study of the Vedas was an integral part. He used to stay with his Guru and was totally dedicated to his Guru, including doing his (teacher's) personal services including tending the cows.

The age for the Upanayana ceremony varied in different times. It varied from 8 years to 12 years. Different ages was prescribed for different Varnas. The upper age limit was also prescribed for different Varnas.

A teacher of high calibre, having very good knowledge of the Vedas, himself pure and capable to build the character of the child, was selected. The guru or teacher was central to this Samskara in the Vedic times because he was trusted without any element of mistrust.

Generally Upanayana used to be done when the Sun was in the Northern hemisphere, which is considered as being auspicious in Hindu philosophy.

Different seasons were prescribed for different Varnas. For example, Upanayna of Brahmin boys was performed in the spring season and that of Kshatriyas in summer. The reason being that the mood and thought process in these seasons matched the duties of the Varnas.

Ceremony: The previous day, a canopy used to be prepared where the ceremony was to be conducted. Lord Ganesha and other goddesses like Lakshmi, Saraswati were worshipped to bring purity and divinity in the environment. The child was supposed to keep silent on that night.

On the next day of Upanayana, the mother and child would eat together for the last time; thereafter they would not be allowed to eat jointly. The idea was to convey to the child that he was no longer the mummy's chum and that he had to take care of himself. The boy was then given a ceremonial bath. He was asked to cover his private parts by a Kaupeena—a sort of grass. The boy would then walk up to the acharya (teacher) and formally announce his intentions to become a brahmachari. The acharya would welcome the boy and formally hand over the clothes to be worn by him. The upper garment used to be of deer skin in Vedic times; however, gradually cotton, silk clothes, pure white or dyed, got introduced to by different communities. A girdle was tied round the waist of the boy with the citation of Vedic verses.

The boy was then given the sacred thread to wear. The sacred thread, which is also called the 'Janoou', had much significance. It was a symbol of purity and strength. The sacred thread was initially of different colours for different Varnas but gradually the yellow colour and cotton material became the standard. Because of great significance attached to the sacred thread, rules were prescribed for its preparation and use in daily life. For example, it was to be spun by a virgin Brahmin girl. Its three cords represented the three gunas viz Sattvik, Rajas and Tamsik from which the universe has evolved, etc. The knot which binds the three threads, is called Brahmgranthi, which symbolically represents the Hindu Trinity—Brahma, Vishnu and Mahesh.

Next a staff was presented to the young man. The staff was a symbol of a traveller. The boy was a traveller in the journey of life and he would pray to Gods to bless him to cover this journey successfully. The staff would also give him a feeling that he was well equipped for his own protection. Different types of woods were prescribed for the staffs of different Varnas.

Next the acharya would symbolically purify the boy by putting water in his jointed hands. The acharya would then touch the heart of the boy and the presiding deity of learning was invoked to unite the heart of the acharya and the student. The union of hearts was important for the total dedication and trust between the boy and acharya. The student was then asked to mount a stone to impress upon him that he has to be firm and resolute in the study period as well as in later life.

The teacher would now formally take charge of the boy. He would pray for his well-being and protection to gods and goddesses by citing the Vedic verses. A round of fire was made both by the teacher and pupil together. Next Savitri mantra was taught to the student by the acharya. The rite of praying the sacred fire was performed by the pupil amidst the recitation of Vedic verses. Agni (fire) was considered a sacred entity in Vedic times. It used to be a witness in all important ceremonies throughout the life. Therefore prayers were offered to fire for bestowing prosperity, happiness and blessings. Next, the student was asked to beg alms from the family members gathered there, thereby conveying a message that he had to survive on charity from society throughout the studentship and subsequently he had to support others in a similar way when he would become economically independent.

The Upanayana ceremony used to be concluded observing the Triratra Vrata, three days of continence period. During these days, the child was asked to refrain from saline food, wine and meat and would sleep on the ground, etc. In the end, Medhajanana ritual—worshipping Sun God—was performed to seek divine blessings for success in the formal education.

Thus, the entire exercise of Upanayana Samskara was to equip the child with necessary items and hand over the child to a able acharya. From then on, the acharya was his friend, philosopher and guide. On the whole, it was thus a great ceremony, emotional, highly spiritual and an extremely important event for the young boy.

However, gradually Upanayana has become a ceremony and not necessarily for the beginning of formal education; it has to be performed at an appropriate age in life but certainly before marriage.

Vedarambha Samskara (the Beginning of Vedic Studies)

In Vedic times, the Vedas were taught to all eligible students. Some rites, vratas, etc. were performed before the study of the Vedas in a formal way. However, gradually the study of the Vedas became confined to Brahmins engaged in spiritual activities and Vedic rituals. The Vedarambha Samskara was introduced to retain the ancient values of Vedic studies by an aspirant. The following ceremony was involved in this Samskara.

An auspicious day was selected. The guru (teacher) would establish the sacred fire. The student was asked to sit on the west of the fire. Ahutis (oblations) were given to the two elements such as Earth, Agni, Vayu, Sky, Sun, Moon, etc. depending upon the Veda proposed to be studied in the beginning. In case the study of all Vedas was planned simultaneously, the above offerings were made together to these elements one after the other. The ceremony used to end with dakshina (cash and kind) to the presiding Brahmin and food to all.

The Keshanta or the Godana Samskara (The Shaving of the Beard)

This Samskara marks the beginning of adulthood for the boy. Beard and moustaches appear and he is reminded of his increased role and responsibility in the society. It envisaged the first shaving of beard and moustaches of the boy when the young man is of sixteen years.

The ceremony of Keshanta was performed on the lines of Choodakarana Samskara since both involve removal of hair. The hair of the beard and of moustaches was removed and buried in bull dung near a source of water, say a pond. A cow was generally offered to the guru; for this reason it is also called Godana Samskara. The boy would take a vow that he would spend a life of simplicity and discipline at least for one full year.

The Samavartana (End of Studentship)

Samavartana Samskara meant the end of studies, end of brahmacharya and returning home of the student from the guru's house. The student was supposed to be well equipped in knowledge and life skills and fit to enter the next Ashram, i.e., Grahyasth Ashram. He was also fit to be married and raise a family.

To begin with, the student would go to the guru and ask his permission to end the studentship. The permission of the guru was essential because he was the only person to certify that he (the student) had acquired the necessary knowledge, skill and maturity needed in life. Before parting from the guru, the student would give Guru Dakshina to the teacher in the form of land, cows, gold, clothes, etc. The guru used to be an enlightened person and he would accept even small things happily (without causing any burden on the child) in case the child happened to be from a poor family, for the Guru, welfare of the child was uppermost.

The following ceremony was observed for this Samskara.

An auspicious day was selected for the ceremony. The student would remain inside a room till noon. Then he would come out and embrace the feet of the guru. He would make an offering to the sacred fire. Eight pitchers were kept full of water which represented eight quarters of the earth. The student would take water from all the pitchers and take a bath amid chanting of Vedic verses. The student would dispose of his dear skin clothes and the staff, cut off his beard and nails, remove locks of hair, etc., i.e., all those items which were given to him at the time of Upanayana. He was now entitled to worldly activities and pleasures. The acharya himself would give the boy new clothes, ornaments, earrings, turban, umbrella, mirror, etc. The boy was permitted to apply scents and fragrance to enhance his physical appeal.

The young man would then proceed to meet the other members of the family and society by riding on an elephant or on a chariot. The acharya would introduce the young 'Snataka' to the assembled guests. The boy would then pay respects in the north and east directions. At night, he would pay respect to the Moon and stars. The ceremony would end with food to all, dakshina to Brahmins and gifts to the guru.

The Vivaha Samskara (Marriage)

The importance of marriage has been recognized throughout civilization since the ancient times. Hinduism recognises the importance of marriage as an important event to develop the person in a wholesome manner. Since Vedic times Grahyasth Ashrama of 25 years from 26 years of age to 50 years of age, has been prescribed, in which the man would marry, raise children, live in a family and then enter the next stage of life. However, starting from Vedic times, there have been several changes in the manner of choosing a boy and girl for the purpose of marriage and the manner in which the marriage is to be formalised. For example, child marriages were quite prevalent among Hindus for a long time for various reasons. One reason was foreign aggression. In order to protect the girls, they were married at an early age. In the Mahabharata, we know that Bheeshma brought by force Amba, Ambica and Ambalika, daughters of king of Kashi, and married Ambica and Ambalika to Vichtraviriya, son of Shantanu and Satyawati. However, this practice was more prevalent among the warrior class. Daiva form of marriage, in which the daughter was given to priests as dakshina, were also practised. Some communities observed polygamy and some polyandry.

Hindu Smirtis mention that eight modes of marriages were practised in different times, which included marrying a girl by force, marrying a girl by offering some money to her father, boy and girl agreeing and marrying each other (Gandhrava marriage), etc. The gandharva style of marriage has been quite popular at all times because it is by consent and liking of the marrying partners.

However, 'Brahma Marriage' had been the most stable form of marriage and it continues till date as the most popular form of marriage among Hindus. In Brahma marriage, the father would give the daughter to a person of choice, a man of character and learning, and without expecting anything in return from the groom's side. Since families are involved in the selection of partners, this marriage was expected to be stable.

We will describe this type of marriage in details as this is popular till date.

Caste and Gotra: Among Hindus, generally marriage occurs within the same caste but outside the gotra. Inter-caste marriages had been existing in society and such marriages are increasingly becoming common in India, specially in cities and among children settled abroad, etc. Whatever may be the caste, the Indian scriptures always advise to marry in families of virtue, i.e. families who are contented, gentlemanly; who are devoid of greed, attachment, envy, pride, and infatuation, etc. It was prescribed to avoid undesirable families in matrimonial alliances, viz, families without great deeds, without exposure to Vedas, suffering from piles, epilepsy, leprosy; families having too tall or too short members; either very white or very black; having extra limbs. Families of disrepute were also to be avoided. The underlying idea was that the subsequent generations shall be virtuous and shall not suffer from serious deficiencies.

Age: The marriageable age has been always a controversy in all societies. At some stage, child marriages were prevalent in Hindu society. Commencement of puberty of the girl had also been the criteria for marriage. The Hindu society has now come of age, child marriages and other old practices are on the wane. The present trend and legal system in India prescribes that girl should be adult, 18 years, at the time of marriage so that she can take a proper decision about her life. It has always been prescribed that the girl should be younger than the husband.

The marriage was solemnised in the following way. The trend, formalities continue to be observed even today with some variations.

Vagdana (Betrothal)

In early times, the proposal to marry a girl used to be given by the groom first. The groom duly dressed in rich clothes and accompanied by his friends and family would go to the bride's place and formally ask her hand in marriage. This was called Vagadana or the oral giving away of wife. If both parties agreed, the marriage was solemnised by feast, exchange of gifts, etc.

Slowly, it got shifted the other way, the girl's father would go to groom's place and present his case. The suitability of the boy and girl, status of the families, etc. were considered and necessary decision to enter in to marriage alliance was taken by both sides. This tradition continues in present times also though boy and girl mutually befriending and then deciding to marry is increasing day by day, specially in cities; nevertheless tradition of both the families to interact and decide the details of marriage is still prevalent.

Marriage Day

A suitable auspicious day for marriage was fixed in consultation with the astrologers. It was considered auspicious when the sun was in the northern hemisphere.

A few days before marriage, the ceremony of Mrdaharna was performed. It consisted of fetching some earth from the north direction to grow sprouts in a pot of clay. The ceremony of Haridralepana, which consists of besmearing the bride and bridegroom with a paste of haldi (turmeric) and oil, was performed one or two days before marriage. This was done basically to improve the looks of the couple, and at the same time it was considered auspicious.

Ganapati, the lord who destroys obstacles, was first worshipped and established in the Vivaha Mandap (nuptial canopy) erected to carry out the ceremonies of marriage. Blessings of Lord Ganesha were invariably sought to make the marriage successful.

In early times when clocks were not available, a water clock used to be established to mark the time of various ceremonies.

On the Marriage Day

Both bride and groom would take the nuptial bath with scented water at their respective homes and amid chanting of Vedic verses. In the evening, the bridegroom would dress himself nicely with ornaments. He would then offer prayers to the family gods and then feed the Brahmins.

A marriage party led by the bridegroom, and his immediate family members, friends and relatives called 'barat' would go to the bride's place in suitable conveyances.

The bridegroom was formally received at the bride's place by the women of the bride's side with lighted lamps, etc. The father of the bride would then ask the groom to sit on a couch of grass. His feet were washed and he was offered water mixed with honey to sip.

In a similar way, the bride was worshipped by her father-in-law with scent, garland, sacred thread and a pair of ornaments. The bride then worshipped goddess Gauri and she would take a seat.

Marriage Ceremony

The groom established the Laukikagni (the sacred fire) because agni was central to Aryans in all sacred activities. The bridegroom then presented the bridal dress to the bride by chanting Vedic verses.

The names of both bride and groom and their gotra, etc. were announced for the information of the gathered guests.

A small pocket containing supari (areca nut), haldi (turmeric), akshat (rice grains), pushpa (flowers), dravya (coins) in the uttriya of the bride was tied to a corner of the uttariya of the groom. This knot was a symbolic way of keeping them united all throughout the life.

The ceremony of Kanyadana (giving away the daughter) followed. The bride was given to the groom in a formal manner. Not all were authorized to do this honour. Generally father, grandfather, brother, mother, etc. were given this honour. The father would give away the daughter pronouncing that he was doing so for the salvation of ancestors.

Among Hindus, Kanyadana is considered extremely auspicious. Many people who do not have daughters, do this great Yajana by adopting girls from poor families, solemnise their marriage and get the spiritual benefit of Kanyadana. Kanyadana is supposed to bring great merit to the person.

Panigrahan: In this ceremony, the groom would hold the right hand of the bride and thus formally take her responsibility. He would pray for a happy, healthy life of hundred years and virtuous children. The couple were then blessed with flowers by all present on the occasion.

Next the groom would ask the bride to tread on a stone. He himself chanted the verses in which he would ask the bride to be firm in her resolves in the married life.

Vows: The groom then was asked to take a few vows before the fire in front of all relatives and friends present there. "I resolve I will always remain soft and tolerant. You will always get my loving words. I will run the household along righteous path on your advice and with your consent etc."

Similarly the bride was asked to undertake the vows. "I will look after your family. I will prepare delicious foods. I will share pleasure and pain with you and never indulge in adultery. I will take care of father in law and others in the family etc."

The vows would put a moral binding on both the bride and groom to respect each other, trust each other, move together in life and share the happy and difficult moments jointly.

Maang Bharna (Applying Sindoor): The groom would sprinkle water on the bride with mango leaves. Dhruva Tara (Pole Star) was shown to them for stability in marriage and love. The groom then puts '– Sindoor' (Vermillion) in the parting of her hair amid chanting of mantras. The married ladies would then sing songs and bless the bride.

Pradakshina: Another important ceremony is Pradakshina, which involved taking seven rounds of the Vedic fire. First 64 ahutis were given to Gods, goddesses and deities. Then seven turns around the sacred fire were taken by both the bride and groom amid ahutis and chanting of Vedic verses. In four rounds, the bride would lead and in three rounds the groom would lead. Pradakshina is a very important ceremony which is a must for a Hindu marriage to be valid and legal even today.

Saptapadi: Following Pradakshina, Saptapadi symbolises that the couple shall move together in the journey of life. The couple would take seven steps together, synchronizing the timing and steps amid chanting of mantras.

The groom would touch her heart symbolically over the right shoulder praying that gods would unite their hearts.

After Saptapadi, the presiding priest would offer the closing ahutis. The groom would give Puranahuti and dakshina to priest. Bhasma was anointed to the couple. The couple would then be led inside and this would mark the end of Vivah Samskara.

The reader would note that the marriage ceremony of Hindus continues to be the same till date. In Vedic times, lot of importance was given to prayers, sentiments and it was a union of souls. At every step the gods were involved and worshipped to make the marriage stable. Both boy and girl were reminded through various mantras, offerings, verses that their union was sacred and they would have to tread together by remaining firm, faithful, respectful, fidelity, mutual trust in life. In present times, in general the sacredness of marriage and associated commitment is missing with the result that disputes, differences crop up very frequently in married life and divorces are becoming common.

Antyeshti Samskara (Funeral)

Disposal of the dead has been a subject matter of discussion among all civilizations. Aryans were a settled race in India and they had evolved a proper procedure for disposal of the dead. Burning of dead body or cremation has been the method of disposal of corpses by Hindus since the Vedic times. One of the reasons could be that Indo Aryans considered Agni as sacred, as the messenger of God on earth and carrier of their oblations to Gods.

Hindus call the cremation ceremony Aurdhvadaihika kriya or the ceremonies that release the soul from the body for its upward journey to heaven. It is believed that till the cremation is done, the departed soul lingers about its past habitation and hovers without consolation and remains in great distress as a 'Preta'. Therefore cremation of dead body at the earliest has been prescribed in Hinduism.

Following method is generally applied in the disposal of dead bodies in Hinduism since ancient times.

- When a person is near his death, he calls his near relatives for a last meeting. Attempts are made to know his last wish and to fulfil the same. The gift of a cow is considered highly beneficial for the peaceful departure of the soul. The cow is called Vaitarni; she is supposed to be the conductor of the dead over the stream of underworld. Gangajal, water of the Ganga, mixed with Tulsi leaves is put in his mouth. The Sri Mad Bhagvad Gita is generally recited near the dying person. All these activities are done so that the soul leaves the body easily, without causing suffering, and so that the departed soul is liberated.
- When the person has expired, the dead body is removed from the bed and placed on the ground with his head towards the North. The body is given a bath and wrapped in new clothes and placed on the 'Arthi.' The arthi is a cot made of bamboo sticks. A small piece of gold is generally kept in the hand of the corpse. New clothes symbolise that the dead is entering a new world. All the family members and friends pay their homage to the departed soul.
- The body is taken to the cremation ground. The funeral procession is led by the chief mourner, generally the eldest son, followed by the bier and then the rest of the mourners. Women were allowed to attend the cremation in ancient times. Name of God, "Ram Naam Satya Hai, Satya Bolo Gata Hai", which means that 'God is Truth. Observance of Truth in life, leads to Mukti' is generally recited by the funeral party.
- At the cremation ground, the corpse is purified by washing it with water. The funeral pyre is prepared. The corpse is placed on the pyre amid the chanting of

mantras; the thread that bind the thumbs are loosened and cords that hold the bier together are also cut off.

The corpus is then covered with sufficient quantity of woods, ghee, samagree, etc. to facilitate proper burning of the body. The pyre is lit by fire all around by the son amidst the chanting of Vedic mantras. When the body has been burnt to some degree, Kapal Kriya is performed; the skull is pierced by a log to facilitate the releasing of the soul. It is for this reason that Hinduism prescribes early cremation of dead, otherwise soul remains trapped inside the body.

- The next ceremony is called the Udakakarma or offering of water to the dead. All the relatives of the dead bathe in the nearest stream and purify themselves and offer prayers to Prajapti. When they reach home, they touch a stone, fire, cow dung, grain, til seed, oil and water to purify themselves before they enter the house.
- Next follows the period of mourning. A period of ten to fifteen days is kept as mourning period so that the bereaved family comes to terms with the loss. Pleasures are forbidden in these days. Relatives and friends visit the bereaved family and offer their condolences, etc.
- The following day, the son and other close persons of the family go to the cremation ground, collect the ash and bones of the dead person in a bag. A small group of persons then go to a river, preferably Ganga, to immerse the remains of the deceased.
- After the mourning period, the family and all relatives, etc. assemble at a place, some Vedic mantra etc. are recited and they return home and normal life is resumed.

Hindu texts prescribe special funeral rites for some cases. For example, a saintly person is not burnt but buried in the ground. Some saints prefer water burial. A feast is generally given to Brahmins and sadhus and holy people when such souls leave their bodies.

Similarly infants or young babies are generally not cremated but buried. The period of mourning is also kept short.

Disposal of the dead is a sensitive matter. Hindu philosophy is to show respect to the departed soul, to seek his peaceful departure, to seek his forgiveness for those left behind and finally seek deliverance of his soul.

Chapter 3: Hindu Scriptures

Vedas

We have mentioned Hindu scriptures briefly in chapter 1. These scriptures are described in this chapter in greater detail. Hinduism can boast of its scriptures, which are an ocean of wisdom and contain time-tested wisdom. The Vedas are the oldest documents of the Hindu religion. They have not been written by a single person but contain the experiences of thousands of *Rishis* (holy people) gathered over thousands of years. These *Rishis* had a craving to know the secrets of such a vast universe around them; what is its origin? Who is its creator? Why has it been created? Why is there so much misery around? What is the way out of 'Samsara' repeated cycle/birth and death? There was no answer outside. They looked inwards to find the answer. They connected themselves with the Supreme through meditation and got the answer. The subtle truth of life as perceived by these great sages over a very long period is documented in the Vedas.

The Rig Veda is the oldest of all Vedas; it dates back to nearly 5000 BC or more. *Rishi* Vyasa compiled the Vedas in the present form of four Vedas out of the Rig Veda. He has been given the honour of being called 'Ved Vyasa'. Ved Vyasa also compiled the Puranas. The Puranas have facilitated the availability of the wisdom of Vedas to the common people through simple stories and dialogues. *Rishi* Ved Vyasa has thus done a yeoman service to mankind by simplifying the Vedas and writing the Puranas, a storehouse of wisdom till posterity. It is for us to emulate the teachings of these great texts. Hindus honour Ved Vyasa by observing fast on his birthday—Puranmasi of the month of Asadha. This day is dedicated to the guru, most Indians honour their respective gurus or spiritual teachers on this day.

Four Vedas

The Four Vedas are

(I) Rig Veda
(II) Sama Veda
(III) Yajur Veda
(IV) Atharva Veda

The Vedas are called Shrutis which means "rhythm of the infinite heard by the soul."

It is not something derived logically but they are poems heard from a divine connection through meditation. That is why the Vedas are called divine and eternal texts. They contain the truth regarding the Creation and the Creator and their contents cannot be contested.

All other Indian scriptures are categorised under 'Smritis'; their contents have changed depending upon the exigencies of time.

Four Sections of a Veda

Each of the four Vedas has four sections viz:

Samhitas

Samhitas portion or Vedas are the collection of mantras. The mantras depict a variety of thoughts of the Vedic *Rishis*. Some hymns are in praise of Gods such as Agni, Surya, Vayu, Indra, etc. Some hymns are in the form of prayers seeking material benefits from the Gods such as cattle wealth, long age, destruction of enemy, etc. Some hymns describe the formation of "Creation." Some later hymns condemn evils like gambling and witchcraft. Each Veda has its own Samhita but Yajur Veda has two, namely Krishna Yajur and Shukla Yajur Veda Samhita.

Brahmanas

The Brahmanas portion of Vedas were written subsequent to Samhitas. They are basically manuals for ritual worship and prayers. Aryans used to worship Gods by igniting sacred fires, and oblations to Gods was given through fire by chanting the mantras. The Brahmanas describe the details of offerings, sacrifices and their inherent meaning to be used on various occasions, say birth in the family, marriage, funeral rites, etc. During the period when Brahmanas were written, there was greater emphasis on rituals; hence priests enjoyed lot of respects in the society in that period.

Arankayas

Arankayas portion of Vedas contain the philosophical and inherent meaning of the hymns of the Samhita and rituals of the Brahmana. They were meant for contemplation by the people who came to forests at the Vanprastha Ashram stage in search for higher knowledge. A grahsth or a householder was already familiar with various mantras of worship and associated rituals. At this stage he was exposed to the inherent philosophical meaning of Samahitas and Brahmanas for contemplation during the forest life. Arankayas are, therefore, a transitional link between the rituals of the Brahmanas and the philosophy of the Upanishads.

Upanishads

The Upanishads are the last portions of Vedas and are also called Vedanta—end of Vedas. The sages have contemplated, concentrated and meditated for centuries to understand the Absolute Truth and presented this priceless knowledge to mankind in the form of the Upanishads. The Upanishads contain the highest truth and deal with the identity of the individual soul and 'Universal Soul'. They teach us the way out to realise the Supreme when Atma (soul) meets 'Paramatma' and individual Soul comes in the state of permanent bliss.

Details of Vedas

The salient contents of four Vedas are given below.

Rig Veda

The Rig Veda is the oldest of all the four Vedas. It is said that the entire Vedic literature, including their last portion, Upanishads, was complete when Buddhism started spreading in India (around 560 BC).

- The early hymns of the Rig Veda were in praise of natural forces as the Gods.
- The first and foremost to be worshipped was Surya (Sun) as God.
- Other prominent nature Gods were fire (Agni), which later became a link between man and Gods for the purpose of worshipping. Agni is addressed in at least 200 hymns in the Rig Veda.
- "Indra" was the God of rains and floods. He occupies a central position in Rig Veda hymns.
- A pair of Ashvins Gods were responsible for dusk and dawn. Soma, the wonder elixir giving a feeling of ecstasy, was equated to that of divine blessings. "We have drunk the Soma, and gained immortality", says the Vedic worshipper in one of the hymns.
- Earth was mother. Parjyana, the Sky, was Father. (In one hymn, the *Rishi* says "My mother is Earth and I am her son. Parjanya is my father; I pray that he may protect us.")
- Yama was the God who controlled the dead and Rudra was the militant God.
- Some of the prominent Goddesses of the Rig Veda period were Aditi, Usha, Saraswati as Goddess of learning, 'Vak' the Goddess of Speech and Aranyani the Goddess of forest.
- The Rig Veda also contains hymns describing Vedic science like meditation, yoga and mantras. Similarly some hymns describe Ayurveda, astrology and astronomy. Weapons used in war such as spears, bows and other war resources such as horses, chariots also find mention in the hymns of this Veda.
- Some Rig Veda hymns mention how the universe was created.

As Aryans settled, these Gods were addressed by the Aryans for protection and mercy as well as to bestow material welfare like wealth, cattle, good health, long age, freedom from diseases, etc. We find some hymns in the Rig Veda praying to Gods for granting these benefits.

- Observing some rhythm and a certain order in the nature, Aryans came to the conclusion that there was one Supreme Power who regulated the universe and

Gods and Deities mentioned in the Veda are manifestation of that Supreme power. Accordingly we find that the later hymns of the Rig Veda are in praise of one Supreme Being.

- The Rig Veda mentions nearly 400 sages including 21 women sages who have enriched its contents. Some *Rishis* like Vishwamitra, Atre, Vashishtha, Brarhaspatya, etc. and their subsequent generations, have made substantial contributions to its contents.

Brahmanas

The Rig Veda has three Brahmanas namely Aitareya,Shankhayana and Kaushitaki.

The Aitareya Brahmana was composed by *Rishi* Aitareya and *Rishi* Shaunaka. It deals with duties of a priest, sacrifices to be performed by Kshatriyas and mutual relationship between Brahmins and Kshatriyas. The Shankhayana and Kaushitaki Brahmana are also similar to Aitareya Brahmana.

Aranyakas of Rig Veda: The Rig Veda has three Aranyakas namely Aitareya, Shankhayana, and Taittiriya.

Upanishads of Rig Veda: The Rig Veda has 10 Upanishads out of which the Aitareya Upanishad is the principal Upanishad. This Upanishad is associated with Sage Aitareya, who taught it to a wider audience of *Rishis*.

Some salient details of the Aitareya Upanishad are described below.

- About the Creation it says that in the beginning there was only Absolute Self, and He, that one Spirit, out of his own will, created the entire universe.
- This Upanishad teaches that man is born again and again till he realises the Atman or 'Self'. After the individual Self meets the Universal Self, man is freed from 'samsara'—cycles of birth and death.

Rishis performing yajna in forest

- This Upanishad gives the philosophical meaning of sacrifices and advocates that inward sacrifices are superior to external ceremonial acts.

Sam Veda

Sam Veda is basically known for its poetic verses and ritualistic description. Almost all its verses have been taken from the Rig Veda. This Veda was compiled so as to accommodate the Vedic rituals and ceremonial chants in a separate document.

It has a Samhita portion which is addressed to various Gods on the lines of the Rig Veda. It has 10 Brahmanas containing the details of various rituals and sacrifices. It has one Aranyaka, namely Jaiminiya. It has 16 Upanishads, out which Chandogya and Kena are the principal Upanishads. Salient details of these two principal Upanishads of the Sam Veda are given below.

Chandogya Upanishad

The Chandogya Upanishad is among the earliest and longest Upanishads. It explains a number of important truths.

- It explains the spiritual importance and benefits of chanting AUM. The syllable AUM is also called "Udgitha." An aspirant who meditates on Udgitha, the syllable AUM, looking upon it as Supreme, has all his aspirations met.
- It explains the doctrine of re-incarnation based on good and bad Karmas or deeds.
- This Upanishad also provides a very important clarification that status of the brahmin (one of the four Varnas) comes from the character, attitude, aptitude of the person not from his family of birth unlike the popular belief that is anybody having the requisite knowledge of shastras and other qualities can be called a brahmin irrespective of his family of birth.
- **"Tat Tavam Asi", "You Are That Self", is one of the four Mahavakyas of this Upanishads which says that Supreme Self—Brahman—is identical with the individual 'Self' and hence man is basically a divine being.**

Keno Upanishad

- This Upanishad is also one of the oldest Upanishads.
- This Upanishad describes Goddess Amba, Ambika or Uma as the Goddess of Jnana (knowledge). She reveals to Indra, the king of devas, the truth about Brahman—that Brahman is Supreme and is the Absolute Truth. All our faculties of hearing, seeing, etc. are due to the grace of Brahma only.

Since we draw our life force from Brahman only, the Upanishad teaches us to withdraw from the world of senses and realise Brahman through Jnana (knowledge), contemplation, meditation, etc. Liberation from 'samsara' should be our motto in life.

Yajur Veda

The Yajur Veda derives its name from Yajus which means "sacrifice". It contains the inherent meaning of sacrifices and rituals. Quite a good portion of the Yajur Veda describes the manner of conducting the rites and rituals on various occasions by a Hindu.

Yajur Veda — Samhita

In Yajur Veda also, most of the hymns have been taken from the Rig Veda and duly arranged ceremony-wise.

- Some hymns of the Yajur Veda are prayers to the Creator praying to bestow the required wisdom to do good deeds and lead a pure life.
- In some hymns, God of Agni is prayed to bestow long life, and provide happiness in general.
- Surya (Sun) is prayed to seek his blessings.
- Lord Rudra is worshipped to grant freedom from diseases and to seek liberation.
- Some hymns contain prayers for bestowing good health, sound mind and good character.
- Some hymns address Vedic scholars to enlighten the people with the knowledge of the Vedas.

Though this Veda appears to be one of rituals and sacrifices it connects the individual with the Creator through rituals.

The Yajur Veda is divided in two portions, namely 1. Krishna Yajur Veda and 2. Shukla Yajur Veda.

Brahmanas of Krishna Yajur Veda: In this Veda, the Brahmanas are not separate but are attached with the Samhita. They are named 1. Taittiriya Brahmana and 2. Anuvakhyana Brahmana.

Aranyakas of Krishna Yajur Veda: There are three Aranyakas of Krishna Yajur Veda, namely

(I) Taittiriya

(II) Maitrayania

(III) Katha Aranyakas.

Upanishads of Krishna Yajur Veda

There are 32 Upanishads of the Krishna Yajur Veda, of which the Katha Upanishad and Taittiriya Upanishad are principal Upanishads. A few salient contents of these two Upanishads are given below.

Katha Upanishad: Katha means story. This Upanishad describes the katha (story) of Nachiketa and Yama, the lord of Death, in which the latter narrates to Nachiketa the profound truth of life.

Annoyed by the behaviour of Nachiketa (who was still a child) in one of the family ceremonies, his father Vajashrava made a remark that he (Nachiketa) should donate himself to Yama-The God of Death, instead of to the priest. It was in the context of a yajna being performed by the king and he was playing to give up his all possessions to achieve bliss of the Lords. Nachiketa was watching the scene and he presumed that he (Nachiketa) would also be gifted to someone.

These remarks annoyed Nachiketa. He immediately left home and went to meet Yama, the Lord of Death. Nachiketa had to wait for three days before he could meet Yama. Pleased with his patience, Yama asked him to ask for three boons. Nachiketa asked for the following blessings.

(i) That Lord Yama should calm down and remove his father's anxieties which was granted by Yama.

(ii) Nachiketa asked Yama to enlighten him (Nachiketa) about that sacrifice by performing of which he would reach heaven and shall be free from hunger, thirst, fear and sorrow. Yama told Nachiketa that **sacrificial fire** is the source of such pleasures and happiness in the world.

(iii) The third question of Nachiketa was "what happens to a man after death, some say he exists and some say he does not?" Nachiketa wanted to know the fate of man after death. This has been hurting man since time immemorial.

This question was highly philosophical and coming from a boy was a bit astonishing for Yama. Yama decided to check whether Nachiketa was really interested to know this profound truth. He said to Nachiketa that it was a difficult question seeing his age; instead, he could ask for other blessings like wealth in the form of gold, horses, elephants, all pleasures of heaven, unlimited amount of land. Nachiketa, however, was very clear in his mind; He insisted on knowing the above truth only and nothing else. Yama was highly impressed and convinced that Nachiketa was a real seeker of Truth. Yama then revealed the following truth to this great seeker.

- A person who is ignorant and immersed in worldly affairs only gets caught in the cycles of birth and death. He therefore dies and takes birth repeatedly.
- Man, however, gets liberated from 'samsara', the cycles of births and death, by knowing the 'Self'. It is, therefore, important to realise the Self. In the world Self is Truth and rest is all 'mayajaal' (illusion).

The Upanishad further explains how to know the 'Self'.

- Brahman or Self is realised when all desires are eliminated; when all the five senses along with the mind and intellect are at rest.
- The knowledge of Self comes not by study, reasoning, intuition or intellect but by looking inwards and through meditation. The wise men, therefore, look inwards, realise the Self and get liberated.
- Self is Supreme. It is imperishable, unborn, eternal, beyond time and space, immutable and pervades the entire universe. It is smaller than the smallest and greater than the greatest. However, it cannot be described fully in words.

After acquiring this knowledge of Self from Yama, the King of Death, Nachiketa was liberated and attained immortality. The Upanishad asserts that whosoever acquires this wisdom of identifying his Self with Brahman will attain Immortality like Nachiketa.

Taittiriya Upanishad: It contains prayers to Gods like Varuna, Indra, Vishnu and Brahman to seek their blessings.

- The Shikshavalli section of this Upanishad deals with the science of meditation to realise the 'Self'. It ontains a prayer on AUM for bestowing prosperity, protection, and finally realisation of Brahman.

- The Brahmanandavalli section emphasises to strive to know Brahman; for the knower of Brahman attains the highest. The entire universe of names and forms has come from Brahman and He alone sustains the universe.
- In the third section called Bhriguvalli, Sage Bhrigu wants to know about Brahman from his father Varuna. His father advised him to meditate to know the answer. On advice from his father, Bhrigu meditated and he realised Brahman, the Ultimate Truth.

Brahmana's of Shukla Yajur Veda

There are two Brahmanas of Shukla Yajur Veda: (i) Shatapatha (ii) Kanva Brahmana.

There is one Aranyaka namely Brihad Arankya of this Upanishad.

Upanishads-Shukla Yajur Vrda: There are 19 Upanishads of Shukla Yajur Vedas of which the Brihad Aranyaka Upanishad and the Ishavasya Upanishad are the prinicipal Upanishads. We will describe the salient contents of these two Upanishads.

Brihad Aranyakas Upanishad: This Upanishad is also one of the earliest and longest. It contains profound philosophical Truths.

- The central message of this Upanishad is that one should meditate with the awareness that one's Self is identical with the Self of all beings and that oneness is called Brahman.
- This Upanishad teaches that Damana, (self restraint), Dana, (alms giving), and Daya, (compassion), are cardinal virtues of life and must be followed in daily life to make life meaningful and blissful.
- About Creation, it says that in the beginning, only Hiranyagarbha existed; He created the Universe and Time and Space.
- Like all Upanishads, this Upanishad analyses the relationship between the individual Self and the Universal Self and concludes that they are identical and this can be experienced by the seeker through meditation.
- It contains the dialogue between *Rishi* Yajnavalkya and his wife Maitreyi and other scholars like Gargi, Kahola, Ushata in a meeting called by King Janaka of Videha. The *Rishi* answers a number of questions of philosophy from various scholars put up in that august gathering.
- In response to one question from Kahola, *Rishi* Yajnavalkya replies that the Self transcends hunger and thirst, grief, delusion, old age and death. Having realised this Self, the seeker gives up the desire for sons, desire for wealth and desire for worldly things, etc and attains liberation from 'samsara'. The conclusion of the discussion is that we are essentially one with Brahman. Man comes in the category of divine and is not to be identified with matter. Man is not a piece of matter but Spirit. Matter is the servant and Spirit is the master.

Ishavasya Upanishad

- This Upanishad is also called Isha Upanishad. Its main teaching is the essential unity of Brahman, which is unseen and is pure consciousness and the outside real physical world .

- Man should live a full life of one hundred years with full zeal, taking interest in all affairs of life while seeing God or the Atman in all the activities.
- Atman, (the Divine Spirit), is in you and me, envelopes everything in the world, though not experienced by senses.
- Self is one and it is everywhere. It is the source of orderliness in nature. By its mere presence, the cosmic energy is enabled to sustain the activities of all living beings.
- A person who has realised the Self, sees the same Self in every being. Because of this realisation, he does not hate an one. For such a person, separateness arising from narrow mindedness goes away. He identifies himself with everybody. He also becomes free from all sorrows and all delusions.

Atharva Veda

Atharva Veda is last of all the four Vedas.

Samhitas – Hymns

- Quite a large portion of hymns of this Veda are common with the Rig Veda.
- There are hymns in praise and worship of Gods and deities like Agni, Surya, Soma, etc.
- The hymns cover a variety of subjects, e.g., love, happy family life, health, longevity of life, etc.
- Contains hymns and mantras which have the power to drive away misfortunes and to destroy enemies.
- Ayurveda—Indian system of medicine—considered as Upa Veda of Atharva Veda, is described in the form of verses in this Veda. There are verses which describe some diseases and their cure. It contains verses which describe the curative power of many herbs and plants and of water.
- Contains hymns for various rituals such as marriage, funeral rites and domestic ceremonies.
- Some hymns teach virtues like kindness, gentleness, effects of good deeds,fearlessness and yoga etc.
- Some hymns mention the bad effects of vices, evil deeds, sensual pleasures, hatred and anger.

Brahmana

- The Atharva Veda has only one Brahmana namely Gopatha, which describes the duties of priests and rituals.
- The Atharva Veda does not have Aranyakas.
- There are 31 Upanishads in this Veda of which following three are the principal Upanishads.
- Mandukya Upanishad

- Mundaka Upanishad
- Prashna Upanishad
- Salient features of the above the three principal Upanishads are given below.

Mandukya Upanishad

- This Upanishad is named after Sage Manduka. It contains only 12 mantras but their spiritual contents are of high order and lead us to path of enlightenment.
- This Upanishad identifies AUM with Brahman.
- It associates the four states of waking, dreaming, sleeping and transcendental consciousness to the three elements of AUM and silence in the fourth ardhmatra respectively. Through intense meditation on AUM, one will reach the fourth stage, which is the ultimate state of Self-realisation and attaining the Brahman.

Mundaka Upanishad

- This Upanishad advocates that higher wisdom, acquired through higher knowledge about Brahman, leads to Mukti. Vedic rituals or worldly knowledge do not liberate the soul.
- An ascetic as well as a householder can realise Brahman, the Supreme truth, through meditation and doing duties in a detached manner. Those who perform actions with attachment and ego are, however, subject to rebirth and caught in samsara cycles of birth and death.
- When a person realises Brahman, he goes beyond the illusory world and sees oneness in all beings.
- On the lines of other Upanishads, it also says that Self or Brahman is formless, pure, transcendental and imperishable. It is the source of everything in the universe. It can only be realised through meditation not by study or intellect.

Prashna Upanishad

Prashna means 'Questions'. This Upanishad discusses some very important aspects of spiritual wisdom like Self, Brahman, AUM, Origin of the Universe, etc. in the form of questions and answers; hence it has been named Prashna Upanishad. Sage Sukesha, Satyakama, Kausalya and Kabandi have put searching questions of great spiritual value and Sage Pippalada has enlightened the *Rishis* with suitable replies. A gist of questions and answers exchanged between the *Rishis* is given below.

Q1: *Rishi* Kabadi asked, "What is the source from which all beings are born?"

Ans: *Rishi* Pippalada replied: Prajpati, the Creator, first created Sun and Moon and all beings have come from them. The *Rishi* then elaborates the reply. Sun is the Energy, the Prana; Moon is Rayi, food or matter. Entire manifested universe has been evolved from Sun, the Prana, and Moon, the matter.

Q2: One of the Bhrigu's family saint asked, "How many Gods support a being, which of these manifest their power through it and who among them is the chief (God)?"

Ans: Saint Pippalada replied: Deities of air, fire, water, space, earth, speech, sight, hearing and mind sustain the beings. But Prana is Supreme and Prana sustains the beings through these deities. All these elements which support a being, draw their power from Prana which is same as Prajapati. The *Rishi* further clarifies that Prana is Sun, the Lord of lights, the rain, Indra, Rudra, the wind, the Earth, the subtle Elements and thus everything manifested and unmanifested.

In verse II.13, the *Rishi* prays to Prana: "You permeate and control the entire Universe. Therefore, protect us as a mother protects her sons. Bestow upon us prosperity and wisdom."

Q3: Kausalya asked "From where is the Prana born? How does it enter the body? How does it reside there? How does it depart from the body? How does it support the external and the internal?"

Ans: *Rishi* Pippalada replied: Prana is born from Self, or Atman.

- Prana enters the body due to actions of the mind, which means that whatever one is thinking at the time of death, he gets that incarnation; Prana and soul enter that body shaped by the last thoughts.
- Prana resides in eyes, ears, mouth and nose. Prana controls the organs of reproduction and excretion; controls the fire and hence distributes food all over the body.
- Atman resides in the heart.
- 'Udana' is responsible for rebirth. It takes the soul for rebirth depending upon the karmic fruit of actions; Virtuous deeds lead to good birth and vice versa.
- The External Prana is Sun.
- The *Rishi* Pippalada concludes that one who understands the various aspects of Prana is enlightened and gets immortality.

Q4: The grandson of Surya asked: "What are organs that go to sleep? Which organ remains awake? Which deity experiences dream? (In deep sleep) who experiences happiness? Into whom do all these merge?"

Ans: *Rishi* Pippalada replied: Just as Sun rays get unified at sunset, all the objects and senses get unified in mind during sleep. Senses are not active in sleep.

- Prana alone remains awake in the body during sleep.
- In the dream state, the mind experiences whatever it has seen or unseen, heard or unheard, real or imaginary, etc. This includes the memories of past, dreams of future, and what not.
- In the dreamless state, all these are merged in the Self, the Supreme Atman, just as birds return to their nests after flying.

Q5: Sage Satyakama asked, "If among men someone meditates on AUM until his death (throughout life), which world will he go to?"

Ans: *Rishi* Pippalada answered: The syllable AUM is the Supreme Brahman. Anyone who meditates on full AUM becomes unified with effulgent Sun. He is freed from sin, (just as a snake loses its skin), and reaches the world of Supreme-Brahman.

Q6: Sage Sukesha asked, "Where does person with sixteen parts dwell?"

Ans: ***Rishi* Pippalada replied:** Person who is called Purusha, from whom sixteen parts arise, dwell inside the body. He created Prana; from Prana He created faith, space, air, fire, water, earth, the organs, mind, food; from food virility, austerity, Vedic hymns, sacrifice the worlds and in the worlds He created forms and names.

All these sixteen parts rest in Him like spokes in the nave of a wheel. An aspirant who attains Purusha, his own identity disappears and he becomes one with Purusha, the Supreme Brahman, the Ultimate Reality, just as a river loses its identity, its name and form disappears, when it merges with the ocean.

Mahavakayas

There are four very important statements from the Upanishads and these are called "Mahavakayas"

These Mahavakayas are:

(I) **Aham Brahmasmi—I am Brahman**

(II) **Tat Tvam Asi—You are That (Brahman)**

(III) **Ayam Atma Brahma—This atman is Brahman**

(IV) **Prajnanam Brahma—Brahman is pure consciousness**

These statements contain profound truths. Brahman is the ultimate reality and it is of the nature of pure consciousness. Atman (soul) is also of the nature of pure consciousness. Therefore this Atman (soul) is one with that Brahman.

Pure consciousnass cannot be divided. There is only one Atman (soul) in all of us.

Summary of Vedas and Upanishad

It would be worthwhile to summarise the teachings of Vedas and Upanishad since entire Hindu philosophy is based on them.

According to Upanishads, Brahman is Supreme. He alone has created this complex universe. Just as a spider creates a web and resides in that, similarly Brahman has created this Universe and He permeates in all things, living and non-living. He is pure consciousness and therefore formless. He is called by various names like Nirgun Brahman, Sagun Brahman, Supreme, Purusha, Virat, Prana, Ishwar, God, Paramatman depending upon the context.

There is unity of soul in all living beings. The same soul is also called Brahman. Man is Divine because of this unity of soul between individual Self and Universal Self.

Upanishads tell us that goal of taking birth as humans is to realise the Self within. Though the same Self is in all beings, man only has the capacity to realise the Self within. Accordingly, those who are busy only in worldly pursuits, they are missing a great opportunity to reach the Brahman. Such worldly people return to this world again and again to reap the fruits of their actions.

The message of the Upanishads is, therefore, very clear. We should adopt teachings of Upanishads namely, acquire higher wisdom through reading and contemplation on scriptures, meditation, control of desires through control of senses and mind, devotion to God and thus strive to reach the ultimate state of 'Self-realisation'. Such a person, becomes free from samsara—the cycles of births and death; he achieves immortality; he is free from pleasures and pains (sukha and dukha) and is in a state of permanent bliss.

The techniques of realisation of Self or Brahman are already described in Chapter 1 of this book. These will be further discussed when we deal with Sri Mad Bhagvad Gita. All Puranas and other Hindu scriptures also cover this subject.

Puranas

By now, we know that the Vedas and Upanishads contain the ultimate truths of life. After the compilation of the Vedas and writing of Mahabharata, *Rishi* Vyasa was still uncomfortable. He had a feeling that common man will not be able to comprehend the philosophy of the Vedas; they are too complex for an ordinary mind to grasp and follow; hence a vast majority of humanity will continue to be deprived of the benefits of these great texts. Accordingly *Rishi* Vyasa, in consultation with *Rishi* Narada, created the Puranas, which contain the wisdom of the Vedas and Upanishads in the form of stories and in a style easily understandable to common man. The Puranas are estimated to have been written between 200 AD to 700 AD. As on today, the following 18 Maha Puranas and some Up Puranas are available. These are briefly described below:

Agni-Purana: This Purana was narrated by the Fire God to Sage Vashishtha who told it to Vyasa. It contains the stories of Mahabharata, Ramayana, astrology, architecture, medicines, meditation, the Bhagavad Gita, etc.

Shri Mad Bhagavata Purana: It is the most popular text dealing with the various Avtaras (Incarnations) of Lord Vishnu. It covers in great detail the life and glories of Shri Krishna. It also contains the story of the Creation of the universe, the story of Sage Kapila, the descent of Ganga on Earth, etc.

Bhavisya Purana: As the name suggests, this Purana contains the prediction of future events which include biblical and modern history, Islam, Buddhism, future kings, etc. It also contains a variety of subjects such as the creation of the Universe, the sixteen Samaskaras, worship of Sun God, importance of Vratas and charity, etc.

Brahma Purana: It describes the process of Creation starting from Manu and Shatrupa and subsequently their three sons namely Vira, Priyavrata and Uttanpada, father of great child devotee Dhruva. It also describes holy places of Puri, Konark and Bhubaneswar. It provides the details of geography of the world, story of Shri Krishna, etc.

Brahmanda Purana: Originally this Purana was narrated by Lord Vayu to Ved Vyasa. This Purana deals with the Creation of Universe, Kalpas, Yugas, Dissolution and annihilation of the Universe, Manavatras, Descent of Ganga on the earth, etc.

Interestingly a copy of this Purana has been found in Bali island of Indonesia, translated in Balinese language.

Garuda Purana: This Purana was narrated by Lord Vishnu to his divine carrier Garuda. This Purana is used to perform ceremonies at death and after death of a person in a Hindu family. It exhorts mankind to perform good deeds as told by the scriptures to avoid the painful journey of "jiva" after death. It also contains Ramayana, Mahabharata, astrology, astronomy, etc.

Kurma Purana: This Purana was narrated by Lord Vishnu to sage Narda in His Avatar as Kurma (Tortoise). It contains details of the churning of the ocean, 1000 names of Paravati, Ved Vyasa and his 28 names, major Vratas, rituals, the 28 incarnations of Lord Shiva, rites to be performed after death of a person, story of Dhruva, story of Vamana and Bali, etc.

Linga Purana: This Purana mainly deals with the worshipping of Lord Shiva. It contains worship of Lord Shiva with "Linga" as His symbol, various Avatars of Lord Shiva in each of the 28 Kaliyugas, one thousand names of Shiva, etc.

Matsya Purana: This Purana was narrated by Lord Vishnu in his incarnation as Matsya (fish). Lord Vishnu told Manu how to save all beings from the impending Pralaya (Dissolution). Manu did as he was told. When Pralaya (day of dissolution) came, Manu asked all beings to board his boat. This boat was pulled by Lord Vishnu in the form of Matsya with a snake as the rope to save all the life forms on earth.

It also contains the details of Creation, various vratas, fruits of giving 'dana' (charity), importance of holy places of Prayag (Allahabad), Varanasi, etc.

Naradiya Purana: This Purana narrates the teachings given to sage Narada by Shankara and others. This Purana is very useful as it contains the summary of all other Puranas. It contains the geography of earth, stories of Mrikandu and Markandeya, Sagara, Aditi's tapas, Vali, Bhagiratha and the descent of Ganga; importance of vratas like Ekadeshi vrata, Pooranmasi vrata, etc.

Skanda Purana: This Purana is the largest of all the Puranas. It is said that this Purana was narrated by Lord Shiva to Parvati, Parvati to Skanda, Skanda to Nandi, Nandi to Atri and Atri to Vyasa. It contains the story of Kartikeya, 180 Teeratha of Venkatachala Hills, importance of places of pilgrimage viz Kashi, Ujjain, Puri, sanctity of Dwarka; questions put to Prahlada by sages, abode of Trinity, Hindu Goddesses and various aspects of worship of Lord Shiva etc.

Vamana Purana: This Purana was narrated by Sage Pulastya to Saga Narda. It gives details of the ten avtaras of Vishnu, specially Vamanavatara. It also contains the ten properties of Dharma, meeting of Prahlada with Nara-Narayana and getting their blessings, importance of Ganga, doctrine of Karma, etc.

Varaha Purana: This Purana gives the teachings of Lord Vishnu in his incarnation as Varaha (the boar) to Bhudevi (the Earth) on the latter's request. Also contains dialogue between Lord Vishnu and Sage Narada, details of Karmas for salvation, installation of various idols, Goddess Parvati, Goddess Durga, Kubera, Kartikeya, Lord Rudra, importance of vrata, pilgrimage, benefits of 'dana' (charity), etc.

Vayu Purana: This Purana mentions the importance of Gaya, as a holy place, details of shraddhas and science of music, etc.

Vishnu Purana- This Purana is extremely popular. The philosophy of the Vedas find a mention in this Purana. This Purana teaches Bhakti Marga as the way for attaining liberation. It also covers the story of Dhruva, Prahalada, end of Yadavas, the Story of Shri Krishna, Pralaya, Creation, etc.

Brahmavaivarta Purana: Deals with the evolution of the universe from Brahma, emanation of Goddess Durga, Lakshmi, Saraswati from the Moolaprakirti, birth of Shri Ganesha and Sanmukha and story of Shri Krishna and His Divine consort Radha, etc. This Purana also touches Ayurveda, sacredness of Tulsi plant, code of conduct for married women and widows, etc.

Markandeya Purana: This Purana contains the replies given by Markandeya to Jaimini on his questions about incarnations of God. Markandeya directs Jaimini to four cataka birds living in the Vindhyachala mountain range. The birds, however, gave the same teachings which was given by Markandeya to Kraustuki. It also contains the story of Harishchandra, birth of Pandavas as the incarnation of deities to relieve Prithvi of her overburden, divine Leela of Lord Vishnu, etc. A very popular Hindu text Devimahatmya (also called Candi and Durgasaptasati) is also contained in this Purana.

Padma Purana: This Purana contains glorifying tales of Lord Vishnu. It has five sections namely.

- Srishti Khand-describes process of Creation, the manifestation of Goddess Lakshmi, origin of deities, etc
- Bhumi Khand-Earth, different types of sins and virtues, propagation of Vaishnavism, etc.
- Swarga Khand-Describes sanctity of holy places such as Bharatvarsha, Jambumarg, river Narmada, Amarkantak, Dharma teertha and sacred bath in Yamuna, Kashipuri, Gaya, etc.
- Patala Khand-contains tales of Sri Rama and Sri Krishna, demon king Ravana, etc.
- Uttara Khand-contains incarnations of Vishnu, dialogues between Lord Shiva and Goddess Paravati, stories of Rama and Krishna, etc.

Srimad Bhagavat Maha Purana

The most popular of all the Puranas is Srimad Bhagavad Mahapurana, popularly called as Bhagavatam. Narada had advised Brahmrishi Ved Vyasa to write a scripture containing the wisdom of Vedas and Mahabharata and at the same time, full of love and devotion towards the Supreme, so that by listening and chanting the name, glories and leelas of Shri Hari, the common man would be spiritually enlightened and attain mukti from samsara. With that noble mission in mind, *Rishi* Vyasa wrote Srimad Bhagavatam Mahapurana popularly called 'Bhagvatam'.

Rishi Shuka, son of Brahmrishi Ved Vyasa, occupies a central place in Bhagvatam. He too was a Brahmgyani (Self-realised) from birth. His piousness and holiness is reflected from the following story mentioned in Bhagavatam.

Shuka, being a born *Rishi* of his Own left home at an early age to live in the forest. *Rishi* Vyasa was following him shouting Putr, putr, putr (i.e. my son, son, son), requesting him to return home. On the way, a number of young women were taking bath in the Ganges, naked, without any clothes on their body. Shuka was also naked, without any consciousness of his body. The women did not bother and continued to take bath in the river. *Rishi* Vyasa, duly clad in clothes, was following Shuka. Seeing Vyasa, the women, however, immediately put on their clothes; *Rishi* Vyasa was amazed. He countered the women. "It is surprising that you continued to take bath in the river when my son Shuka passed from here but became conscious of your body when I passed though I am old and very well clad." The ladies replied, "O Sage, you have body consciousness, but Shuka does not, so we also had no body consciousness in his presence."

Sage Shuka was the first to listen to Bhagvatam from his father *Rishi* Vyasa. Shuka then narrated it to King Parikshit, the grandson of Arjuna at Hastinapur. King Parikshit was to die in a week's time under a curse, because of insulting sage Sameeka. Shuka narrated Bhagvatam to the king in his last seven days so that he is liberated from 'samsara'. At that time Sage Suta was also present along with many other holy people. Sage Suta later narrated the Katha to other holy people at Nemisharanya. This way Bhagvatam spread to the common man.

Originally Bhagvatam was completed in seven days by Sage Shuka. Since then, it is being completed in seven days in religious discourses. Though its recitation can be done any day, the months of Bhadrapada, Ashvin, Kartik, Margsheersh, Poha and Shravan (roughly August, September, October, November, December and January) are specially recommended. It is further advised that the Yajman (chief sponsor) should invite as many people as possible to get maximum benefit of the Katha for himself and others. The devotees are expected to observe celibacy and practise purity of thoughts and actions during the course of attending the discourse. The venue of Katha can be home/a hall or a calm and quiet place like a forest, mountain or the bank of a river.

Srimad Bhagavatam contains the wisdom of the Vedas and Upanishads; hence it has been given the status of a fifth Veda. This holy book contains 18000 Slokas in 12 Skandhas (sections). Each Skanda contains various chapters which cover different topics, e.g., chapter 3 of Skanda 1 covers various Incarnations of Lord Vishnu; chapter 1 of Skanda 2 contains the techniques of meditation and description of "Virat Swaroop" of God, etc.

Story of King Parikshit

Bhagvatam starts with the story of birth of King Parikshit. After the Mahabharata war was over, Ashvatthama, the son of Guru Dronacharya stealthily killed the five sons of Draupadi in the dead of night when they were sleeping in a tent. Draupadi, all the Pandavas and Shri Krishna were extremely angry by this ghastly act of Ashavatthama. Arjuna with the help of Shri Krishna located and caught Ashvatthama. Out of extreme fear, Ashvatthama launched his "Brahmastra" to kill the five Pandavas and the unborn son of Queen Uttara from Abhimanu. Arjuna also launched his "Brahmastra". Everybody was now afraid of the likely annihilation those weapons were to cause. Suddenly Ashvatthama's missile started heading towards Pandavas and Queen Uttara. Then on the request of Kunti and Uttara, Lord Krishna neutralised both the weapons and saved the Pandavas and baby Parikshit in the womb of Uttara. In due course of time, Uttara gave birth to Parikshit. It was forecast by the scholars that he would be a virtuous and brave king and that he would uphold the idealism of the Kaurava dynasty.

After the war, Yudhishtira ruled Hastinapur for some time observing Dharma while performing the duties of a king. Shri Krishna went to Dwarka. Entire Yadava clan perished by mutually killing each other at Prabhash Kshetra because of the curse of a *Rishi* and that of Gandhari. Shri Krishna too left his earthly body and went to Vaikuntha Dhama.

Sensing the shape of things to come in near future, after the demise of Shri Krishna, Yudhishtira immediately gave the throne of Hastinapur to his surviving grandson Parikshit and left for the Himalayas along with the other Pandavas and Draupadi. All the brothers and Draupadi perished on the way and Yudhishtira alone reached the gates of heaven with his physical body.

Sage Shuka narrating Bhagvatam to King Parikshit and other Rishis

This is how Parikshit became the king. He ruled Hastinapur for many years. He was an illustrious king full of virtues. The people of Hastinapur were very happy in his kingdom. One day when King Parikshit was out for hunting, he felt thirsty and entered the cottage of Sage Shamika and asked for water. The sage was in deep meditation and continued meditating. As bad luck would have it, King Parikshit felt insulted. He came out of the cottage in a bad mood and extremely angry. He lost his wisdom and put a dead snake, which was lying outside, around the neck of Sage Shamika. This act of Parikshit did not annoy

Sage Shamika but infuriated his son Sage Shringi. Shringi cursed Parikshit that he too would die on the seventh day with the bite of snake 'Takshaka'.

King Parikshit realised his mistake. He should not have insulted the Sage Shamika, that too when the later was in meditation. However, there was no going back. He decided to renounce the world and spend the seven days of his life in the company of *Rishis*, sages and contemplating on God. He gave the throne to his son Janamajaya. Leaving behind everything, he went to the bank of River Ganges and was soon surrounded by holy people. By the grace of God, Sage Shuka happened to reach the place while roaming in the forest. All the assembled sages and King Parikshit received Sage Shuka with great honour and delight. Parikshit requested Sage Shuka to bestow on him the necessary knowledge so that he is liberated from 'samsara'. Then Sage Shuka, who was a born "Brahm Giani" (knower of Self), narrated the Bhagvatam to Parikshit.

Contents of Bhagvatam

Bhagvatam is an ocean. It contains the philosophy of theVedas, stories of virtuous kings and divine people, stories of Creation, etc. It is not possible to cover all these topics in a small book. Only a few stories and few philosophical teachings have been mentioned to give an idea of its relevance and sacredness.

The Question Asked by King Parikshit

The first question King Parikshit asked Brahm *Rishi* Shuka was "O great master, as you have blessed me with your holy presence, I pray you to teach me as how men who are mortals, should conduct themselves in the world? What they should hear? What should they meditate upon and worship, etc.?

Shuka said to King Parikshit:

(I) "O king, you are great as you have desired to know the Truth to be practised to live in the world. Most of the people waste their life in earning bread and butter, seeking worldly comforts, wealth, etc. They totally forget the Almighty. A wise man, though living in the world, is not attached to it. He keeps his senses away from the worldly pleasures. He leads a simple life. He does actions but is not attached with its fruits or the sense of doership. He does everything in the name of God.

(II) Shuka continues, "The very purpose of human birth is to seek God. God is the only Truth. The visible world, its attractions, its comforts, are a great illusion. One should practise detachment from all these worldly attractions. The three-letter AUM is very powerful; it should be chanted with proper understanding. AUM is nothing but God only. The devotee should thus absorb himself in the Almighty. He will then get the heavenly bliss."

(III) Shuka then concludes, "Do thou, O king, therefore meditate on Him and identify with Him for He is the ultimate Truth."

Bhagvatam mentions about Creations — Brahma was the first born, Swaymbhu or self born. He was meditating as to how to create the Universe. His own self divided itself into two; one half became man and the other half became woman. The man was called Manu and woman Satarupa and entire mankind has come from them.

Two sons Priyavrata and Uttanpada and three daughters namely Akuti, Devahuti and Prasuti were born to Manu and Satarupa. Devahuti married Saint Kardama and gave birth to Kapila.

Kapila was born as a free soul, endowed with divine powers and wisdom. He is the father of 'Sankhya Philosophy' (Sankhya means Cosmic Wisdom) of Hindu philosophical thoughts which we have briefly mentioned under Hinduism in Chapter 1. His mother Devahuti too had a strong quest for spiritual life.

Bhagvatam narrates the discourse between *Rishi* Kapila and his mother Devahuti. It is a unique example of Hindu philosophy that a mother is asking the son to enlighten her about the purpose of life.

To begin with, Devahuti asks son Kapila, "Kindly tell me the knowledge which shall lead me towards freedom from the bondage of the world."

Kapila replied to the mother: "O mother, mind is responsible for our bondage to the world. Attachment to the worldly objects through senses and mind is the cause of bondage and misery. Give up the idea of doership like I, me and mine. Divert the mind to the devout men. Such men live in the company of God; their hearts are united with God. By living in such atmosphere, the devotee develops love for God. He no longer gets attracted towards worldly objects and forms, and becomes an enlightened soul and is freed from the bondage of the world.

Devahuti further asks, "Tell me son how I may love God which will lead me to freedom from bondage."

Rishi Kapila said: "Mother, I am the God, the lord of universe. I am Self in all beings. All natural forces like Sun, wind, clouds, fire draw their power from Me. Yogis worship Me. These people love Me and meditate on Me to attain salvation. (Note: Kapila is a Brahm Giani and he addresses his mother in first person as God to bring home the point.)

"Therefore, O, mother love the Almighty. Meditate on Him. Those who love Him, have affection for Him like their own children, have respect for Him as that of their Guru and surrender to Him, they become one with him."

Kapila continues: "Mother, feelings of love are of different degrees in the individuals. People have hatred, jealousy, anger and pride in their life but pretend to show love to God; such love is impure and such people are called "tamasika" devotees. Some people worship God and show their love for Him mainly to get the fulfilment of their material enjoyments; this love is called "rajasika" love. The real love is to love God for love alone, no desires are involved, that love is called "Satvika" love. Divine love is when the love, the lover and the loved have become one; when the devotee sees Him in all beings and loves all equally. The devotee then becomes united with Brahman."

"Mother, Now I will tell you how to reach to this ultimate stage of love towards divinity:

- Perform the duties of life without expectation of awards.
- Worship the God through Japas, meditation, discourses, kirtans, etc.
- Train the mind to see God in all beings; He is the Self in all beings; therefore love all and serve the God in the beings.
- Be kind to the poor and needy. Do charities regularly.
- Respect the holy people.
- By this way of life, the heart of devotee gets purified and he gets the vision of God."

Devahuti, then asked Kapila to enlighten her about Yoga of Meditation.

Kapila replies: Mother I will tell you about Yoga of Meditation, by following which mind gets absorbed towards God. This Yoga has several stages to be followed and practised to attain the highest .

The first stage is purification of mind by following the prescribed techniques. The aspirant should learn to:

- Control the mind and senses, practice detachment from the world.
- Observe non violence by thoughts, words and deeds.
- Observe celibacy.
- Study the Scriptures, speak the Truth, Respect the holy people, be contented.
- Do the yoga asanas and practise sitting in an erect position for a long time to facilitate meditation.
- Do charities and observe vratas (fasts).
- By the practice of above techniques, mind becomes pure and steady.
- Then yogi should concentrate on the beautiful image of God and feel His divinity.
- The yogi then meditates and fixes his mind on Him till mind gets fully absorbed in the God.

At this stage, all beings look equal to him; he sees Brahman in all and he is in a state of permanent bliss.

O Mother, it is very unfortunate that a worldly person wastes his precious life in obtaining wealth in the form of wife, children, house, cattle, etc. These possessions are only temporary and they are subject to decay and loss. In the process he unknowingly commits lot of sins in order to maintain himself and his family. Ultimately, he becomes old. He develops lots of health problems; he is totally at the mercy of people around him .He suffers in old age as per his fruits of action. Now he remembers God and prays to God for deliverance from the world but then it is too late. Human beings should remember that whatever good or bad a man does to maintain the family, he has to bear the fruit of those deeds by himself alone and nobody else.

Kapila further enlightens Devahuti as to how a Jiva (soul) takes birth in the human yoni; how by the union of a woman and man, life is conceived, how the embryo develops, how it gradually gets the senses, mind, intellect and soul; how the Jiva cries from pain and prays to God for deliverance. The baby brings with him the 'samskaras' of previous birth, the fruits of which have to be borne in this and subsequent births.

Kapila concludes, "Mother, those people who do their duties with the observance of Dharma, unattached, and dedicate the actions to God, their minds are purified gradually, and ultimately they realise the Brahman. The realisation of Brahman, the unity of individual Soul with the Universal Soul is the ultimate goal of human birth otherwise one is caught in the 'samsara', the painful cycles of birth and death.

Devahuti was enlightened with the knowledge imparted by her son *Rishi* Kapila; She followed the teachings of Kapila and was liberated from 'samsara'.

Teachings on the lines of Kapila are covered in Bhagvatam under various stories of saints, holy people, *Rishi* Narda and at times of Brahma himself coming down to earth and explaining the ultimate Truth of life for the benefit of the individual devotee and people.

Bhagvatam also contains the story of child devotee Dhruva who was given divine status by the Lord. It also contains the story of King Pruthi, a descendent of Dhruva. Pruthi was a noble king; Lord Vishnu himself appeared before him when he performed a yajna and taught him the wisdom which leads to salvation. Later Sage Santkumara taught him the divine wisdom. Equipped with divine wisdom, he practised meditation and realised the divinity within.

It also contains the story of Prachetas. They were virtuous persons, who renounced the world at a later stage of life. Sage Narada enlightened them with divine wisdom and told them of the path of liberation from 'samsara'. They followed the teachings of Narada and got united with the Supreme.

In the fifth book, Bhagvatam contains the story of Priyavarata, second son of Manu. He was a noble soul and devoted to the love of God. He wanted to leave the world at a very early age but his father Manu and the Lord Himself prevailed upon him to rule the earth and serve humanity. He did that duty towards the mankind and later renounced the world and got united with the Almighty.

In the seventh Skanda, Bhagvatam contains the story of the child Prahlada, who was a devotee of Vishnu since childhood. His father, Hiranakashipu, was the king of Daitays (demons). Hiranakashipu became the ruler of three worlds and he ordered the people to worship him only and not the Supreme, Lord Vishnu. But Prahlada, true to his conviction, continued to regard only Vishnu as the ultimate reality. Hiranakashipu was greatly annoyed by his son. He tried all methods, persuasion or coercion to make Prahlada not to worship Vishnu but of no avail. Once during such events, Hirankashipu challenged Prahlada asking whether Vishnu existed in a pillar. To which Prahlada said that Vishnu existed in the pillar also. The king was infuriated and rushed to kill Prahlada. The Lord Vishnu immediately appeared as Narisimha—half man and half lion—from the pillar and killed Hirankashipu. Prahlada was then made the king and after his earthly existence, he was united with the Supreme.

In the eighth Skanda, Bhagvatam contains the story of asur king Bali and how his pride was humbled by Lord Vishnu in the guise of a dwarf as a Brahmin. Bali had undergone penance for thousands of years and was blessed by Lord. He defeated Indra and became the monarch of three worlds. Lord Vishnu then took birth as son to Kashyap and Aditi but in the form of a dwarf. Once Bali performed a yajna and invited all Brahmins to participate. Vishnu, the dwarf too attended the yajna. Bali was much pleased with his presence. Then the Brahmin (Vishnu) dwarf requested Bali to grant him three steps of land. Bali was amused and requested for more land as three steps were too small. Dwarf insisted for only three steps. The boon was granted. In first step, the dwarf covered the Earth; in the second step, he covered the heaven and rest of the universe. Now nothing was left to be covered in third step. Bali realised the dwarf's divinity and was humbled. Bali offered his head to dwarf for the third step. The Lord was pleased; He placed the third step on Bali's head. Bali was thus humbled but united with God.

It also contains the story of Raj *Rishi* Rishbhdeva who was a noble king and at the same time was an enlightened soul. He was a Brahmgiani (knower of Brahma) from birth. He was son of Nabhi and grandson of Priyavarta. He taught his sons the highest Truth. He gave the kingdom to his elder son Bharata and became a 'sanyasi'. He did meditation and got united with Brahma.

In the seventh Skanda, Bhagvatam contains a dialogue between Narada and Yudhishtira. Narada enlightens Yudhishtira about the four Varnas, four stages of life, purpose of life, the duties of a householder and how a man should conduct himself in life so that he is relieved from 'samsara', etc.

Through such stories and dialogues, Bhagvatam brings spiritual wisdom to the devotees so that they develop love and devotion towards Shri Hari and attain 'mukti' (Liberation) – freedom from cycle of birth and death.

Throughout the texts, Bhagvatam narrates the glories of God, various incarnations of Vishnu in which He came to earth, acted for the welfare of devotees, mankind and all beings. A brief purpose for which God came on earth in various incarnations is given below.

- 1st Incarnation was of four Sant Kumars. In this incarnation Lord revived the knowledge of Self among the saints and holy people.
- 2nd Incarnation was of The Boar or Varaha and killed demon Hiranyaksha for the welfare of beings.
- 3rd Incarnation was born as Narada and spread the message of virtues like 'Nishkama Karmas'.
- 4th Incarnation was born as Nara-Narayna for the propagation of Dharma.

- 5th Incarnation was born as Kapila from Devahuti, the daughter of Manu. In this incarnation, Lord as *Rishi* Kapila revived Sankhya philosophy — Cosmic Wisdom which was getting extinct.
- 6th Incarnation was born as Dattatreya from Sage Atri and wife Anasuya and taught Brahmvidya. He was purity personified.
- 7th Incarnation was born as Yagyadeva, son of Ruchi Prajapati and Aakoothi.
- 8th Incarnation was born as Sage Rishabhdeva, son of Sage Nabhi and Merudevi for establishing the norms of Grihasthashrama.
- 9th Incarnation was born as Prithu who milked (extracted) from the earth in the form of cow, various nutrients like cereals and pulses, etc. to save all beings on earth when there was severe drought which could have killed all life forms.
- 10th Incarnation was born as Matsya and protected the life of all beings of the world from the deluge, floods, which were caused by the great 'pralaya' – (dissolution). Manu saved all beings by putting them in his boat; the boat was pulled by Lord Vishnu, Incarnate as Matsya
- 11th Incarnation was born as Kurma (Tortoise). Lord Vishnu turned 'Kurma' facilitated 'samundramanthan'– churning of the Ocean by holding the Mandarachala mountain on his back when the mountain started sinking.
- 12th Incarnation was born as Dhanvantri and revealed the medicines for the welfare of living beings. Dhanvantri is said to be the first physician. He brought medical science on earth. Indian system of medicine called Ayurveda based on herbs is his gift to mankind.
- 13th Incarnation was of enchanting beauty Mohini. Vishnu incarnated as Mohini lured the demons and took possession of "Amrita" nectar bowl and handed over to same to devas, when ocean was churned jointly by devas and demons.
- 14th Incarnation was of Narasimha (Man-Lion) who came out of a pillar and protected Devotee Prahlad from the tyranny of his demon father Hiranaykashipu.
- 15th Incarnation was of Vamana (the Dwarf), a Brahmin, who humbled the pride of asura Bali by asking for three steps of land.
- 16th Incarnation was of *Rishi* Parashuram, born as son of sage couple Jamdaagni and Renuka, to eliminate Kshatriya kings on the earth as their acts had become highly immoral and thus restored the welfare of holy people and Brahmins.
- 17th Incarnation was born as *Rishi* Vyasa from the union of *Rishi* Parasher and Satyawati. Brahmrishi Ved Vyasa compiled the Vedas, wrote the Mahabharata and the Puranas for the welfare of humanity.
- 18th Incarnation was born as Lord Rama to rid the earth from the most notorious demon Ravana and other demons.
- 19th Incarnation was of Lord Krishna who was magical, did superhuman deeds, always helped his devotees in need. He established 'Dharma' by assisting the

Pandavas in the killing of mighty Kauravas in the battle of Kurushetra. To the Hindus, He is de facto, Supreme God.

- 20th Incarnation was born as Balarama—elder brother of Lord Krishna, did deeds for the welfare of mankind individually and with Shri Krishna.
- 21th Incarnation was born as Gautam Buddha; did severe 'Tapasya', got divine enlightenment through meditation; thereafter propagated eight fold path as a way to eliminate sufferings of the people.
- 22th Incarnation is forecasted that the 22nd Incarnation shall be of Kalki, son of a Brahmin named Vishnuyasha, for liberating the earth from sinners in Kaliyuga.

Shri Krishna and his Divine Deeds

Shri Krishna was the most magical of all incarnations. He performed superhuman deeds and killed many cruel demons like Kansa, for the welfare of mankind. His noble deeds are widely discussed and narrated in religious discourses throughout India. In the entire Bhagvatam, His leelas have been mentioned in various contexts. Any write-up on the Bhagavatam will not be complete without mentioning the glories and divine acts of Lord Krishna. Therefore, some salient welfare deeds done by Shri Krishna are described below.

Birth of the Lord: When Lord Krishna was born as their eighth baby, Devki, his mother, and Vasudeva, his father, were in the prison of Kansa at Mathura. It was forecast that the eighth baby of Devki and Vasudeva would kill Kansa; since then Kansa had put Devki and Vasudeva in prison. Both Devaki and Vasudeva were worried that cruel king Kansa would kill baby Krishna also. However, Lord Krishna, as a baby told the anxious parents not to worry and told them what was to be done. Father Vasudeva acted as told by the baby Krishna. As per divine will, suddenly, the prison gates opened automatically and the guards went to sleep. Vasudeva could escape and carried the baby to Gokul across the River Yamuna to Nand Baba's house. He exchanged the two babies and brought the baby girl of Yashodha and Nand Baba and gave it to Devki. The gates got closed and guards woke up from sleep as if nothing had happened the previous night. This is how Lord Krishna got himself saved from the cruel hands of Kansa.

Redemption of Pootna: Kansa was suspicious and vigilant about his potential killer in Mathura and around. He deputed Pootna, a demoness to kill all new-born babies in and around Mathura. Pootna had powers to change her size, shapes, etc. She poisoned her breasts and went to meet the child at Nand Baba's house. She started feeding the baby from her poisoned breasts. Lord was not affected by the poison on the breasts; instead Pootna felt extremely uncomfortable. Ultimately she collapsed at the site revealing her real form of a demoness. Nevertheless Lord Krishna did his divine duty and gave Pootna salvation.

Universe in the mouth: One day Krishna was lying down and Yashodha was helping him to sleep. Shri Krishna happened to yawn which Yashodha was watching. She was amazed to see the entire universe in the mouth of Krishna. She saw the galaxies, the stars, the Sun, Moon, the earth and other planets, all forms of living beings, the mankind seas, rivers, and mountains and what not.

Demon Bakasur: Demon Bakasur, brother of Pootna, in the form of a crane bird, lifted child Krishna in its beak to kill him. Krishna tore open the beak up to his throat and killed the crane. Bakasur was however, liberated by the Lord.

Demon Aghasura: Kansa sent demon Aghasura to kill Krishna. Aghasura turned himself into a huge python and sat in the usual path of cowherds. His mouth was so huge that it looked like a cave. Boys fell into his trap. They went inside the mouth of the demon along with their cattle and got trapped. Krishna knew the game plan but he arrived late at the scene. To save the children and cattle, he went inside the mouth of python. He expanded his own size so much that it killed the python Aghasura and saved the children also.

Kalia: Serpent Kalia had polluted the village pond with his venom. The village animals were not able to drink its water. One day while playing with other children, Krishna hit the ball to the pond knowingly. He then jumped in the pond under the pretext of recovering the ball. He dived to the bottom of pond where serpent was hiding. He caught hold of Kalia and squeezed it very forcefully. Kalia begged for life. Shri Krishna spared Kalia on the condition that he would vacate the pond. Kalia had no option and left the pond for good.

Shri Krishna and Kalia

Goverdhan mount lifted by krishna'

Mount Goverdhan: Lord Indra ordered torrential rains over Braja area with the bad intention of flooding it. Everybody in Vraj was in panic. Shri Krishna understood the intentions of Indra. He lifted mount Govardhana on his little finger and asked the people to come under the mountain along with their cattle. The rains continued for seven days. Indra realised his mistake and he descended from heaven and begged pardon from Lord Krishna.

Krishna fulfilled the extreme desire of the Gopies when he danced with hundreds of them together in what is called a divine dance, 'Rasa leela'. It was the intense craving of each gopi to possess Him. Through His 'maya'(divine power), He made each gopi experience as if, Krishna was dancing with her only physically.

Raas Leela

Once Krishna and Balarama were dancing and singing with gopies in a night-long celeberation. Demon Shankhachoora came and grabbed a few gopies and fled away. Krishna and Balarama ran after the demon. They overpowered him. Krishna hit the demon on his head and killed him.

Demon Vyomasura entered in their group disguised as a shepherd boy and started taking away the sheep. He would hide the sheep in a cave. Krishna could sense his secret activity. He killed the demon and thus saved the sheep.

King Kansa hatched a plan to eliminate both Krishna and Balarama in a dual fight. He sent Akroora, a common relative, to bring both Krishna and Balarama to Mathura to participate in the local sports. Both Krishna and Balarama came to Mathura along with many Yadavas knowing fully that Kansa had a plan to eliminate them. Still they went to the wrestling competition. At the gate of the stadium, they were stopped by an elephant. The 'mahavat' (driver of elephant) made the elephant attack them. Shri Krishna swung sideways, grabbed the elephant by its tusks and killed it. Later on they were asked to face two giant wrestlers. Shri Krishna wrestled with Chanoor and Balarama with Mushitika. Both Balaram and Krishna killed their opponents with severe blows.

Seeing the failure of his plans, Kansa was infuriated. He was screaming out of rage and in his frustration he ordered his people to kill Krishna and Balarama. Shri Krishna was already very alert. He ran towards Kansa, caught hold him by his hair and punched him in his chest till the cruel king died. Shri Krishna installed Ugrasena, on the throne of Mathura. People of Mathura were thus relieved of the cruel Kansa.

➤ When Kansa was killed, his two wives Asti and Prapti became widows. They were the daughters of Jarasandha, the powerful king of Magadha. Jaransandha was highly annoyed with Balarama and Krishna. To take revenge, he attacked Mathura seventeen times to kill Krishna and Balarama and other prominent Yadava people but every time he was defeated. Later Jarasandha made an alliance with Kalyavana to attack Mathura with greater force. Krishna was already prepared. He shifted the entire population of Mathura to a new capital at Dwarka. When Kalyavana attacked Mathura, Krishna challenged him in a one on one battle. He very cleverly took Kalyavana to a cave where Muchukunda was sleeping. Muchukunda was his enemy and got extremely angry when disturbed from sleep and killed Kalyavana by emanating a strong beam of fire from his eyes. Mathura was a ghost town now and Jarasandha had to go back empty-handed.

➤ Rukmini, princess of Vidurbha, wanted to marry Krishna but her brother Rukmi wanted to marry her to his friend Shishupala in a 'swayamawara'. Rukmini sent a message to Krishna and told Him of her wish Shri Krishna made a plan and abducted Rukmini when she was on her way to the temple to worship the deities. Rukmi, the brother of Rukmini, was defeated by Shri Krishna when the former opposed his carrying away of Rukmini. Shri Krishna brought Rukmini to Dwarka and formally married her. In a similar way Lord Krishna married Satyabhama and Kalindi. He also married princess Mitravinda who chose Him in a swayamvara and defeated her brothers when they protested. Shri Krishna wed Princess Satya of Kosala in a 'swayamvara' by fulfilling the condition of the swayamvara of yoking seven rough and tough bulls at a time. In all these alliances, Shri Krishna respected and fulfilled the desires of these women.

- Lord Krishna relieved 16000 princesses from the clutches of demon Bhaumasura by riding on his carrier Garuda and adopting aerial attacks. Later, on their wishes, He married these 16000 princesses and provided them individual palaces, etc. in Dwarka.

Aniruddha was the grandson of Krishna. Aniruddha happened to fall in love with Usha, daughter of demon Banasura. Banasura managed to hold Aniruddha captive. Banasura had the protection of Lord Shiva. Shri Krishna and Balarama raided Banasura, defeated him and his army and brought Aniruddha and Usha to Dwarka and arranged their marriage.

Krishna freed twenty thousand kings in the prison of Jarasandha, the king of Magadha. It was difficult to engage Jarasandha in a fight, etc. He took Bhima, the Pandava, and went to Jarasandha in the guise of a Brahmin and begged for a wrestling duel with Bhima. The duel continued for 27 days but results were not coming. Krishna then revealed to Bhima the weak part of Jarasandha's body. Acting on that tip, Bhima tore apart Jarasandha in two pieces. The 20,000 kings were freed and resumed ruling their kingdom. These kings later supported Yudhishtira in the Mahabharata war.

Shri Krishna with Sudershan Chakra in the assembly of kings

Sishupala misbehaved, rather insulted, Shri Krishna and Bheeshma beyond limits in the august assembly of kings and elders called by Yudhishtira on the occasion of Rajsuya Yajna ceremony in their new capital at Indraprastha. Shri Krishna did not want to spoil the decorum of the Yajna; He initially warned Shishupala that he would be excused up to 100 invectives but not a word beyond. Shishupala did not pay heed to the warning and continued his onslaught. Shri Krishna then beheaded Shishupala with His 'Sudershan Chakra', (divine weapon) when all the invited kings were in full attendance.

Draupdi being maltreated in Kauravas assembly'

Shri Krishna saved the honour of Draupadi in the Kaurava assembly when she was dragged and was being undressed by Dushashan. Everybody, including the Kaurava patriarch Bheeshma and the mighty Pandavas, expressed their helplessness to protect the honour of Draupadi on the pretext of

Dharma. Draupadi then remembered Shri Krishna. Lord of the Universe then appeared and extended the saree of Draupadi infinitely. Ultimately the cruel Dushashna got exhausted and fell on the floor and the honour of Draupadi and of entire womankind was saved.

Shri Krishna played a decisive role in the war of the Mahabharata. But for his blessings, the Pandavas would not have won the bloodiest battle in the world in which millions were killed. Shri Krishna became the charioteer of Arjuna. He guided Arjuna and managed to kill all the Kauravas' great warriors such Bheeshma, Karna, Dronacharya, Salya and lastly Duryodhana.

Krishna and Arjuna in war

However, before the war started, Arjuna saw on the opposite side all his elders, cousins, friends, relatives, etc. He was overcome by grief at the thought of killing all those near and dear ones. He gave up the Gandeeva bow and told Shri Krishna that he did not want to be party to that bloodshed. Shri Krishna knew that without Arjuna, the war could not be won and in any case the Kauravas had to be killed to establish Dharma. Shri Krishna then gave Arjuna (in the midst of battlefield) His highly philosophical discourse which is famously known as Srimad Bhagavad Gita. He taught Arjuna the basis of existence, duty of individuals, paths which lead to salvation, etc. and thus motivated him to only fight and not to think otherwise. Arjuna was enlightened. He lifted the Gandeeva bow, blew his conch and announced his readiness to fight. He decimated the Kauravas and secured victory for the Pandavas.

Sudama, childhood friend of Shri Krishna, was extremely poor, virtually having no income to survive. On the advice of his wife, Sudama went to Dwarka to meet Krishna. He was quite hesitant to face the Lord of Universe. On getting the news of Sudama's arrival, Shri Krishna rushed to the gates setting aside all protocols, hugged Sudama, brought him inside the palace, washed his feet and served him food in His presence. Sudama hesitantly could not ask anything from the Lord. Apparently, Sudama took leave empty handed, but when he reached home, his hut had disappeared and a palace was standing there. Sudama's wife and children were very well dressed and extremely happy with the grace of Lord Krishna.

In the 11th Skanda, Bhagvatam describes the end of the earthly life of Lord Krishna. Entire Yadava clan met their end at Prabhas Kshetra in the presence of Shri Krishna. Sri Krishna too left for his heavenly abode 'Vaikuntha Loka'. He was lying under a tree and was hit by the arrow from a hunter by the name Jara. Lord gave his parting message to His great friend and devotee Uddhava. The last message of Shri Krishna is popularly called 'Uddhava Gita'.

By reading and listening to the Bhagvatam regularly, devotees are exposed to the leelas (glories of God), the various divine deeds done by God for the welfare of the beings, etc. The devotee starts believing in the divinity of God and becomes a God lover, and continuing their journey further, reaches Shri Hari.

Humanity is grateful to *Rishi* Vyasa. The Puranas have fulfilled their objectives. Day in and day out Indians are attending to the discourses, based on Puranas, to satisfy their spiritual quest and to lead a pure life.

Hindu Scriptures – Ramayana

Ramayana is a very popular epic of Hindus. The original epic was written by *Rishi* Valmiki around 5th century B.C. in the Sanskrit language. Since then Ramayana has been translated in many languages but Ramacharitmanas written by Saint Goswamy Tulsidas in Brajbhasha has been the most popular. Ramacharitmanas is basically a document of devotion; Tulsidas has poured his heart out in glorifying Shri Rama through this writing. He has very beautifully portrayed Vishnu incarnate Shri Rama as a human being doing his duties as a son, brother, husband and king in an ideal manner; at the same time Shri Rama is God, the Supreme being, the Universal Soul of Vedas. The common man has been greatly benefitted by Ramacharitmanas. Day in and day out, discourses, kirtans, based on Ramcharitmanas are held all over India. Recitation of Sunderkand Path (chapter) of Ram Charitmanas is generally done on important occasions such as marriage in a Hindu family. Ramayana belongs to Treta Yuga (which came after Satyuga).

Kands of Ramayana (Ram Charitmanas)

Ramayana has eight sections called Kands. These are:

Bal Kand: This Kand deals with the birth and childhood of Shri Rama and other brothers in the family of Dashratha, king of Ayodhya; their training by Sage Vishvamitra, the marriage of Shri Rama with Sita, preparation for the coronation of Lord Rama for the kingdom of Ayodhya.

Ayodhya Kand: This Kand deals with the grief of Dashratha over sending his virtuous son Rama to exile to keep his promise given to queen Kaikeyi. Shri Rama proceeds to exile for fourteen years along with Sita and Lakshmana.

Aranya Kand: This Kand describes the life of Shri Rama, Sita and Lakshmana in the forest and abduction of Sita by demon king Ravana.

Kiskindha Kand: This Kand describes Rama meeting Sugreeva, the Vanara king (monkey king) of Kiskindha and Hanumana. Sugreeva pledges support to Rama to trace Sita.

Sunder Kand: This Kand describes about Hanumana flying to Lanka, locates Sita in Ashok Vatica imprisoned by Ravana. Hanumana burns Lanka and returns with the proof of meeting Sita.

Lanka Kand: This Kand describes the war between Rama and Ravana. Rama raids Lanka with Sugreeva, Hanumana and their monkey sena. Rama kills Ravana, Kumbha

Karna and Meghnada, brother and son respectively of Ravana, and recovers Sita. Rama returns to Ayodhya with Sita and Lakshmana and asumes the throne of Ayodhya.

Uttar Kand: It describes the coronation of Lord Rama. His kingdom was the ideal, popularly known as 'Ramarajya'. Sita is abandoned and goes to *Rishi* Valmiki's ashram. Rama performs Ashawmedha Yajna.

Lava Kush Kand: It describes the birth of Lava and Kusha in the ashram of Valmiki. Lava and Kusha intercept the Ashvamedha Horse and defeat everybody in battle. Sita is accepted by mother Earth and Lord Rama too goes to His heavenly abode.

The Story of Ramayana

King Dashratha with his four sons

- Dashratha was the king of Ayodhya. He had three wives, namely Kaushalya, Kaikeyi and Urmila. He belonged to the Suryavanshi dynasty, which was famous for their virtues. For a long time, the king did not get a child from any of the queens. He was frustrated. On the advice of Guru Vashishtha, he did the Putreshti Yajna with the help of sage Shringi. With the blessings of *Rishis*, in due course of time, Kaushlaya gave birth to Rama, Kaikeyi to Bharata and Urmila to the duo Lakshmana and Shatrughana. Shri Rama was first to be born on Navami (ninth day) of Shuklapaksh (bright fortnight) of the Chaitra month of the Hindu calendar. Guru Vashishtha did the Naamkarana ceremony of all the four babies. He also told Dashratha that all the four shall be virtuous sons. Dashratha was a happy person now.
- One day Kaushlaya gave a bath to baby Rama and placed him in bed to sleep. She then sat for her morning 'pooja' in her private temple and offered to the deities some sweets as 'prasadam'. She happened to go to kitchen for some work. When she returned to the temple, she found baby Rama eating the sweets. She hurried to the bed and found Rama sleeping. She again came to the temple but she again found Rama eating the sweets. She was shocked and amazed.
- **Seeing her predicament, baby Rama showed her his divinity. Kaushlaya saw the entire universe, the galaxies, the stars, the oceans, the mountains, the rivers, all living beings, the creatures, the Sun and Moon and what not. Kaushlaya was stunned and speechless. Rama comforted her and turned himself again into small baby, thereby giving Kaushalaya, a great relief. Rama asked her not to disclose the incident to anyone.**
- All the four princes were trained by *Rishi* Vashistha in the knowledge of Vedas , other scriptures, political science, administration, economics, etc. They were also trained in the techniques of warfare and archery by different experts of the subject.
- At that time, *Rishi* Vishwamitra was living in the forest. The *Rishi* and other holy people

in the Ashram were engaged in spiritual activities but there was always the nuisance of demons, specially Mareech and Subhahu. Vishwamitra decided to take the help of Rama to eliminate these two demons; He knew that Lord Vishnu had already taken birth as an incarnation in Rama to eliminate these monsters from earth.

Vishwamitra taking away Rama and Lakshmana

- Accordingly one day *Rishi* Vishvamitra went and requested Dashratha to send Rama and Lakshmana to forest to eliminate the demons. As a first reaction, Dashratha offered an army to handle the demons because the princes were too young for the job; but the *Rishi* knew that God incarnate Rama only can finish them. On the intervention of guru Vashishtha and with a heavy heart, Dashratha sent Rama and Lakshmana with the *Rishi* Vishvamitra. On the way, a she- demon 'Tadka' pounced upon them. Rama was already alert and he killed Tadka immediately. Later Lakshmana killed demon Subhau and Rama made demon Mareecha fly hundreds of miles away to the sea. With the killing and driving away of these demons, peace returned to the forest. The *Rishis* completed their Yajnas properly.
- Sita was the daughter of King Janaka of Mithila. When she was of marriageable age, Janaka announced her wedding through a 'Swayamvara' choosing the groom by her self. *Rishi* Vishvamitra was also invited and he took Rama and Lakshmana to Mithila to attend the Swayamvara. On the way, fell the statue of Ahalya, wife of Sage Gautma. Visvamitra told Rama the story of Ahalya, how she was cursed and was turned in a stone. On the advice of *Rishi* Vishvamitra, Rama touched the statue; Ahalya immediately appeared in full elegance. She prayed to the Lord for her deliverance. Rama blessed her and Ahalya was liberated.
- **Story of Ahalya:** Ahalya was the wife of *Rishi* Gautama. She was beautiful as well as pious. Lord Indra fell in love with her. He played a trick One day he transformed himself as Gautama and slept with her. When Gautama returned from the meditation in the morning, he found Indra in the hut. *Rishi* suspected his wife's fidelity. Indra escaped but *Rishi* cursed Ahalya and turned her to a stone.
- *Rishi* Vishwamitra along with Rama and Lakshmana reached Mithila. King Janaka welcomed the *Rishi* and received them with full honour. They were made to stay in a most comfortable palace. Next day, Rama and Lakshmana went to the palace garden to pick up

Ahalya coming to life

flowers for the morning pooja (worship). At that time, Sita too was on her way to the Gauri temple as part of her morning ritual. Sita's close friends happened to see both the brothers. They were awe struck with the divine beauty of Shri Rama. Sita also saw Him stealthily and was struck by his grace. From that moment she and all her friends prayed for Rama's victory in the Swayamvara.

- On the day of the Swayamvara, the stage was set for the event. The invited guests took their seats as per their status. *Rishi* Vishvamitra and Lord Rama and Lakshmana too were seated. Sita came to the venue with a garland in her hands. She was a divine beauty, who cannot be described in words. The devas welcomed her by showering flowers and the celestial dancers danced in sheer joy. A formal announcement was made regarding the conditions of the Swayamvara – that whosoever lifts, strings and breaks the bow of Lord Shiva, shall win the hand of Sita in marriage. Unfortunately no one among the invited kings and princes could lift the bow. All the assembled kings were feeling highly embarrassed over their inability to break the bow. King Janaka and queen mother of Sita were repenting for having put such a severe condition for Sita's marriage; a fear gripped them lest Sita should remain unwed throughout her life. There was, therefore, an uneasy calm in the entire assembly. Lakshmana was agitated and wanted to prove his might but he was restrained by Rama and he remained seated. Then on the advice of *Rishi* Vishwamitra, Rama moved forward and went where the bow was kept. He very comfortably lifted the Shiva bow, strung it and broke it. He did these acts so swiftly that nobody could see him lifting the bow, putting the string and breaking it; the assembly only witnessed that Rama approached the bow and it was in two pieces. The entire scene changed. Janak and queen mother expressed gratitude to *Rishi* Vishwamitra. An inwardly jubilant Sita garlanded Rama as a token of accepting Him as her husband. Devas, *Rishis* showered blessings on the couple from heaven.

Sita's Swayamvara

- Amid this jubilation, *Rishi* Parshuram appeared on the scene. Parashuram is said to be 16th Incarnation of Vishnu.; He took birth to save earth from the tyrannies of kshatriyas and restore the Dharma and dignity of Brahmins. He was anger personified and would eliminate his enemy under the slightest pretext. Knowing his nuisance value

Parushurama on the occasion of Swaymvara

and to ward off any unpleasant happening, every body including King Janaka and his queen Sita, Rama and Lakshmana and other kings offered their salutations to him. On his asking, every thing was explained to him but it did not satisfy him. Habitually he said "how dare any one break the bow of Shiva; he has to suffer from my hands". King Janaka and others pacified him but he was hurling out abuses, insults and openly boasting of his power of destruction. Lakshmana too got angry and wanted to fight with Parashuram. Shri Rama, however, kept His calm and asked the *Rishi* to forgive Lakshmna. Parashuram did not pay heed and continued his onslaught unabated. Shri Rama then clearly told Parshurama "we, the Raghuvanshi, are not afraid of any king or battle like a true kshatraiya, come what may, even if we have to lay down our life". Parashuram decided to test the courage of Shri Rama and asked Shri Rama to break the bow of Vishnu (which he was holding). The *Rishi* then offered the bow to Rama. To every body's surprise, the bow itself started moving towards Shri Rama. Parashuram was taken aback. He realized the divinity of Shri Rama. He begged his pardon from the Lord and started shouting slogans in His praise and went away. Every body was relieved as an ugly face-off got averted.

- King Janak sent the news of Rama winning the hand of Sita to Ayodhya through two ambassadors. There were jubilations in the palace as well as in the city. An imposing marriage party consisting of Dashratha, Bharata and Shatrughana, *Rishi* Vashishtha and other prominent family members, friends and citizens, chariots decorated with jewels and gems, extremely swift and elegant horses, smart and handsome riders, lots of gifts of all types was were arranged and set out for Mithila.
- There were all good omens when the marriage party led by Dashratha started from Ayodhya. A nevla, a crow, and a Neelkantha, all signs of good omen, were sighted. The wind was intoxicating, cool, and was blowing gently. The marriage party was received by King Janaka accompanied by his ministers, guru, relatives amid beating of drums, musical instruments, dancers and auspicious songs sung by the women dressed in their colourful best. Devas too joined the celebrations as 'Baratees' in the guise of Brahmins.
- Sri Parvati, Lakshmi, Saraswati and Indrani were watching, enjoying and blessing Shri Rama and Sita. They joined the inner circle of the family in the guise of well- dressed women of respectable families, which no body could recognize, because of prevailing excitement.
- The marriage party was made to stay in palaces having heavenly comforts. Needless to mention that they were looked after well and were served with delicious food having variety, and taste. On the auspicious day and time, the marriage between Rama and Sita was solemnised by the royal priests in the presence of both the kings, queen — Sunaina (mother of Sita), Guru Vashishta, *Rishi* Vishwamitra, Lakshmna, Shatrughana, Shatananda (head priest of King Janak), other close relatives of both sides. The couple was blessed by all present there. On the same occasion King Janaka proposed and Dashratha agreed and Lakshmana married Urmila, sister of Sita; Bharata married Mandvi and Shatrughana married Shrutikriti, both cousins of Sita.

- On the insistence of Janaka, Dashratha stayed for a few days more as the royal guests. On the appropriate time and day it was decided by Dashratha to return to Ayodhya. Janaka gave lakhs of horses, elephants, maids, servants, huge jewellery, etc. as gifts to Dashratha. All the *Rishis* and Brahmins were also ceremoniously respected with gifts.
- King Dashratha, Rama and the three brothers and their brides were received in Ayodhya among beating of drums, dances and lot of excitement. Aarti (worship) of the brides with all Vedic rituals was performed by the queens and they were led inside the palace.
- On the other side, Ravana was the son of Brahmrishi (knower of Self) Vishrava and a demon mother Pushotkata. Ravana was very ambitious and power hungry. He did tapasya (penance) for a thousand years while standing on one leg to acquire extraordinary powers. Lord Brahma was extremely pleased with his devotion. Brahma granted a boon to Ravana that none among devas, demons, gandhravas, snakes, ghosts will be able to kill him; however, he could be killed by a human. Because of a boon Ravana could also assume any form without any body detecting it. Because of his superhuman powers, Ravana was chosen as their kings by the demons. Thus blessed with massive powers, Ravana started giving trouble to devas and other demons.
- Rama was eldest of the brothers; at the same time, he was virtuous, brave, expert in war and in the affairs of the state. He was also very popular among the people. At appropriate time, it was decided by King Dashratha to hand over the kingdom of Ayodhya to Rama, after due consultations with the ministers and Guru Vashishtha. There was joy and jubilations in entire Ayodhya and in the palace of king Dahsratha. All houses, markets, palaces were decorated to mark the occasion. All preparations were made for the coronation ceremony as per the Vedic rituals.
- However, Lord Vishnu incarnated as Rama had some other duties to perform before he could become the king of Ayodhya. Some time back queen Kaikeyi had saved the life of king Dashratha in a war with demons; She had driven the king and his chariot to a safe place when he was badly injured. Pleased with the queen, Dashratha had given her two boons which could be fulfilled any time. Manthara, the crafty maid of Kaikeyi, instigated the queen by these provocative words "once Rama becomes the king, Kaushalya would become all powerful and that she (Kaikeyi) will be reduced to nothing; she may have to live like a maid or may be even thrown out of the palace." Kaikeyi loved Rama a lot and she was happy that a virtuous person like Rama was being coronated, but Manthara's words created uncertainty and insecurity in her mind. She fell in to her trap. She asked Manthara, "What is the way out?" Manthra had already thought of the plan. She suggested the queen to ask Dashratha to fulfil those two boons. Accordingly on the eve of Rama's coronation, Kaikeyi asked Dashratha to grant those two boons. She asked Dashratha to send Rama to exile for 14 years and make Bharata, her son, the king of Ayodhaya in place of Rama. King Dashratha was totally shattered. He did not have the slightest inkling that Kaikeyi would be so cruel in getting those wishes fulfilled on such an auspicious occasion and that too in sending Rama to exile of 14 years. It was bizarre. Rama came to know of these development next day when coronation ceremony was to begin. He understood the predicament of the king. In

keeping with the ideals of the Raghukul, his dynasty, and to avoid any embarrassment to his noble father, Rama himself announced his decision to go to forest for 14 years. He gave up his royal dress and met mother Kaushlaya and Dashratha and all others elders and proceeded to the forest along with Sita and Lakshmana. At that time Bharata and Shatrughana were away at their Naunihal (parents of mother).

- Rama and the party slept under a tree on their first night in the forest. Next morning, Rama took a bath in Prayagraj—confluence of the three rivers Ganga, Yamuna and Saraswati—and proceeded further. He first went to the ashram of *Rishi* Bhardwaj and paid his tributes to the *Rishi*. They then went to Shringverpur on the bank of River Ganges and requested the boatman to drop them to the other bank of river. Kevat, the boatman, agreed to ferry the trio across Ganges but insisted that he would first wash the feet of Lord Rama. Very innocently, Kevat clarified that he was afraid that the dust of the feet of Lord could turn the boat in to a woman as it happened in the case of Ahalya and that he cannot afford to lose his bread earner, the boat. With a smile, Lord Rama accepted the wish of Kevat. Lord also blessed Kevat for salvation in life.

Kevat and Rama on the banks of Ganges

- Rama, Sita and Lakshmana were moving from place to place in the forest, serving the holy people. On the way people were extremely impressed by their divine beauty. Some were even cursing King Dashratha and Kaikeyi for not doing justice to Rama. The trio came to the ashram of *Rishi* Valmiki. *Rishi* Valmiki received them with great honour. Valmiki showered praise on Lord Rama. *Rishi* suggested them to settle on Chitrakoot mountain which was full of lively flora and fauna; the holy Mandakini river was also flowing nearby. Shri Rama decided to stay on Chitrakoot mountain. Devtas, disguised in the form of local tribes people, came along with the celestial architect Vishavakarma and built two beautiful, comfortable huts for their stay. Sita was enjoying the company of Shri Rama and she forgot the discomforts of forest life.

- Sumanta, the minister deputed to persuade Shri Rama to return to home, returned empty handed after leaving Rama, Sita and Lakshmna in the forest. He met the king and queen Kaushlaya. They were anxiously waiting for him. Dashratha was in a bad shape. All his hopes of meeting Rama were shattered. Dashratha narrated to Kaushlaya the story of Dhruva and the curse of his parents, which was responsible

Dashratha grieving and crying Rama–Rama

for this tragedy. Shravana, a child devotee, was going on a pilgrimage carrying his blind and old parents in a palanquin. He was taking water from a pond in the forest. At that time King Dashratha was out for hunting. That day the king could not get any target. He was tired and was taking rest under a tree. The king heard a sound and took the sound of water and that of the pitcher as though some animal was drinking water. He shot an arrow in the direction of sound. The arrow proved fatal for Shravana. When Dashratha went to the spot, he found Shravana fatally wounded. King was repentant and told Shravana the real story. Shravana forgave the king but requested him to go and offer water to his parents. Dashratha reached Shravana's parents. He offered them water and told them how Shravana was killed. The old couple could not bear the loss of the son. They died wailing for the son and cursed Dashratha that he too would die while grieving for his son. Narrating this, Dashratha died uttering Rama's name. The palace and entire Ayodhya plunged into grief. Guru Vashishtha preserved the body of the king in oil to be cremated later and sent for Bharata and Shatrughana to return immediately from the maternal home.

- When Bharata came back from his maternal home, he found gloom in the city and the palace. Kaikeyi, however, welcomed Bharata and narrated the whole story. Bharata was extremely annoyed for what Kaikeyi had done. He went to the extent of saying "When you had such a bad intention, why did you not kill me at the time of birth? Why did your heart not fail when you asked for the boon? Your tongue deserved to be rotten. You deserve to be infested with insects, etc." He used the word 'tu' to show his extreme resentment towards Kaikeyi. Meanwhile, Manthara came richly dressed and in a triumphant mood. Shatrughan got annoyed on seeing her; he gave a strong blow on her back; she fell crying and suffered lots of injuries. Leaving them there, Bharata went and met Kaushalya. It was an emotional meeting between the two.
- All along Bharata was disturbed by the thought that palace inmates, the queens and people of Ayodhya could think that he too was part of this conspiracy. Bharata then clarified to all the queens that he was absolutely clean on the matter. He vouched that God may give him the worst punishment applicable to a sinner (who has committed the worst crime like murder of parents, guru, a woman or a Brahmin), in case he had any role in this plot of sending Rama to exile and rule Ayodhya.
- Next day king Dashratha was cremated with full state honours and following the Vedic rites. Holy people, Brahmins and poor were given food and gifts in the form of land, gold, clothes, cows, etc. as per the rituals. On the request of Bharata, the three queens did not resort to 'Sati' (the tradition of self-immolation on the pyre of dead husband).
- After the mourning period of ten days, it was time for serious business. Guru Vashishtha, Kaushlaya and other ministers asked Bharata to commence

Bharata on his way to meet Rama

his duties as a king but Bharata was still uncomfortable. He clarified that his late father wanted only Rama to be crowned; therefore, he would first like to meet Rama in the forest and persuade him to come to Ayodhya and be the king. These feelings of Bharata were welcomed by everybody. Next day, Guru Vashishtha, wife Arundhati, the three queens, Bharata and Shatrughana accompanied by prominent Brahmins and many citizens of Ayodhya started early in the morning to meet Shri Rama in the forest. They first met Nishadraj Guha. He took Bharata and the group through the same route which Rama had gone before settling in Chitrakoot. He showed them the Ashoka tree where the trio had slept on their first night in forest. Seeing the tree and bed of grass, Bharata was taken over by grief thinking that Rama, a divine figure and king of Ayodhya, had to face such hardships. Guha then brought them across Ganges and Bharata met *Rishi* Bhardwaj. Bhardwaj counselled Bharata; "It was not time to indulge in grief; Kaikeyi was not at fault; it was divinity's will to happen that way for the larger good and therefore you should respect the divine will."

☛ Bharata and group ultimately met Rama at their ashram. Vashishtha broke the news of death of Dashratha. Lord Rama and others plunged into grief on hearing this news. That day everybody took bath in holy Mandakini and kept a fast --'nirjala' (without water). Rama did all other rites and rituals under the guidance of Vashishtha for the departed king. The group stayed with Shri Rama for a few days. All along Bharata was under lot of pressure as to how to initiate the talks. One day, however, Guru Vashishtha called a meeting of all and initiated the dialogue. With great respect and courage, Bharata requested Rama to accept the kingship and return to Ayodhya with Sita; instead either Bharata and Shatrughana can go to forest or the three brothers go to forest but Rama alone must rule Ayodhya. Rama had other thoughts and he did not respond; he kept mum. Meanwhile Janaka, accompanied by wife Sunaina, and other prominent family members announced their coming from Mithila.

☛ Guru Vashishtha, Janak and Bharata were individually thinking and thinking and thinking to find a solution acceptable to both Rama and Bharata. Ultimately, these three great souls went to Lord Rama and requested him to take a final decision because He is the upholder of Dharma and all have great faith in His divinity and wisdom. Lord Rama then true to his divinity said the following.

☛ "O, Bharat, You are familiar with the customs of Suryavanshi race and you know very well that our father was very affectionate and truthful. You also understand the traditions of our family and that of the gurus. You very well understand the inner feelings of friends and foes at this critical moment."

"You know the duties of everybody and the Dharma of mine and yours."

"Our father has died prematurely but we have been saved by our Guru and Mithileshwar (Janaka)."

"All the affairs of state, our honour, our virtue, all these our guru's glory will defend us and the end will be all good."

"The blessings of Guru are our protector. Obedience to one's father and mother, guru and master upholds all righteousness as Sheshnag (lord of serpents) upholds the earth."

"Therefore, dear brother, obey their commands and help me to do the same and thus be the saviour of our race. For the aspirant, obedience is the only means for attainment of glory, power and salvation."

"Reflect upon this and make your subjects and kinsfolk happy. My afflictions have been shared by all but you will carry the maximum stress and that too for entire period of 14 years."

"I know you are tender hearted and my words are harsh but hold these evil times responsible for this, I had no choice. In an emergency situation like this, noble souls like you can only be depended upon."

- Bharata understood what Shri Rama had in mind and did not press the matter further. The controversy was settled. On the advice of *Rishi* Atri, Bharata dug a well near a sacred place and water of all Teerathsthanas (holy places), which had been brought for the coronation, was poured in that well. The well was named after Bharata as "Bharatakoop". Later Bharata and his group also went around the Chitrakoot mountain and enjoyed its beauty and sacredness.
- After staying for nearly six days, both the group led by Bharata and other one led by Janaka took leave from Rama and returned to the respective city. It was a tearful farewell. Rama sent everybody with due respect. Everybody was feeling sad. Bharata returned to Ayodhya with the sandals of Rama on his head. He put the sandals on the throne of Ayodhya. He did his duties after ceremoniously consulting Rama and Guru Vashishta on all important matters of state. He did not stay in the palace; instead he made a hut in Nandigram, a place outside Ayodhya; He wore bark of a tree, had matted hair and lived as an ascetic.

Charan Paduka

Aranya Kand-Forest Period

- The trio Ram, Sita and Lakshmana were moving in forest and meeting the holy people. They met *Rishi* Atri and his wife Anusooya. *Rishi* Atri formally worshipped Lord Rama by citation of Vedic mantras. Anusooya blessed Sita for observing the Dharma of a woman by moving with Rama in hard times. Then they met *Rishi* Sharbhang, Sharangpani and *Rishi* Agastya in their respective ashrams. All the munis received them with due honours. *Rishi* Sharbhang after the 'darshan' of Lord Rama, invoked his yogic powers and left his earthly existence.
- At some spot, Rama saw a heap of bones; he was told by the accompanying ascetics that the bones were of holy people killed by the demons. Rama was greatly moved; raising his hands and took a vow "I will rid the earth of demons."

- Upon the advice of Sage Agastya, they started living in Panchavati in Dandak forest. Here they met Jatayu, the king of vultures. When they were comfortably settled in Panchvati, one day Lakshmana requested Rama to explain to him the Bhakti Marg through which the devotee becomes dear to Lord. Rama explained the essential of Bhakti Yoga by which the individual soul, "Jiva", meets "Universal Soul", Parmatma.
- One day, Shurpnakha, the sister of Ravana, happened to see Rama while she was roaming in the forest. She was greatly attracted by His sublime personality. She turned herself into a beautiful woman and approached Rama to marry her. Rama declined stating that he was already married and sent her to Lakshmana. Lakshmana too declined the offer. In frustration, she adopted an ugly shape and attacked Sita. An alert Lakshmana rushed to her and cut her nose by a knife. Disfigured and bleeding Shurpnakha ran away and narrated the incident to her demon cousins - Khar and Dushana.
- Khara and Dushana came with an army of 14000 demons to take revenge. Rama sent away Sita with Lakshmna and single-handedly fought with the large army of demons. The demons were extremely frightening, disfigured, shouting in a horrifying voice. Lord Rama faced them boldly. At one stage, Rama used his powers of illusion and made each demon feel that the other demon was Rama and thus they killed each other. Ultimately Rama killed Khar, Dhushana, another powerful demon Trishura, and a few left out, fled away.
- After this incident one day in the absence of Lakshmana, Rama told Sita that the time had come to fulfil his purpose of taking a human birth—eliminating the demons. He asked her to merge herself in 'Fire'. Sita disappeared in Agni and placed a duplicate Sita with Rama having the same beauty and attributes. Obviously, Lakshmana was not aware of this divine plan.
- A humiliated Shurpnakha, later met her brother Ravana in Lanka and narrated the whole incident. Ravana was furious and took the bad treatment meted to Shurpnakha as a challenge to his might. He thought of a plan to abduct Sita. He flew in his plane 'Pushpak' and met his uncle Mareecha in the forest and asked him to execute his plan. Mareecha tried to explain to Ravana that Rama was God incarnate and that he (Ravana) was inviting death with his plan. Ravana got extremely angry and threatened Mareecha with serious consequences in case his instructions were not followed. Mareecha knew that by not following the plans of Ravana, he was sure to die. He preferred to die at the hands of Lord Rama than by the crafty and cruel Ravana. Therefore, as desired by Ravana, he went near Rama's cottage in Panchvati disguised as a deer of gold and started playing around. Sita was greatly attracted by the beauty of Mareecha turned deer and asked Rama to catch it for her. Rama knew the reality but went out to catch the deer mainly to please Sita. The deer ran and ran and took Rama far away by his playful tricks. Ultimately Rama shot an arrow which killed the deer. While dying the deer turned into Mareecha and gave an agonising cry 'hai Lakshmana, hai Lakshmana' but from inside he remembered Rama. While dying, Mareecha showed his demon form and Lord Rama blessed him. Sita heard the cry of Mareecha as if Rama was hurt; she got worried. She insisted that Lakshmana should go and provide help to Rama.

Lakshmana persuaded Sita that nothing would happen to Rama but Sita did not agree. Very reluctantly Lakshmana left in the direction of the sound. He drew a line around the hut with a divine arrow and asked Sita to remain within the boundry of line; that way she would be safe. Ravana was already watching the scene happening at the hut. As soon as Lakshmana left, Ravana presented himself in the guise of an ascetic at the hut of Sita and asked for the bhiksha (alms). Sita was bound not to cross the line but Ravana insisted that he would take the bhiksha only when she comes out of the hut. Sita fell in to the trap of Ravana. As soon as she came out of **Lakshmana Rekha** (line around the hut), she was forcibly lifted by Ravana. Ravana disclosed his identity and then put her in his Pushpak vahan (plane) and fled towards Lanka.

- A helpless Sita cried for help. On the way, she dropped her ornaments/clothes to facilitate identification of the route by which she was being carried away. King of vultures, Jatayu, a friend of king Dashratha, heard her wails. He flew quite high and attacked Ravana to release Sita but could not succeed. In a fit of rage, Ravana chopped off his wings and Jatayu fell on the ground, fatally wounded. While returning on the way towards the hut Rama met Lakshmana. Lakshmana told Rama how he was forced by Sita to leave the hut. Both of them realized that it was some big game plan and hurriedly proceeded towards the hut. On the way they met Jatayu who was moaning and was nearing his death. Jatayu told them that Ravana had flown with Sita towards South. Jatayu worshipped Rama--by citation of mantras and then breathed his last. Rama blessed Jatayu. Rama cremated Jatayu with his own hands. Jatayu belonged to the lowest category of birds (vultures --those who feed on the corpses) yet he went to Brahmloka because of his devotion to Lord Rama and he died in the act of serving Lord Rama. Interestingly, Rama requested a dying Jatayu that he should not disclose to King Dashratha in heavens that Sita had been abducted instead let it be told by Ravana himself when he would die at the hands of Lord Rama.

Rama and Jatayu

- While on the move, Rama and Lakshmana came to the ashram of Shabri, a tribal woman. She was a great devotee of Rama. She welcomed them wholeheartedly and gave water, forest fruits, etc. to eat. Shabri offered them pretasted berry (jhuthe ber to ensure that they were testy) out of sheer love and respect but Rama ate them with equal love. Shabri then requested Rama to tell her about Bhakti Yoga by following which she could unite with Him. Rama explained to Shabri nine types of devotions.
- "The first type of Bhakti is to remain in the company of saints,
- Second type of Bhakti is to enjoy listening to kathas related to Me
- Third type is to serve the Guru in a selfless manner,

Shabri

- The fourth type is to sing and narrate my leelas/ virtues with a pure heart,
- The fifth type is to repeat (japa) My name and have abiding faith in Me,
- The sixth type is control of senses, develop sweet temperament, refrain from too much of activities and have a pure conduct befitting the saintly people,
- The seventh type is to see Me (God) in everything,
- The eighth type is to be contented in whatever you have and not find fault with others even in dreams,
- The ninth type is to be simple and understanding in behaviour, have faith in Me even during an adversity, behave with equanimity in both 'sukh and dukh' (pleasure and pains)
- "O dear Lady, whosoever is following even one of these nine forms of devotions (Bhakti), he or she is dear to Me. You are observing all the nine Bhaktis, therefore you are very very dear to Me." concluded Lord Rama Shabri was grateful to Lord. She invoked her yogik powers and burnt her body in the presence of her Lord and went to Brahmloka. Before leaving the world, Shabri told Rama that He should meet Sugreeva who would help them to track down Sita. Both the brothers then proceeded towards Pampa Lake to meet Sugreeva, the monkey king.

Kishkindha Kand

Rama meeting Sugreeva

- Rama and Lakshmana went towards Rishyamook mountain where Sugreeva was staying. Seeing them, Sugreeva sent Hanumana in the guise of a Brahmin to find out who they were. Shri Rama told Hanumana the purpose for which they were roaming in the forest. Hanuman was a great devotee of Shri Rama. He now saw his Lord face to face. His joy knew no bounds. He put Rama and Lakshmana on his shoulders and took them to Sugreeva. Both exchanged their stories and a formal friendship took place. Sugreeva narrated his tale as how he was made to run away by Bali, his real brother from the kingdom. Sugreeva narrated "Bali is my real brother. He was the king of monkeys. We loved each other. One day demon Maayaace attacked us and we faced him boldly. The demon ran away and hid himself in a cave. Bali too went inside the cave to fight. Bali sent me back with the instructions that you wait for me for 15 days, if I do not return, I may be assumed dead. I waited for a month and Bali did not turn up. One day a stream of blood came from inside the cave. I thought that demon had killed Bali. I came back. I was made the king. One day however Bali appeared. Bali thought that I had declared him dead to grab the kingdom. He attacked me. I ran away to save my life. Bali also took my wife."

- Lord Rama was moved by his story. He assured Sugreeva that Bali would be killed. Sugreeva then disclosed that he had seen a multi-headed demon carrying a woman who was weeping and crying for help. Sugreeva presented to Shri Rama some clothes and ornaments which were dropped by Sita and came to the possession of the monkeys. Rama was extremely delighted by this authentic proof of abduction of Sita.
- Rama, Lakshman and Sugreeva came to Kiskindhapuri where Bali was staying. Sugreeva with assurance from Rama challenged Bali for a fight. Bali attacked Sugreeva very fiercely and Sugreeva had to flee. He complained to Rama as to why he did not kill Bali. Rama clarified that he couldn't recognize Bali because of his strong resemblance with Sugreeva. Sugreeva was again sent for the fight; this time by putting a garland given by Rama. It was a terrible fight. They used big trees and stones as their weapons. Shri Rama was witnessing the fight from behind a tree. At appropriate time, He shot an arrow and killed Bali, however Lord Rama blessed a dying Bali. Sugreeva was made the King of vanar kingdom of Kiskindhapuri with Angad, Bali's son, as Yuvraj—the Crown Prince Sugreeva also got united with his wife.
- Shri Rama and Lakshmna stayed atop mount Rishyanook for some time. Some time passed but there was no news from Sugreeva about the whereabouts of Sita. Hanumana reminded Sugreeva to take care of Rama's work. Sugreeva then summoned all the monkeys with instructions to go to each corner across mountains, forests and locate Sita in a month's time.
- Since Ravana had taken Sita towards South, a strong team consisting of Hanumana, Neel, Angad and Jambvant (the king of bears) were sent towards South for search. An extensive search was made but there was no clue of Sita. Once they were sitting and sharing stories of Lord Rama, the story of Jatayu came up in their discussion. Sampati, the brother of Jatayu, was staying in a nearby cave. He heard their discussion. He came out and introduced himself. He was briefed about Jatayu, how he was killed by Ravana. Sampati became very sad; he then went to the ocean side and did the ceremonies connected with last rites of Jatayu. He informed them that Ravana had taken away Sita and that she had been kept in Ashoka Vatika in Lanka. It was decided that Hanumana should go to Lanka and locate Sita since he alone was capable of crossing the ocean. Shri Rama had already given Hanumana his personal ring to show to Sita as a proof that he was the messenger of Rama. Hanumana then remembered his Lord, blew up his body and flew towards Lanka across the ocean.
- In Lanka, Sita was having a tough time. She was surrounded by demon woman round the clock. These demon women had very frightening looks. Some were blind by one eye; some were having three eyes; some were having three breasts; some were having

only one leg; some were having a long protruding tongue. They used to frighten Sita and persuade her to accept the wishes of Ravana and become his queen. Once Ravana himself came, well dressed, covered with rich ornaments. He started to induce Sita by promising a very royal, regal life with hundreds of servants, woman attendants, big palaces at her disposal, if only she accepted him. A determined and pious Sita did not budge instead reminded Ravana to behave properly else he would be doomed. Ravana went back fuming with anger.

- Hanumana crossed the ocean and entered Lanka by killing few guards at the entrance of Lanka. He turned himself into a small creature to avoid detection and went around Lanka but could not locate Sita. In one house, however, he saw a Brahmin reciting the name of Lord Rama. Immediately Hanumana went inside and met Vibhishana, Ravana's younger brother. Vibhishana was a devotee of Shri Rama. Vibhishana informed Hanumana that Sita had been kept in Ashoka Vatika.
- Hanumana went to Ashoka Vatika and spotted Sita sitting under an Ashoka tree. She was in a bad shape and was continuously remembering Rama. Hanumana was greatly moved by her condition. He met her and presented her the ring given by Shri Rama. He assured Sita that Shri Rama and Lakshmana were fine and they would very soon attack Lanka and liberate her. This was a very momentous occasion for Sita.
- Later Hanumana destroyed Ashoka Vatika by uprooting trees, destroying plants to show his anger and strength to Ravana. Hanumana killed Ravana's son Akshay Kumar who was sent to arrest him. Meghnada, another son of Ravana was, however, successful in arresting Hanumana by invoking the Brahmastra. Hanumana was presented to Ravana. Ravana ordered to wrap Hanumana's tail with flammable materials like cotton, ghee and oil and set it on fire. Hanumana's tail was thus wrapped in flammable material and set on fire. Instead of feeling sad, Hanumana was jubilant. He jumped from building to building and set on fire various palaces and houses. The whole of Lanka was burning like wildfire in a matter of minutes. He, however, took care that house of Vibhishana remained safe. Finally Hanumana jumped in to the sea to extinguish the fire. He again presented himself to Sita in diminished size. Hanumana took one jewel of Sita as a proof of having met her and started his return journey. The damage caused by Hanumana was a great blow to Ravana's power.

Hanumana with Sita in Ashoka Vatika

- Rest of the monkeys returned empty handed. An extraordinarily happy Hanumana joined his colleagues Angad, etc. waiting on the bank of ocean on other side of Lanka. They immediately went to meet Rama who was anxiously waiting with Sugreeva and told them the entire story. Rama was extremely relieved to know that Sita was fine. A delighted Rama blessed Hanumana for his great personal service to the Lord. He asked Sugreeva to make preparations to attack Lanka. Sugreeva mobilised a huge army of millions of monkeys and bears. It was an ocean of monkeys and bears full of energy, motivation and a common purpose of winning the battle with the demon king of Lanka and thus make the mission of Lord Rama successful.

- There was panic in Lanka after Hanumana had gone. Mandodari, Ravana's wife, tried to counsel Ravana to release Sita and thus save Lanka from destruction. Ravana did not move and sent her away saying that she was a coward lady. Vibhishana, the younger brother of Ravana and a devotee of Lord Rama, was also thrown out of Lanka by Ravana for the same reason. Pride had overpowered Ravana and his end was, therefore, quite near. Vibhishana left Lanka and got united with Lord Rama. Vibhishana's entry was an important and extremely useful addition in the army of Rama to defeat mighty Ravana. Lord Rama specially blessed Vibhishana because the later continued to be His devotee in such an hostile environment prevailing in Lanka. He formally coronated Vibhishana as the king of Lanka in advance by applying Tilak on his forehead.

Hanumana burning Lanka

- Ravana had sent a few demons to spy on Rama's army. These demons got caught and were thrashed badly by the monkeys. Sugreeva ordered to mutilate their face by cutting their ears and nose but they cried, "We in the name of Rama, the king of Kosala, appeal to you not to cut our noses and ears". Lakshmana was watching the scene. He took pity on them and let them go. He however, gave them a message to be delivered to Ravana. The message read "Give up your pride, release Sita honourably, take the blessings of Shri Rama whom the entire world worships and thus avoid your own death and destruction." The spies came back and narrated the immense strength of monkey army and their power of devastation. Suka, one of the messenger and also a devotee of Rama, advised Ravana in very clear terms that Rama's army was invincible and surrendering to Lord was the best option. Ravana kicked him out of Lanka. Ravana was now internally shaken but pretended to be unmoved. A cornered Ravana ordered to make preparations for the war.

- Now the biggest challenge for Rama was how to cross the ocean with a huge army of millions of bears and monkeys. Rama meditated and prayed to the Sea deva to help them cross the ocean. There was no response from Sea deva for three days. Rama lost his calm. He decided to dry the ocean by his divine arrows. The Sea deva realized his mistake, appeared and begged pardon from Him. Rama had no intention to

Rama praying to Sea god at Rameshwaram

dry the water because that would have meant a bad death for millions of water animals like fish, snakes, alligators etc. Sea deva suggested that a floating bridge could be constructed over water. To accomplish this, he suggested that two monkeys viz Nala and Neel, in His own monkey army had the blessings of a *Rishi*; that any stone, which they would touch and put on water, would start floating. Accordingly Nala and Neel were deputed to construct the bridge with the labour provided by all the monkeys and bears. The bridge was prepared in a record time. Shri Rama established a Shivalingam and worshipped Lord Shiva before he left towards Lanka.

- Shri Rama and entire monkey army, duly guided by Vibhishana, entered Lanka by crossing the ocean over the bridge. They settled at Mount Subel. When Mandodari and one of Ravana's son, Prahast, came to know that Shri Rama had landed in Lanka, they again pleaded with him to release Sita. But Ravana ignored their pleas; instead he went to a gathering of dance and music arranged at a mountain top. Shri Rama was assessing the scenery of Lanka that night. He witnessed clouds, some sorts of lightning and sound at a distance in the southern direction. Vibhishana explained to Shri Rama, "What you are seeing is not clouds and lightning; it is scene of Ravana attending an evening of dance and music atop the mountain. There is a dark coloured big-sized royal umbrella over his head which is appearing to you as a cloud; what you are seeing as lightning is actually the movements of earrings of Mandodari and the sound is of the musical instruments." Shri Rama shot an arrow in that direction to warn Ravana that he should forget the luxuries and be prepared for the war. The crown of Ravana and earrings of Mandodari were dislodged by the arrow and fell on the ground. Everybody got scared, Mandodari the most. This was the beginning of Ravana's end.
- Shri Rama sent Angad, son of Bali, as an ambassador to Ravana as a last attempt to release Sita amicably without war. There were heated arguments between Angad and Ravana in his court. Angad advised Ravana to settle the matter amicably else he would be destroyed but Ravana was all along boasting his power and ignored his advice. While exchanging heated arguments, Angad struck both his arms on the floor; the ground was shaken violently. Ravana too was unseated for a moment; some of his crowns fell on the floor. Angad gave the crowns a blow; they flew off and fell at Shri Rama's camp. Shri Rama immediately understood that it was Angad's feat and valour in the court of Ravana in Lanka. Subsequently, Angad put his foot down and challenged Ravana, "If you can even move my foot, Sh Rama will turn back." Ravana was furious and out of control. He ordered to throw Angad on the ground. Indrajeet, Ravana's son and some of Ravana's best strongmen tried but they could not lift the foot of Angad. Ravana was feeling humiliated; out of sheer rage, he got up and rushed towards Angad to lift his foot. Angad immediately withdrew the foot. He uttered, "O, Fool, you should touch Shri Rama's foot; he can only save you not me." Ravana had no words. Angad returned back and attack on Lanka became inevitable.

Battle on Lanka

- Lord Rama now attacked Lanka on a full scale on all the four sides. Both sides started killing the army of opposite side in a big way. The monkey army armed themselves with big boulders, stones, trees and attacked Ravana's men. Demons were in large numbers; they were having frightening looks; they were armed with swords, arrows. Both sides caused heavy casualties of the other side. When half of Ravana's army was dead, he got worried. He sought the advice of ministers. Ravana's Nana (mother's father), Malyavant, also counselled his son in law- Ravana -- to return Sita to Shri Rama and save Lanka. But Ravana was in no mood to listen. Ravana now sent his son Meghnada to turn the battle in his favour.

- Meghnada fought fiercely. His main strength was 'Maya, illusion'. He rose high in the sky and started throwing fireballs; he made ghosts appear on the scene, who started making frightening sounds. He threw poisonous snakes in the form of arrows on Rama and Lakshmana. At one time, both Ram and Lakshmana became unconscious. The monkey army got demoralized. Lord Vishnu then sent Garuda to help Rama. Garuda made the snakes disappear. Both the brothers recovered immediately. The monkey army again swung in to action.

Hanumana bringing Sanjeevani

- Lakshmana and Meghanada then fought on one to one basis. Once Lakshmana destroyed his chariot and horses. Meghnada was agitated. He then let his powerful javelin fly towards Lakshmana; it pierced his breast and Lakshmana became unconscious; it was a very tense moment for Rama. On the advice of Vibhishana, an experienced physician by the name Sushena was lifted by Hanumana from Lanka. Sushena advised to bring Sanjeevini herb from Himalaya before daybreak. Again Hanumana was deputed to bring the herb. Hanumana, ever ready to serve Shri Rama, immediately flew towards Himalaya. Ravana came to know of this development. He deputed demon Kalnemi to create conditions to block Hanumana from bringing the herb. Kalnemi prepared a water pond and a garden en route and sat on its bank as an ascetic. Hanumana happened to see that lovely place. He was attracted and came down to take some rest as well as to drink water. Hanumana entered the pond to take a bath, a female crocodile pulled him inside. Hanumana managed to kill her. She was, however, relieved from a curse; she told Hanumana that the ascetic actually was demon Kalnemi in disguise. Hanumana got angry and killed the demon. Hanumana reached the Himalayas but he could not recognize the herb. He lifted the entire mountain and started his backward journey towards Lanka. When he was crossing Ayodhya, Bharata happened to see him; Bharata thought that he was a demon. Bharata shot an arrow towards Hanumana. The arrow struck Hanumana and he fell on the ground remembering Lord Rama. Bharata realized his mistake. He prayed to Lord Rama to revive Hanumana;

Rama answered the call of Bharata and Hanumana was revived. Bharata was sad to learn that Lord Rama was passing through a difficult time. Hanumana managed to reach Lanka in time. Lakshmana was revived by the Sanjeevani herb. Everybody was relieved that a tragedy was averted.

- Lakshmana was again in the battlefield. Ravana decided to depute Kumbhkarna, his brother in the battle field. Kumbhakarna was of the size of a mountain. He used to sleep for six months in a year. At that time he was asleep. Lot of beating of drums, blowing of conch shells and trumpet call of elephants was done to wake him up. Kumbhakarna was briefed about the whole development. Kumbhakarna was not happy what Ravana had done; it was unwise and unethical on the part of Ravana. Nevertheless the damage had already been done. At the same time, Kumbhkarna thought it was wise to get killed at the hands of Shri Rama, at least he shall be liberated. Very reluctantly, Kumbhakarna joined the battle. He was killing the monkeys and bears of Rama's army in thousands. He spread terror in the monkey army. Shri Rama sensed the panic in his army. He shot an arrow which chopped off one arm of Kumbhkarana, another arrow chopped off another arm and then his head was chopped off. His head was carried by the arrow and fell at Ravana's feet. Kumbhkarana was dead. Lord Rama, however, blessed him. Death of Kumbkarana was a great blow to Ravana.
- Recovery of Lakshmana infuriated Meghnada. He Again appeared on the scene and started causing heavy casualties. He started doing Yajna to make himself invincible. Vibhishana warned Shri Rama of his intention. Shri Rama deputed Lakshmana, Sugreeva, Vibhishana to spoil his Yajna. They could manage to destroy his Yajna. Meghnada then disappeared himself and used hypno-illusion powers and showered arrows on the monkey armies by remaining invisible. Lakshmana used telepathic powers and shot arrows in the direction of Meghnada which pierced the chest of crafty Meghnada; he and his chariot came tumbling down from sky. Meghnada was dead.
- It was now Ravana's turn to face Shri Rama. Ravana appeared on the scene. Initially there was one to one fight between Lakshmana, Hanumana and Ravana. Needless to mention they all were great warriors. There was a deafening noise caused by the cry of elephants and horses. Swords of demons were glittering as if lightning had struck. Soon there was a rain of arrows from both sides. Warriors were falling down as if a crop was being harvested by a high-power machine. Ravana used his illusive powers, ghosts, witches appeared on the site to frighten the monkey army. Vultures were hovering in the sky. Headless bodies were roaming; similarly heads without body were crying lying on the ground. It was a doom's day caused by humans and other beings. In desperation, Ravana also attempted to do the invincible Yajna but that was also spoiled by the monkeys led by Hanumana and Angad.

Lord Rama now himself concentrated on Ravana. He formally challenged him for a fight. Ravana was shooting hundreds of powerful arrows but they were neutralized by Shri Rama. At one stage, Shri Rama shot 30 arrows which chopped off Ravana's twenty arms and ten heads but the demon got them again. Shri Rama did this act of chopping his heads and arms several times but every time he got them replenished due the boon of

Lord Shiva. Ravana created as many of his type---through his power of illusion--equal to the number of monkeys and bears, thereby frightening the army of Shri Rama. Sh Rama then released divine arrow from his Sharang bow and destroyed the illusory 'Ravanas'.

Vibhishana then told Shri Rama "O Lord, there is a pool of nectar in the navel of Ravana which is his support for life." Shri Rama got the clue. He shot thirty-one divine arrows, one arrow dried up the nectar in the naval and the balance thirty smote his twenty arms and ten heads and carried them away. With the drying of nectar, Ravana's had lost his life support; his headless and armless body was now dancing violently. Shri Rama cut his body in two and Ravana was finally dead. Lord Rama blessed Ravana. The whole universe resounded with cries of triumph. The devas showered flowers on Shri Rama from heaven. Their purpose was served by the Lord.

- The arms and heads of Ravana fell near Mandodari. She was terrified; she was weeping but she took control of herself because she knew the outcome of war since Ravana was on wrong side. Vibhishana did the last rites of Ravana as per rituals and with full state honours.
- Lord Rama installed Vibhishana on the throne of Lanka in a ceremony attended by Lakshmana, Sugreeva, Hanumana, Angad, etc. Mandodari and other women of the palace were assured of a good treatment and there was nothing to worry about. Lord Rama then sent Hanumana to inform Sita about the victory. Sita was overjoyed and greatly relieved. Lord Rama then sent Vibhishana, Hanumana, and Angad to fetch Sita. Sita took a ceremonious bath, wore royal jewellery and came and met Shri Rama. It was a tearful union between the two.
- On Shri Rama's asking, Lakshmana prepared a blazing fire from a heap of woods. Sita addressed the fire, "In case I had some other person than Shri Rama during this period in my thoughts, words or deeds, you turn cold and soft as a sandal wood paste." Saying this, she entered the fire. The fire became soothing like a sandalwood paste. The mirror image of Sita, however, got burnt; Lord of fire appeared and he personally handed over actual divine Sita to Shri Rama.

Agnipariksha of Sita

- It was now time for Lord Rama to start back for Ayodhaya; the period of exile was over. To begin with Shri Rama blessed all the monkeys and bears and requested them to return to their places.
- Shri Rama, Lakshmana and Sita then flew to Ayodhaya along with Hanumana, Sugreeva, Nal, Neel, Angad, Vibhishana and others. Shri Rama showed Sita the place in the battlefield where Ravana, Meghnada and Kumbhkarana were killed. He showed her Rameshwaram Dham where the bridge was prepared over the ocean and Shivalinga was established. Shri Rama and Sita sought the blessings of Shiva while passing over Rameshwaram. Shri Rama got down at Dantak forest and went and met *Rishi* Agastya,

Bhardwaj and other holy people and sought their blessings. He and Sita took bath in Triveni. He crossed Ganga and met Nishadraj Guha. Meanwhile he dispatched Hanumana, in advance, to inform Bharata of his arrival in Ayodhya.

Uttar Kand

On hearing the news of arrival of Rama, Bharata's joy knew no bounds. Bharata ran and met them at the outskirts of Ayodhya. Bharata prostrated before Shri Rama. They came to the palace and met with the queens and Guru Vashishtha. Shri Rama specially went and met queen Kaikeyi to convey that he had not lost respect for her. The citizens of Ayodhya were happy and welcomed Shri Rama from the balconies of their houses. The people had come out and lined up in streets to greet their king. Shri Rama ascended to the throne of Ayodhya in a ceremonial way. There was celebration by the Devas in heavens. A few days after the coronation, Shri Rama held a special session of the royal court. He addressed the gathering. He specially thanked Sugreeva, Vibhishana, Angad, Hanumana for their big role in this war against demons. He did not consider it proper to hold them at Ayodhya for a long time. He requested them to go to their respective kingdom and resume the service of their people. Vibhishana, Sugreeva and Angad also took leave from Shri Rama. Hanumana expressed his desire to stay with Shri Rama to serve the lord for the rest of his life. As a proof of his devotion towards Shri Rama, he tore open his chest and showed to everybody present that Rama and Sita were present in his heart. People present there praised Hanumana for his extreme devotion towards Shri Rama.

- Thus the reign of Rama began in the Kaushal kingdom. Rama's kingdom known as "Ramrajya" was an ideal kingdom where everyone including animals, the poor, and holy people lived happily and peacefully. It was the kingdom where nobody would suffer from diseases.
  - People loved each other and observed the teachings of Vedas in practical life.
  - The wild animals roamed in the forest without fear.
  - The air was always cool and pleasant. There were always good crops. The rains were plenty, there was never a condition of drought. The water of the rivers was pure, sweet and refreshing.
  - All people had reasonable income. Nobody suffered from poverty.
- As a king, Shri Rama was using agents for gathering the information about subjects of the kingdom. For him, the people's perception about the king was very important. Once a spy brought information that a washerman had disowned his wife, suspecting her fidelity because she had stayed one night in some other person's house saying, "I am not like Rama who accepted his wife though she remained away from home for years." The comments of the washerman disturbed Shri Rama. He wanted to uphold the highest standards of morality in public life.
- Next day when the court started, he narrated the incident to his brothers. They tried to belittle the matter but Shri Rama did not budge. He ordered Lakshmna to drop Sita at an undisclosed place in the forest, left to her fate. Lakshmana complied with a heavy

heart. All along Sita was at a loss to understand the unreasonableness of Shri Rama. She became unconscious and lay unattended in the forest. *Rishi* Valmiki happened to pass by her at that time. He took Sita to his ashram. Sita was pregnant at that time. She gave birth to twins who were given the name Kusha and Lava. The life of Sita changed dramatically. She became busy in bringing up the children. Valmiki gave them the necessary training in Vedas, other scriptures and advanced archery skill, etc. Valmiki also composed a poem on the life and fate of their mother Sita. They would recite this poem in a very musical style. They used to call Sita as Goddess of Forest. The name of Shri Rama as their father was not disclosed to them.

- Shri Rama now decided to perform Ashavmedha Yajna to claim his superiority in the entire kingdom. An auspicious day was selected and kings, Brahmins, and saints were invited. Sugreeva, Vibhishana, Neel and Angad were specially invited. Preparations were made for the Yajna as per Vedic rituals under the guidance of Guru Vashishta. A golden statue of Sita was kept to represent Sita. Necessary pooja was performed and the horse was released to roam about in the territory. Shatrughna was appointed as the defender of the horse. All the kings en route accepted the supremacy of Shri Rama. One demon, Lavanasura, stopped the horse. He was routed in thr fight with Shatrughna.

Ashvamedha Yajna by Rama

- The horse reached near the Valmiki ashram. At that time Lava and Kusha were practising archery in the forest. They noticed that beautiful horse and read the contents of Ashwamedha Yajna. They stopped the horse and tied it under a tree. The soldiers of Shatrughna came and asked them to release the horse. Lava and Kusha did not release the horse; instead challenged them for a fight. The army was defeated very badly. Then Shatrughana himself came but he too was defeated. Matter became serious as two young boys were unmanageable by the accompanying army. Shri Rama then deputed Lakshmana to defend the horse but Lakshmana also got defeated. Shri Rama then deputed Bharata and Hanumana with monkey army but they also suffered serious defeat. Lot of soldiers and monkeys got killed.

- The result was that Shri Rama had to come himself to fight the young warriors and save the honour of Yajna. He took with him Sugreeva and Vibhishana and other good fighters. He saw the young and handsome boys and was greatly attracted towards them. He requested them to release the horse but they were not in a mood to give up so easily. He asked them for their introduction. The

Fight between Lava, Kush and Rama and his army

boys told him that they were the sons of Sita and have been brought up by *Rishi* Valmiki. They also informed that they were not knowing their father. Knowing that they were his own sons, Shri Rama chose not to fight and left it to the army. Lava challenged Shri Rama but Shri Rama maintained his strategy not to play offensive. Kusha was successful in making Hanumana fall on the ground and tied him with a rope and took him to the ashram. Kusha told Sita the story and showed her his prize catch. Sita was aghast. She immediately asked the boys to release Hanumana. She requested *Rishi* Valmiki to mediate and avoid the fight between father and sons. *Rishi* Valmiki assured her that the boys had done no wrong. It was their natural act to catch the horse and fight with the army as it was a Yajna horse; it was good they got a chance to display their war skills.

- Valmiki then reached the battle scene along with Sita. Valmiki told Shri Rama that Lava and Kusha were his sons. The sage narrated the entire story of Sita after she was abandoned in the forest. Both the boys paid respect to Shri Rama and he accepted them as his sons. Valmiki indirectly vouched for the purity and faithfulness of Sita; Lakshmana asked her to accompany them to Ayodhya but Sita wanted Rama to personally invite her to Ayodhya. Shri Rama chose to ignore her. She felt humiliated and decided not to go to Ayodhya as an unwelcome person. She then addressed both the sons to obey their father and help him in the discharge of his duties. She then moved towards Sarayu river. She prayed on its bank, "Mother Earth, I have never entertained an idea of any other person than Shri Rama as my husband in my thoughts, words and deeds; in case this is true, give me refuge in your bosom." Immediately there was an upheaval; lightning struck; clouds thundered and the earth split into two parts beneath Sita's feet. Sita was accepted by mother Earth. Shri Rama and others witnessed the event with awe and among the screaming of the boys for their mother.
- Shri Rama, Bharata, Lakshmana and Shatrughna along with Lava and Kusha returned to Ayodhya with the horse. The Yajna was completed after worshipping the horse. All the invited guests including the holy people were seen off with appropriate gifts.
- Shri Rama ruled the world for eleven thousand years from Ayodhya. His kingdom was an ideal kingdom.
- Time had now come for Him to depart from the world. Due to the curse of sage Durvasha, Lakshmana left for his heavenly abode first. After the departure of Lakshmana, Shri Rama called a meeting of the royal court. He announced his decision to give up his earthly existence. Guru Vashishtha declared Kusha as the king of Ayodhya. Shri Rama accompanied by Bharata and Shatrughna and other citizens proceeded towards Sarayu River. He worshipped Lord Shiva first. Then He entered the river and released His soul by submerging in the water. Bharata and Shatrughna followed him.
- Before leaving the earth, He blessed Hanumana, "Dear Hanumana, You will always be present wherever there is recitation of my name or any other ceremony concerning me. You will be people's protector from fear." Thus Hanumana, his staunch devotee, was immortalized by the Lord Rama.

- Ramayana thus sets very high standard of character in family and public life. Rama was an ideal king having high values of morality, doing justice in an impartial manner. His kingdom was an ideal kingdom, following justice and Dharma, uniformly for all. Bharata was an ideal brother. He had no eye on the throne of Ayodhya. Lakshmana had love for brother Rama and he accompanied Rama and Sita in the forest. Sita was an ideal woman and an ideal wife. She was not at all attracted by the incentives of Ravana. She accompanied Rama in the exile period, embracing the tough life of forest and dropping the luxuries of the palace. God of fire vouched for her purity.
- The epic also lays emphasis on the value of commitment. Promise given shall be honoured, howsoever, trying may be the circumstances. Shri Rama chose to go to forest mainly to uphold the highest virtues in the society. Dasharatha gave up his life but fulfilled the boons given to Kaikaiyi.
- Ramayana tells us that righteous not the ritualistic life leads to Mukti. It teaches the Bhakti yoga for reaching God. Dedication to God through thoughts, words and deeds brings the devotee closer to God. The devotee should contemplate on God, feel ecstasy and joy while doing pooja or recitation of bhajans, prayers, lead a pure life free from attachment, hatred, jealousy, anger. He should see same God everywhere, then he is merged in Supreme and attains God's bliss.

Goswami Tulsidasa

- Any write-up on Ramayana will not be complete without crediting Goswami Tulsidasa for his valuable contribution in writing this epic in people's language, thereby spreading the message of love, respect, devotion and selfless service for generations to come.
- Goswami Tulsidasa was born on the seventh day of the bright fortnight of Shravana month of Hindu calendar in 1543 in Rajpur village of Banda district in Uttar PradeShri His father's name was Atma Ram Dubey and mother's name was Hulsi Devi. There were peculiar symptoms when he was born. He did not weep, instead he spoke 'Rama'; he had all the 32 teeth at the time of birth. His parents were a bit disturbed at his unusual features at the time of birth. His mother, therefore, sent him with Chunia—a maid, to her in-laws within a week of birth and mother unfortunately passed away the very next day. His foster mother Chunia, the maid, also died when he was nearly six years old.
  - He was then picked up by Swami Narharyanand and he named him as Rambola. He also taught him glories of Shri Rama. Tulsidas, then came in contact with Shri Sheshsanatan ji; there he learnt all the Vedas and Upanishads for 15 years and became a scholar of Indian wisdom.
  - He was married on the thirteenth day of bright fortnight of Jayeshtha month of Hindu calendar to Ratnawali. He was greatly attached to his wife. It is said that once his wife went to her home. Because of infatuation, Tulsidasa also followed her. She got annoyed She said, "You have such a great attachment for the flesh and bones of my body; if you had even half of that (attachment) in God, you would been very very successful". These words gave a blow to

Tulsidasa's consciousness; he immediately turned left the house of his in-laws; he straightaway went to Kashi—Varanasi and turned himself into an ascetic.

➤ In Kashi, Tulsidasa started preaching Rama Katha. It is said that Hanumana in Ayodhya and Shri Rama in Chitrakoot gave him Darshan (appearance). *Rishi* Bhardwaj and Yagyavalkya in Magh mela in Prayagraj also gave him Darshan (appeared to him). One day he saw Lord Shankar in dreams. He immediately got up from sleep. Lord Shankar and Parvati too gave him Darshan (appearance). Shankar then told him, "You go and stay in Ayodhya and write in Hindi. I bless you that your poems will flourish like Sam Veda". Tulsidasa then immediately came to Ayodhya.

➤ He started writing Ramacharitmanas from Ramanavami—the birthday of Lord Rama. It was completed in two years, seven months and twenty six days. He then went to Kashi and narrated Ramacharitmanas to Lord Shankar and Annapurna Devi. At one night he kept Ramacharitmanas in the temple of Vishwanath—Lord Shankar in Kashi. To the surprise of everybody, "Satyam Shivam Sundaram" was found to be written on this book in the morning.

➤ Tulsidasa went to the abode of God on the third day of dark fortnight of Shravan month in 1623.

★ Jai Shri Rama ★ Jai Shri Rama ★ Jai Shri Rama ★

Mahabharata

The Epic of Mahabharata is a monumental work of *Rishi* Ved Vyasa. It has rich contents and has been given the status of fifth Veda. It has influenced the philosophical thoughts of Indians for centuries. Its story and philosophy is discussed, interpreted and applied by all Indians routinely in their day to day life. It is said that whatever is present in the world, is also contained in Mahabharata and whatever is not mentioned in Mahabharata, is nowhere to be found.

The holy book Shrimad Bhagvad Gita forms the core of the Mahabharata. The philosophy of Gita is independent of any religion and is followed the world over by people of all faiths for spiritual attainment.

Central theme of Mahabharata is that "Dharma always triumphs". It analyses very critically the observance of Dharma in the wheel of life; be it pursuit of money (Artha); pursuit of pleasures (Kama); or pursuit of liberation (Moksha). The Katha ends with the triumph of Dharma, represented by Yudhishtira, over Adharma, represented by Duryodhana, when Pandvas won the bloodiest ever battle of the world fought in the plains of Kurukshetra. Pandavas suffered a lot in their life but got the highest reward, the Moksha--liberation--from 'samsara' because they followed Dharma throughout their lives.

Lord Ganesha acted as the scribe in writing the epic. He, however, put the condition that His writing should not stop even for a moment. Ved Vyasa accepted His condition with the stipulation that He (Ganesha) would not write anything without understanding the inherent meaning of the text. This strategy gave *Rishi* Vyasa some time to think whenever required. *Rishi* Vyasa completed this epic in three years' time. The epic contains nearly one lakh verses divided into the following eighteen sections called 'Parvas'.

(I) Adi Parva—Birth and bringing up of Pandvas and Kauravas

(II) Sabha Parva—Game of dice and Pandavas go to forest for 12 years

(III) Vana Parva—12 years of Pandavas in exile

(IV) Virata Parva—One year of exile of Pandavas in disguise

(V) Udyoga Parva—All possibility of reconciliation failed and decision taken to go to war

(VI) Bhishma Parva—First 10 days of war with Bhishma as Commander in Chief of Kauravas

(VII) Drona Parva—War with Dronacharya as Commander in chief of Kauravas

(VIII) Karna Parva—War with Karna as the Commander in Chief of Kauravas

(IX) Salya Parva—War with Salya as the Commander in Chief of Kauravas

(X) Sauptaka Parva—Killing of sons of Draupadi by Ashwathama

(XI) Stri Parva—Women of Kauravas including Gandhari visit the battlefield and their grief

(XII) Shanti Parva—Bhishma's advice to Yudhishtira on all aspects of life, duties of kings, etc.

(XIII) Anushasana Parva—Bhishma gives final instructions to Yudhishtira

(XIV) Ashvamedhika Parva—Yudhishtira becomes the king of Hastinapur and performs Ashvamedika Yajna

(XV) Ashrama Vasika Parva—Departure of Dhritarashtra, Gandhari and Kunti to forest

(XVI) Mausala Parva—Yadavas go to Prabhash Kshetra and their total annihilation as cursed by Gandhari

(XVII) Maha Prastharika Parva—Yudhishtira gives up the throne to Parikshit and Pandavas go to Himalayas. Only Yudhishtira reaches the gates of Heaven in person.

(XVIII) Swargarohana—Yudhishtira meets Shri Krishna, Arjuna etc in Divyalok.

The Complete Story of Mahabharata

Mahabharata is the story of "Puruvanshees", rulers of Hastinapur. They belonged to the dynasty of king Dushyant and Shakuntala. There have been very prominent kings from this dynasty. However, we are starting this saga of Kurus when Shantanu and Satyavati were the king and queen of Hastinapur and their grandchildren from Dhritarashtra and Pandu fought the famous war of Mahabharata at Kurukshetra.

Satyavati was the daughter of chief of fishermen. Once Satyavati was out in the river for her daily routines when *Rishi* Parasara saw her and was immensely attracted by her beauty. He asked Satyavati to make love with him. Satyavati tried to persuade *Rishi*

Parasara but *Rishi* did not accept her pleadings. *Rishi* assured her that her virginity will be restored after giving birth to their child. *Rishi* Parasara filled the atmosphere with fog to make themselves invisible to others and made love with her. Then and there, Vyasa was born out of that most unlikely union. As promised by the *Rishi*, Satyavati regained her virginity.

Vyasa was brought up by *Rishi* Parasara. Vyasa is also called Dvaipayana--born on an island of Yamuna river. He is popularly called Ved Vyasa because he later compiled the four Vedas.

The kingdom of Hastinapur in the times of King Shantanu, was very prosperous and all beings including poor and animals were happy. Shantanu was very much fond of hunting. Once the king happened to go to the banks of Ganga for hunting, he spotted a beautiful woman. She was Ganga. King was bewitched by her beauty. He approached her and requested her to marry him. Ganga was also attracted towards him. She said "I can marry you but I have a condition. You will not ever question me in whatever I do and if at any time, you object to my doing anything, I will leave you." Shantanu, lost in her beauty, agreed to this stringent condition.

In due course of time, Ganga gave birth to seven sons but each time, she would throw them in Ganga River immediately. Shantanu was perplexed but did not object for fear of losing her. When their eighth son was born, Shantanu could not resist and objected to her drowning this baby also. Ganga retorted, "You have broken your promise. I will leave you now. I shall take with me our son also; however, you do not have to worry for the boy; I will return him after giving complete training; This boy will be a great person; He will bring honour to you."

Ganga named the boy as Devavrata. Ganga kept her words. After sixteen years, she again met Shantanu at the riverside with Devavarta and handed him over to the king. Ganga further informed the king that Devavrata was a fully trained youth and well-groomed for handling the affairs of kingdom.

Shantanu was now a satisfied king. He declared Devavrata as "Yuvaraja", heir to the throne. On some other day, he had gone to the riverside on his usual round of hunting. He got a very pleasant fragrance. He followed it up and saw Satyavati with her boat. The king fell in love with her also. As advised by Satyavati, the king went to her father and sought her in marriage. Her father, the king of fishermen, agreed for the marriage on the condition that their only child would be made the king of Hastinapur. Shantanu could not accept this condition as the first claim to the throne was of his dear and promising son Devavrata. Unfortunately, Shantanu could not forget the beauty of Satyavati. He started remaining sad and gradually became disinterested in the affairs of kingdom.

Devavrata noticed the deteriorating condition of his father and as a responsible son, found the cause of the king's sadness. Devavrata met Satyavati's father. He gave word to Nishad Raj that "I would never stake any claim for Hastinapur kingdom and that Satyavati's child from Shantanu, would only be made the king". Satyavati's father countered Devarata "your own children can stake a claim for the throne, how does he take care of that possibility?" Then and there, Devavrata took a vow which changed the course of history of the Kaurava family and that of Hastinapur kingdom. Devavrata vowed, "I shall never marry. I shall never be with a woman. I shall never produce children." It was a terrible (bheesham in Hindi language) vow (to give up throne and remain celibate/ brahmchari throughout life). Thereafter, he was given the name Bhishma. Devtas and other celestial gods showered flowers on Devavrata. Devavrata brought Satyavati home. Shantanu was extremely pleased with his rare gesture. Shantanu, in turn, blessed Devavrata that death will not come to him, instead, he will have the option of choosing his time of death; i.e. he was blessed with "Ichhamrityu."

Bheeshma taking a vow in presence of all with Nishad Raj

King Shantanu was having a great time in the company of Satyavati. In due course of time, Satyavati gave birth to two sons who were named Chitrangad and Vichitravirya. Elder son, Chitrangad was made the king of Hastinapur but he was killed at an early age. Younger son Vichitravirya was then made the king of Hastinapur. Both Satyavati and Devavrata decided to marry king Vichitravriya with the noble and beautiful daughters– Amba, Ambika and Ambalika—of king of Kashi. Devavrata of his own, went to their swayamvara. He abducted all the three brides and brought them to Hastinapur. (Later Amba was freed as she had already decided to marry king of Shalva.) Vichitravirya married both Ambika and Ambalika. As bad luck would have it, Vichitravira also died early without having any heir to the throne. In spite of repeated requests of Satyavati, Bheeshma, declined to accept the throne of Hastinapur very forcefully quoting his vow. He will not do anything against "Dharma" come what may.

Now Satyavati virtually had no option. She remembered her son Vyasa from Shri Parasara. Vyasa immediately presented himself to Satyavati. Satyavati told *Rishi* Vyasa the entire development and requested him to provide princes from the two queens to maintain the Kaurava dynasty. Vyasa fulfilled the desire of Satyavati. In due course of time, Ambika gave birth to Dhritarashtra and Ambalika gave birth to Pandu from the union with Vyasa. However, Dhritarashtra was blind and Pandu was pale-looking from birth. Though Satyavati got heir to the throne, yet she was not happy with the birth of deficient princes. Satyavati arranged a second time union between *Rishi* Vyasa and Ambika. Ambika was afraid of complexion and figure of *Rishi* Vyasa and was not prepared to repeat her experience. Without informing Satyavati, Ambika sent her maid to the *Rishi* at the fixed time and place. The maid had a successful union and gave birth to a normal child who was named Vidura. *Rishi* Vyasa informed Satyavati that Vidura is a holy soul and the incarnation of Lord of Dharma.

The house of Kauravas was full of activity and joy after the birth of Pandu and Dhritarashtra. Bheeshma taught the princes their "kshatriya" duties. They were trained in techniques of war and were also taught the Vedas, Puranas and other scriptures.

Since Dhritarashtra was blind from birth, Pandu was asked to rule the kingdom in his name under the guidance and care of Vidura and Bheeshma. Bheeshma arranged Gandhari, the daughter of the king Subla of Gandhar as bride for Dhritarashtra. Ghandhari agreed to marry the blind king, however, as an ideal Indian woman (Pativarta), she decided to cover her eyes with a folded cloth throughout her life so as to suffer equally as the husband. Pandu won Kunti as his wife in a "Swayamvara". Pandu also married Maadri, daughter of king of Madra Desha as his second wife. Daughter of king Devak was chosen as the bride for Vidura.

When Kunti was a child, *Rishi* Durvasha had come to stay in her home. She took great care of the *Rishi*. A pleased Durvasha gave her an incantation telling whenever she would recite it thinking a certain Deva, he would come to her. Kunti was happy as well as curious to know about the power of the incantation. One day, she invoked Sun God by reciting the incantation. Sun God came. Kunti had a union with him though unwillingly and gave birth to a child who was born with a Kavacha and Kundala. He later became famous as Karna. Since Kunti was still a virgin, she wrapped the child in a cloth, put him in the basket and let the basket go in the river. The basket with the child was lifted by a couple who was a charioteer and Karna was brought up by them.

King Pandu had a liking for hunting. Once during hunting, he killed a deer couple while they were making love. The couple happened to be a *Rishi* and his wife making love in the form of animals. *Rishi* was greatly annoyed with the cruel act of Pandu. He cursed him that he would also die whenever he would approach his wife to make love. Pandu now was a shattered man. He decided to live in the forest for the rest of his life. Kunti and Madri also went and stayed with him in the forest.

Pandu started living sadly in the forest. He could not produce children to continue the dynasty. Kunti could sense his predicament; she narrated to him the boon of *Rishi* Durvasha. On Pandu's request, Kunti invoked Lords of Dharma, Vayu and Indra, who gave her three sons, namely Yudhishtira, Bhimsena and Arjuna respectively. Kunti also taught the invocation to Madri, Pandu's second wife. Madri gave birth to Nakula and Sehdeva by invoking the two Ashvini Kumaras. In due course of time, Gandhari gave birth to hundred sons and one daughter (by the name Dussala) from Dhritarashtra.

Pandu, Kunti and Madri enjoyed the company of their children for 15 years while living in the forest. One day when weather was fine, Pandu was attracted towards Madri. He forgot the curse of the *Rishi*. As soon as he approached Madri to take her, he fell dead. Madri was feeling guilty; she also died with him on the funeral pyre. Kunti returned to Hastinapur with the five well grown, healthy and handsome children.

Bheeshma deputed Kripa and Dronacharya to teach the five sons of Pandu and 100 sons of Dhritarashtra in the use of arms, weapons and related skills. Arjuna turned out to be the most favourite disciple of Drona. He was declared to be the greatest archer on the earth by Guru Dronacharya.

Yudhishtira was Yuvraja. He was extremely popular among the people. Duryodhana and Dhritarashtra were now jealous of the growing popularity of Pandavas. In their heart of hearts, they wanted to eliminate the Pandava children so as to capture the throne permanently. To materialise this, a plan was hatched by Duryodhana; it was decided to send Pandavas away to Varnavarta and eliminate them there.

As planned, Duryodhna deputed Purochana to build a grand palace in Varnavarta made from highly flammable material like wax and lac and asked him to store lots of similar flammable material in the palace. The plan was that the Pandavas will be asked to stay in that house; at appropriate time, the house will be set on fire, thereby killing all the Pandavas. Pandavas went to Varnavarta and stayed in the house which was named "SIVA".Vidura had warned Yudhishtira indirectly to be careful from fire etc. while living in Varnavarta. Pandavas stayed in the lac house Siva, outwardly unsuspecting but inwardly careful for any mis-happening. A person was deputed by Vidura to dig a tunnel connecting this home with the bank of river Ganges. At appropriate time, Pandavas themselves set the whole house on fire and escaped to Ganges via the tunnel. A tribal woman was a regular visitor to the palace for getting food from Kunti. That day she got late and her entire family of six (mother and her five children) were allowed to sleep in the palace on that night. That tribal woman and her five children got burnt in the fire; it was concluded by the people that Pandavas and Kunti have perished in the fire.

Draupdi Swayamvara

Pandavas escaped to the other side of Ganges and stayed in the house of a brahmin. During their stay, Bhima killed demon Bakasur who had terrorised the people of the village. Later hearing the news of Swaymvara of Draupadi from a guest of the brahmin, Pandavas started towards the city of Kampilya in Panchala kingdom of King Drupada, to try their luck for getting Draupadi. Pandavas reached the Swayamwara of Draupadi and seated themselves among the galaxies of kings, and princes. Shri Krishna and Balarama were also present there. The condition of Swayamvara was to hit a rotating fish placed at the ceiling of hall and bring it down with the available bow and five arrows. All Kauravas including Duryodhana, Karna, Jarasandh, Sishupal tried but could not hit the target. Finally Arjuna dressed as a Brahmin got up, walked up to the target, lifted the bow and in quick succession released five arrows which pierced the revolving fish and brought it down. There was a commotion in the hall because a brahmin could pierce the target and not any of the kings and kshatriyas.

Draupadi accepted Arjuna as her husband and garlanded him. The Pandavas brought Draupadi home. As soon as Yudhishtira entered the house, he said, "Mother we have brought bhiksha for you." Without seeing anything, Kunti said, "Sons, share the bhiksha among all of you." When she came out, she saw beautiful Draupadi standing there with the Pandavas. Kunti had never imagined that bhiksha was actually the bride they had won. It was a very embarrassing situation. Finally it was decided that Draupadi shall marry all the five Pandavas. Draupadi later married the all the five Pandavas in a formal manner at her father's palace.

There was unrest in Kaurava camp at Hastinapur for obvious reasons, Pandavas had not only survived from their planned death in Varnavarta but they also managed to marry Draupadi. Even Dhritarashtra was not happy. Dhritarashtra and Duryodhana were worried about the kingdom of Hastinapur. Time had now come to give Pandavas their share of the kingdom. Matter was debated intensely in the family and it was decided by Dhritarashtra that a portion of kingdom called Khandavaprastha may be given to Pandavas. Yudhishtira accepted the offer of blind king to settle the matter amicably though he knew that it was not a fair offer as Khandavaprastha was a totally barren land. Shri Krishna deputed Vishvakarma, the divine architect of Lord Indra, to construct the city. Vishvakarma turned Khandavprastha in to a very elegant city. The city was renamed as Indraprastha. At the same time Arjuna married Subhadra, half-sister of Shri Krishna.

Pandavas were now happily settled in Indraprastha. Maya, the great architect, built a palace named as Mayasabha for the king Yudhishtira. It was comparable to all great palaces of the time and was matching in beauty with the palace of Lord Indra. Subhadra gave birth to Abhimanyu. Draupadi gave birth to five sons, one from each of the Pandavas. They were named as Prativindhaya from Yudhishtira, Sutasoma from Bhima, Srutakarman from Arjun, Sataneeka from Nakula and Srutasena from Sahadeva. Yudhishtira also performed Rajsuya Yajna and established his supremacy on earth. On this occasion of Rajsuya, Shri Krishna killed King Sisupala as the latter had gone beyond limits in criticising and insulting prominent kings including the five Pandavas and Shri Krishna present there. Shri Krishna gave Sishupala enough space and time to behave properly but he did not budge and there was no other option left to Shri Krishna but to finish him.

After the Rajsuya was over, Duryodhana and party (Karana, Dushasana, etc) took a round of the palace. They were amazed by its grandeur. Duryodhana had to lose face on a number of situations; he hit upon a wall which was looking like a gate; he fell in a pond of water which looked like a plain surface; he adjusted his dress thinking it was water though it was a plane surface. Draupadi and others happened to watch Duryodhana in these situations and laughed openly over his embarrassment.

Kauravas playing the game of dice

Duryodhana was in extreme anger seeing the rise of Pandavas. He again started thinking to eliminate them. A plan was hatched to invite Yudhishtira to play the game of dice with Sakuni, maternal uncle of Duryodhana and an expert of the game. The game of dice also happened to be the weakness of Yudhishtira. Vidura was sent to Indraprastha to invite Yudhishtira for the game in the name of entertainment.

Yudhishtira and other Pandavas came to Hastinapura for the proposed 'entertainment'. The die was cast. The game began. Sakuni played on behalf of Duryodhana. In the first round, Yudhishtira announced his stakes namely his jewels, his precious stones and his wealth. Duryodhana announced, "I am laying my wealth against yours." Sakuni threw the dice first time and he shouted "won". Subsequently Yudhishtira lost his wealth, land, army, slaves, horses, etc. in successive rounds. A losing Yudhishtira put at stake his brothers, one by one, starting from Shahdeva and including himself and he lost all brothers and himself. Finally he put Draupadi at stake and lost her also. This meant that all Pandavas and Draupadi and their entire kingdom were now under the control of Kauravas. There was hilarious joy in Kauravas camp. The evil plan of Duryodhan was successful.

Draupdi Cheer haran (disrobing)

Draupadi was the worst victim of this development. She was dragged to the assembly hall in full presence of all elders by Dussasana. It was humiliation of worst order to the daughter-in-law of the famous Kuru dynasty. Duryodhana, Karna hurled indecent language at her; she was asked to go to harem of women and choose some other husband, etc. Dussasana started disrobing her. She prayed to everybody including Bheeshma, Dhritarashtra to stop this insult but there was no response. Finally she prayed to Lord Krishna to protect her honour. Lord answered her call. The 'saree' of Draupadi increased to indefinite length and Dussasana could not disrobe her. He fell on the ground exhausted. Bhima could not bear the insults of Draupadi. He vowed to kill Dussasana in the war and drink his blood. Bhima also vowed to break the thigh of Duryodhana and kill him in the war. Arjuna vowed to kill Karna in the war, come what may for insulting Draupadi in the assembly.

Though Dhritarashtra was initially happy with the defeat of Pandavas but seeing the anger of Pandavas, he sensed that these developments could have serious implications for his sons. He salvaged the situation. He asked Draupadi for two wishes. In the first boon, Draupadi asked Dhritarashtra to free her husband Yudhishtira from bondage. In the second boon, she asked to free all other Pandavas from bondage. Those wishes were agreed to by Dhritarashtra. Pandavas were freed and they returned to Indraprastha with the bitterness caused by cheating and humiliations in the game of dice and extreme humiliation of Draupadi.

Freedom of Pandavas irked Duryodhana. All his plans to rule Hastinapur on a permanent basis were again spoiled. He expressed his unhappiness before Dhritarashtra. He asked Dhritarashtra to invite Pandavas again for the game of dice. This time, however, the stakes were a twelve years exile and 13th year as period of disguise to the loser; however, in case of identification in the period of disguise, there would be another period of 12 years of exile. Pandavas were again invited for the game. Yudhisthra knew that he stood no chances to win but he had no option to decline the invitation. Pandavas again lost in the second session. They went to the forest with Draupadi to spend 12 years of exile and one-year period of disguise. Kunti, however, stayed behind in Hastinapur.

To begin with, the Pandavas settled in Dwaitavana forest. *Rishi* Vyasa, Lord Krishna, *Rishi* Markendya, etc. came and met them. They were all very sorry by the treatment given to Pandavas but assured them victory in the forthcoming war which was foreseen. 12 years was a long period. In this time, Arjuna did the penance of Lord Shankara and got Pasupata Astra from Him. Lord Sankra told him the incantation to release the astra and how to withdraw it. Arjuna also met his father Lord Indra and got his Astras. Arjuna learnt music and dance from a Gandhrav named Chitrasena during his stay with Indra. Yudhisthara went on Teerathyatra (pilgrimage) with other brothers. They had holy dips in the Ganges, Saraswati, Yamuna, Godavari. They also visited Mount Kailash. There Bhima had a chance meeting with Hanumana, the Lord of monkeys. Hanumana assured his help in the forthcoming war by sitting on the flagstaff of chariot of Arjuna; his cry would frighten the enemy but embolden Pandavas army.

Nothing untoward happened in these 12 years except that Pandavas had a tough time. Duryodhana and his team Karna, etc. decided to meet Pandavas and make a mockery of them because of their bad condition. They went to Dwaitavana forest under the pretext of inspecting the cows. They decided to take bath in a lake nearby where Pandavas were staying. Already some Gandharvas—celestial people--were taking bath in the lake. There was a fight between Gandharvas and Kauravas as to who will take bath in the lake. Gandharvas were very powerful; they overpowered Duryodhana's army and were taking them away. Karna who was very proud of his skills, fled from the scene. Pandavas were nearby and they were informed by somebody as to what had happened with Kauravas. Soon Arjuna and Bheema arrived at the scene and encountered the Gandharvas. Gandharvas knew Arjuna. They told Arjuna the entire story. Duryodhana was handcuffed and brought to Yudhishtira in that condition and later released on orders from Yudhishtira. It was a big humiliation for Duryodhana and Karna.

In another incident, Jaydhartha, husband of Dussala, the only sister of Kauravas, was out on his way to Silva. He happened to see Draupadi in her ashram and was fascinated by her beauty. He forcibly took her and ran away. Soon Pandavas came to know about the plight of Draupadi. They located Jaydhartha. Jaydhartha had to flee from the scene. His life was spared on the intervention of Yudhishtira, being the son-in-law of the Kaurava family.

Yudhishtira with Yaksha at lake

There was also another interesting event. Once Pandavas were hunting in the forest. They sat at a place for some rest. Nakula was sent to fetch water from a nearby lake. As Nakula started to drink water, a voice came from the lake asking him not to drink water before giving answers to a few questions. Nakula ignored the voice and proceeded to drink water and he fell dead immediately. Sahadeva was sent to fetch water and he also met his death. Later Arjuna and Bhima went but they also met the same fate. Yudhishtira now had to go by himself. He was surprised to see all his brothers dead. He was also restrained by the same voice advising him not to take water before answering the questions. Yudhishtira was a man of restraint. He asked the voice who it was. The voice said that "I am the Yaksha and I control the lake. Your brothers did not care to listen to my conditions and hence met their death". Yudhishtira was a wise man. He did not confront the Yaksha. He answered satisfactorily many questions of Yaksha. The Yaksha was very much pleased by the wisdom and mature behaviour of Yudhishtira. He not only allowed Yudhishtira to drink water but also gave life to all the four brothers. The Yaksha was none other but Lord Dharma, the father of Yudhishtira. Both father and son were happy to meet. Lord Dharma gave Pandavas his blessings for victory in the forthcoming war.

Thus came the end of 12 years of exile of Pandavas and one year of disguise period started.

Pandavas decided to spend the disguise period i.e. the 13th year in Virat in Matsya kingdom considering high stakes in case they got identified during this one year period. It was decided that each of the five Pandavas will meet the king and present himself to the king justifying that his addition as an aide would be an asset to the king. Hopefully the king and queen will accommodate as both of them were nice and highly considerate. All Pandavas met the king and queen individually and pleaded their case for accommodating them in suitable jobs in the palace. Yudhishtira named himself Kanka and he was deployed as assistant to the king for political matters. Bhima called himself Valala and was engaged as a cook and also was the in-charge of the gymnasium. Arjuna called himself Brihanala and presented himself as an eunuch and was engaged for teaching dance and music to the king's daughter Uttara. Similarly, Nakula called himself Damagranthi and was engaged for the upkeep of horses. Sahadeva called himself Tantripala and was engaged for the upkeep of cows. Draupadi named herself Sairandhri and got a job as a maid to the queen Sudeshna. All the Pandavas proved to be very useful to the king and queen. In turn, they were also having a good time. One day queen's brother, Keechaka, who was also Chief of the Army, saw Draupadi and was fascinated by her beauty. He insisted on marrying Draupadi. All advice from Draupadi and the queen could not convince him. Finally Bhima and Draupadi hatched a plan and he was killed by Bhima in a lone fight at midnight in the presence of Draupadi.

Arjuna teaching Uttra and Draupadi in the attendance of Queen

On the other side, Duryodhana was restless to find the whereabouts of Pandavas in the disguise period of one year; He was desperately keen to locate them so that the exile period is again extended by 12 years which will virtually bring the end of Pandavas. From the news of murder of Keechaka, the Chief of Army of Matsya kingdom and brother of the queen Sudeshna, Duryodhana guessed that Pandavas were hiding in the Matsya kingdom. He started stealing the cows of kingdom and attacked Matsya with a large army in the hope that the Pandavas would be detected. All great warriors including Bheeshma, Drona, Karana, Aswatthama, etc. were present in the attack. A second army led by Susarma, king of Trigartas, opened another front of war with the Virata kingdom. Yudhishtira, Bhima and King Virata himself went to counter Susarma. Susarma had to flee. On other side, prince Uttara Kumara went to defend the attack with Arjuna in the disguise of a woman as his charioteer. Prince was too young to handle the situation. Seeing the huge army of Kauravas, he fled from the scene. Arjuna had foreseen this possibility. He was prepared to take control of the situation. He went to Sami tree and got his Gandeeva bow and arrows which were kept hidden there. He single-handedly fought with the entire Kaurava army led by Bheeshma. From the casualties and fighting skill, Bheeshma, Drona etc. concluded that he was none other than Arjuna himself. Arjuna was not afraid as the 13th year was already completed. King Virata came home and on the other side Prince and Arjuna came victorious. Then, the real identities of Pandavas became known to the king. There was a shower of praises and gratitude on the Pandava brothers by the king, queen, Uttara Kumara and others. In gratitude, King Virata gave the hand of Uttara to Abhimanyu — son of Arjuna. The marriage was celebrated with great fanfare and was also attended by Drupada—father of Draupdi, Shri Krishna, and Balarama.

By this time it was obvious that war could not be avoided. Accordingly, preparations for the war started at the back end by both sides. Surya, the father of Karna, appeared to Karna in dream. He cautioned Karna that Lord Indra shall come to him in the guise of a Brahmin and would ask him to part with Kavacha and Kundalas. Surya advised Karna not to lose Kavacha and Kundalas as they would serve as his protective shield in the forthcoming war. Karna told father Surya that he (Karna) is bound by the oath that he would not refuse a brahmin. Next day Indra came to Karna and asked for his Kavacha and Kundalas. Karna argued that these were his protection for life and he could ask for any other thing. But Indra as Brahmin insisted on those two items only. Karna then removed Kavacha and Kundalas from his body and gave it to Indra. In turn Indra gave Karna his weapon 'Shakti', which will serve as a protection but with a rider that it can be used only once to kill the enemy. Indra blessed Karna that he would be remembered till posterity as the greatest giver *Dani* on the earth.

After the wedding ceremony of Abhimanyu with Uttara, it was time for serious discussion. Shri Krishna, Balarama, Panchal King Drupada, King Virat, Satyaki and all the Pandavas deliberated about the next course of action to get the lost kingdom. It was decided that a mature brahmin from the court of king Drupada, would be sent with a message to Dhritarashtra to return half of the kingdom to Pandavas. The brahmin went but returned empty handed. Dhritarashtra sent Sanjay to impress upon Yudhishtira to forgo the demand of kingdom and continue to live in forest for the remaining life as Duryodhana was beyond control and he was in no mood to return the kingdom and that Yudhishtira being mature and wiser can salvage the situation and avoid the war. It was a great shock to everybody in the Pandava side. The Pandavas never wanted war. They had taken recourse to diplomacy only to avoid war. Sanjay was sent back with a strong message that Pandavas do not want war but at the same time they were not afraid of war. In order to avoid large-scale killing of people on both sides and kith and kin, they wanted their fair share of kingdom; "Give them half of kingdom, if not half; give them five cities, even five villages will do". Duryodhana, however, was adamant. Duryodhana announced that he is not afraid of war and he will not give land even equal to the tip of a needle.

Shri Krishna decided to go himself as an ambassador as a last-minute effort to avoid war and resulting annihilation. He went to Hastinapur. He was given a warm welcome. He presented the case of the Pandavas in the presence of all who mattered in the Kaurava kingdom. Duryodhana, however, was adamant. Ignoring the advice of everybody, he reiterated that so long as he was alive, he would not give even an inch of land not to speak of the five villages. According to Duryodhana, Pandavas were suffering because of their own deeds and that he was in no way responsible for their misfortunes. To add insult to injury, Duryodhana decided to take Shri Krishna captive so that Pandavas would be totally demoralized. Hearing this plan of Duryodhana, Shri Krishna was extremely annoyed. He showed his Virat Swaroop to all present in the assembly hall. Brahma, the Creator could be seen on his forehead; eleven Rudras, Indra, Kubera, Varuna and Yama, 12 Adityas, Maruts, all the gods of heaven, Balarama, Arjuna, five Pandavas, etc. could be seen in that form. Bheeshma, Vidura understood the divine form of Shri Krishna and they worshipped Him. Lord Krishna gave vision to Dhritarashtra to enable him to see that form; the blind king was grateful to Him.

Later Shri Krishna met Karna in person. He told Karna the background of his birth and requested him to join Pandavas as they were his brothers from Kunti. Karna, however, declined citing his eternal friendship and loyalty to Duryodhana. He said that he knew the outcome of war (defeat of the Kauravas) but he would like to face Pandavas specially Arjuna for the sake of Duryodhana.

Kunti was now sad on the thought that Karna, her son, will be fighting on Duryodhana's side. She decided to go to Karna and ask him not to fight against Pandavas. She went and met Karna early in the morning when he was worshipping Sun after a bath in the Ganges. It was a great union which Karna was longing for throughout his life. Both mother and son wept remembering the agony of a lifetime's separation caused by fate. Karna, however, reiterated his stand. He said, "Mother, it is too late. I am indebted to Duryodhana; it was Duryodhana who gave me name and identity by making me Angraj, King of Ang Pradesh, when everybody else rejected me, insulted me by calling Sutputra." Karna recalled the humiliation meted out to him throughout his life.

Nevertheless Karna knew the sentiments of a mother. He did not want that his mother would go empty handed. He gave her a promise that he will not kill any other Pandava brother except Arjuna; in that case either he will survive or Arjuna and thus she will have five sons in any situation. Kunti returned home after embracing Karna.

Now the war became inevitable. Diplomacy had failed to avert the war. Both sides started preparing for the war. Dhrishttadyumna, brother of Draupadi, was chosen as the commander of the Pandavas's army. Bheeshma was chosen the commander of the Kaurva army. Shri Krishna was chosen by Pandavas but His army will fight from the Kauravs side. Balarama did not join any group. Rukmi, the brother of Rukmini was rejected by either side to join as he was too proud of himself. River Hiranwati was chosen as the line of demarcation between the two sides.

Rishi Vyasa met Dhritarashtra. He gave Sanjay divine vision by which he could see all that was happening in the battle field; Sanjay would even come to know the thoughts of the warriors. Everyday he would go to the battlefield, see the events and narrate them to Dhritarashtra at night.

The army of both sides assembled at Kurukshetra to decide the fate of the kingdom. Rules of the war were decided mutually. Yuyutsu, son of Dhritarashtra from another queen, changed sides and came to the Pandava side when an announcement was made giving a choice for anybody to change sides.

Krishna and Arjuna in the midst of battle

Shri Krishna brought the chariot of Arjuna in the middle of the battlefield. Arjuna scanned the entire army of both sides. He saw Bheeshma, Guru Drona, Karna, Duryodhana, Dussasana, etc. He saw other friends, teachers, uncles, and their children. He thought he was expected to kill those friends, relatives and elders with whom he had grown up. He became nervous and confused. His famous bow, Gandeeva, slipped from his hands. His mouth became dry. He said, "I cannot fight. I cannot kill these cousins, elders, friends and their sons. Even if I get victory, I would not enjoy at the cost of death of these people who had been so close to me." He started weeping. Shri Krishna was amazed. He knew that Arjuna had to be motivated otherwise war could not be won. He then told Arjuna the great philosophy of life and death, which is famously known as Sri Mad Bhagavad Gita. Gita combines the philosophy of Vedas, Upanishads and other Hindu scriptures. Shri Krishna explained to Arjuna:

"Those who are born must die. Death invariably follows birth. However the Soul does not die. It only changes shape. It acquires new body with every death. Soul is eternal. These people whom you are afraid to kill, have already died many many times and have taken births an equal number of times; therefore, by killing them, you are not incurring any sin.

“By fighting, you are doing your duty. It is a war between ‘Dharma’ and ‘Adharma’. A righteous war is a great occasion for a kshatriya. You are lucky. You should not miss this chance. You are destined to go to heaven by performing your duty as a warrior. Further your right is only to do your duty. You have no right to the fruits of action. Dedicate all work to me. Give up the idea of doer-ship, attachment like me, mine and I. This is the divine way of doing work.

Similarly inaction is not your right. Everybody is bound to carry out his duty. Even gods are eternally engaged in their duty of running the universe. To remain inactive is a sin; therefore, do your assigned duty and dedicate the work to me.

“Do not have attachment with the sense objects. They are not permanent. They lead to painful cycles of birth and death. Control your mind and senses. Aim for salvation. The purpose of life is to attain salvation.”

“I will tell you a great secret. I have assumed this human form. So fools do not recognise me as the Lord of all beings. I am the Supreme. I am the Father of Universe. I am the Sun. I am the Moon. I am the Vedas. I am the AUM. Those who meditate on Me and worship Me and only Me, will reach Me in the end.” In other words the whole universe, beings and non-beings, seen or unseen, is HIM only and whatever He says is Truth only.

Shri Krishna continued. “I am the Time, destroyer of all. Bheeshma, Karna, Duryodhana, Drona, etc. have already been slayed by Me. You are just the instrument of their death; therefore, kill them and win name, fame and heaven.”

Arjuna wanted to see His divine form. Krishna granted Arjuna divine eyes and revealed to Arjuna His divine form. Arjuna saw the universe in all its manifestation. He told Shri Krishna, “My Lord, I am seeing Brahma and all the *Rishis*. You are infinite. There is no beginning and no end. I am seeing the sons of Dhritarashtra, Bheeshma, Drona, Radheya and other great warriors rushing in to your mouth and perishing rapidly.”

Arjuna was enlightened. He understood his duty and purpose of life. He understood that by killing all those, he will be performing his duty, and kshatriya Dharma and thereby attain Mukti, Liberation, also. Strength returned to his mind and arms. No illusion of any kind, no attachment to worldly people and things was disturbing him. His mind was calm and serene. He lifted his bow, Gandeeva, and announced his readiness to fight by blowing his conch. A happy Shri Krishna moved the chariot towards Bheeshma, the commander of the Kaurava army.

And the Great Historic War began at Kurukshetra.

The first nine days passed without any major casualty. Few sons of Dhritarashtra were killed. Ghatotcatch, son of Bhima from Hidimba, fought from Pandavas’s side and terrified the Kauravas. His war skill, his bravery astonished everybody. There were encounters between individual warriors time and again. Bheeshma played havoc and caused great casualties on the Pandavas side. However, both Pandavas and Duryodhana were frustrated as nothing substantial was being achieved which could bring the war to an end. Duryodhana was time and again alleging Bheeshma that not enough was being done. Bheeshma told very clearly to Duryodhana that he was doing his best and made clear to Duryodhana that he would not kill any of the Pandavas. On the other side Pandavas were also getting frustrated. They discussed among themselves and came to the conclusion that unless Bheeshma was killed, war would not be won. Accordingly they met Bheeshma on the night of 9th and 10th day of the war. They sought the blessings of Bheeshma to win the war. Bheeshma said that he was invincible; however, he loved the Pandavas. He told them a way out to kill him. He told them that Shikhandi was a woman in previous birth. Let Arjuna fight with Shikhandi in front, Bheeshma then would not fight seeing a woman and shall give up the weapons; this will give Arjuna a chance to kill the Kaurava patriarch.

Next day was the 10th day of war. The strategy as suggested by Bheeshma was adopted by Yudhishtira. Shikhandi was on the chariot of Arjuna. Kauravas were taking all precautions not to leave Bheeshma alone without adequate protection. Therefore, Bheeshma was surrounded by other great warriors like Drona, Duryodhana, Dusassana, etc. However, at some time Shri Krishna spotted Bheeshma alone and immediately directed Arjuna to finish the job. Arjuna lost no time and under the cover of Shikhandi, showered a rain of arrows on Bheeshma. The great warrior happily accepted the anger of Arjuna and fell on the ground with arrows pierced all over his body.

The falling over of Bheeshma was a great misfortune for the Kuru house. The great soul Bheeshma had nurtured the Pandavas and Kauravas and the kingdom of Hastinapur. There was pin-drop silence in that colossal noise. All the Pandavas and Kauravas gathered around Bheeshma. Bheeshma asked for a pillow. Everybody brought highly comfortable pillows. Bheeshma was not happy. He asked Arjuna to provide him with a pillow. Arjuna, understood what Bheeshma wanted. Arjuna shot an arrow in the ground near the head of Bheeshma and his head now rested on the arrow as a pillow. Bheeshma was thirsty. He asked for water. He looked at Arjuna. Arjuna shot an arrow in the ground. A stream of water erupted from the ground and fell directly in the mouth of Bheeshma. The stream was not ordinary water but it was Ganga herself, the mother of Bheeshma.

Karna came to meet Bheeshma at midnight. He begged pardon from the great scion of Kauravas for words of anger, indecent arguments, that both had had on various occasions. Bheeshma assured Karna that he was fond of him, he loved him and he was sorry for Karna that he (Karna) did not get his due in spite of taking birth in a royal family. Bheeshma assured Karna that he did not carry any ill feelings towards him. He embraced Karna and blessed him for earning name and fame on the earth. Karna forgot the ill feelings and returned with a light heart.

Bheeshma was blessed with Ichhamrityu, i.e., he could choose his day and time of death. Bheeshma announced that he will give up his body when the Sun will be in Uttarayana.

Drona was appointed as the next commander of the Kaurava army. Drona assured Duryodhana that he will capture Yudhishtira as early as possible. Pandavas, therefore, took all precautions not to leave Yudhishtira alone. Heavy casualties were inflicted by both sides. Bhagadatta, the king of Pragjyotisha, caused panic in the Pandava army. There was a duel between the various Maharathikas (stalwarts) of both sides.

Abhimanyu fighting alone in Chakravyuh

On 13th day Drona arranged the Kaurava army in what is called 'Chakravyuha'–a war technique to trap the enemy. Duryodhana was at the centre of the arrangement. He was surrounded by a first layer of protection, given by Karna, Dussasana and Kripa, etc. Seeing the Chakravyuha, Yudhishtira was in a fix. Only four persons Arjuna, Abhimanyu (the son of Arjuna from Subhadra), Shri Krishna and Pradyumana, son of Krishna, knew how to enter the Chakravyuha. Arjuna and Krishna were busy fighting somewhere else. Abhimanyu knew how to enter the Chakravyuha but he did not know how to come out of that. Pandavas had virtually no option. It was decided to send Abhimanyu to break the Chakravyuh with the plan that he will be supplemented by Bheema and Yudhishtira at appropriate time. Abhimanyu entered the Chakravyuha. He astonished everybody in the Kaurava camp with his bravery and war skill. No Maharathi including Karna could face him in a one to one fight. He was killing the enemy by thousands. Abhimanyu had reached the centre of the Chakravyuha where Duryodhana was placed well protected. Fury of Abhimanyu came to such a stage that Kaurava Maharathis decided to attack him together. Accordingly Drona, Kripa, Aswathama, Karna, Kritvarma and son of Dussasana together attacked Abhimanyu. Radhey (Karna) cut his bow from behind; Drona killed his horses; Kripa killed his charioteers. They broke his sword and shield. Abhimanyu then started fighting with the wheel of his chariot. He was totally alone. Nobody else could join Abhimanyu as Jaydhartha was successful in blocking the arrival of Pandavas to aid Abhimanyu. Ultimately Abhimanyu fell on the ground. Son of Dussasana rushed towards him and killed him with the blow of a mace.

There was gloom in the Pandava camp. The Maharathis of Kauravas namely Drona, Karna, etc. had cornered a boy of 16 and ruthlessly murdered him. Arjuna was furious. He took a vow that he would kill Jaydhartha by sunset next day or else kill himself. Pandavas including Shri Krishna were worried that Jaydhartha must be killed otherwise they will lose Arjuna. Kauravas wanted to protect Jaydhartha so that Arjuna is eliminated automatically. Next day Arjuna killed the Kaurava army as if harvesting a crop. Sun was about to set but Jaydhartha could not be killed. Krishna was also worried. He played a trick. He blocked Sun with his Chakra, thereby temporarily causing darkness, giving the impression that Sun had set. Kauravas started shouting about their victory that Jaydhartha could not be killed. For a moment Jaydhartha was alone and unprotected. Shri Krishna immediately asked Arjuna to finish Jaydhartha with his Pasupata astra (which was given by Lord Shankra). Arjuna knew his job very well. Next moment everybody saw the head of Jaydhartha up in the sky. The bright disc of Sun God again appeared proving that sun had not yet set. Now the Kauravas were gloomy and Pandavas were jubilant.

It was 14th day of the war. There was a tough fight between Drona and Dhrishtadyumna. Ghatotkacha used his *mayaiu* tactics and harassed the Karuavas. The casualties caused by Ghatotkacha were so terrible that it became necessary to kill him at any cost. Ultimately Radheya (Karna) used his Shakti Astra (which Indra gave him in lieu of Kavacha and Kundalas) and killed Ghatotkacha. With the use of Shakti Astra, Karna lost everything. Now he had no astra to kill Arjuna. He became powerless. Bheema was sad because his son Ghatotkacha died. But Shri Krishna told Arjuna, "It is the happiest day in my life. Now Shakti astra has gone back to Indra and that there is no fear from Radhey. With the loss of Shakti, Radhey has been reduced to any other human being and he is sure to be killed." Frustration of Duryodhana was increasing. He had an altercation with Drona. They exchanged harsh words because Pandavas were advancing and the war was going in their favour. Drona was fed-up with the blames of Duryodhna.

Next day, the 15th day of war, Drona was emanating fire. In no time he killed Virata and his (Drona's) long time enemy Drupada by throwing javelins. There was a spectacular fight between Guru Drona and his most loved student Arjuna. They were displaying their unmatched war skills. Drona was, however, advancing and annihilating the Pandava army. He was using divine astras and causing casualties by thousands at a time. Krishna decided to kill him by a trick. He asked to kill an elephant by the name Ashwatthama. Bhima did it and shouted that Ashwatthama has been killed. Drona heard the words of Bhima. He did not believe it. He asked Yudhishtira to confirm that Ashwatthama had been killed. Shri Krishna forced Yudhishtira to tell a lie otherwise it was difficult to eliminate the great war veteran. For the first time Yudhishtira spoke a lie. He said "Ashwatthama is dead" and softly added "the elephant called Ashwatthama". It is said that chariot of Yudhishtira sunk in the ground because of this lie; otherwise it always used to remain above the ground.

Ashvatthama was Drona's son. News of the death of his 'son', was a great shock to him. Drona was now frustrated. He continued to fight but with a heavy heart. Bhima abused Drona of violating all ethics of a Brahmin and causing such a large-scale casualties of humans, especially when his son is dead. The words of Bhima struck his conscience. He gave up his arms. Immediately, Dhrishtadyumna who was waiting for the right moment, cut off his head with the sword and Drona fell on the ground.

Radhey was now nominated the next commander of the Kaurava army. It was the dream of a lifetime of Karna to head the Kaurava army. Radhey assured Duryodhana that he would definitely kill Arjuna though in his heart of hearts, he knew that he was powerless and it was impossible to kill Arjuna and win the war. But he decided to sacrifice his life for Duryodhana as gratitude for giving his love, identity and status. The 16th day of the war started with Radhey as the commander of Kaurava army. Radhey advanced towards the Pandava army. He was destroying it ruthlessly. There was fight between Radhey and Nakula. Ashwathama fought with Bhima. Shikhandi was fighting with Kritvarma. Duryodhna fought with Yudhishtira. The war went on routinely. Duryodhana met Radhey and reminded him about his vow to kill Arjuna. Radheya assured Duryodhana that tomorrow either Arjuna will survive or Radhey. Radhey, however, requested that Salya be made his charioteer as a help on the same lines as Shri Krishna was helping and guiding Arjuna. Salya was a senior warrior but agreed to act as Karna's charioteer seeing the requirement of a fast deteriorating situation.

At night, Radhey could not sleep. He remembered the curse of *Rishi* Bhargava that he would forget the incantation of Brahmastra at a critical time of war. He remembered the curse of a brahmin that the wheel of his chariot shall sink in war and he would die helplessly as his (Brahmin's) cow died, whom Radhey happened to kill unintentionally. His Kavacha and Kundalas had already been taken by Indra. The Shakti astra given by Indra in lieu of Kavacha and Kundalas was spent in killing Ghatotkacha. Death was, therefore, a fate accompli for Radhey; he had no option. Nevertheless he did not want to dishearten Duryodhana for whom he (Radhey) was the only hope to win the war.

The 17th day of war started. Bhima came across Dussasana. His only aim was to kill Dussasana and drink his blood in order to fulfil his promise to Draupadi when she was humiliated in the Kaurava assembly. Bhima caught Dussasana and held him on the ground. He cut his right hand and threw it because he had caught Draupadi by her hair using his right hand. Bhima then cut open the chest of Dussasana and drank his blood oozing from the chest.

Radhey asked Salya to take him straight to Arjuna. Radhey met Yudhishtira and showed Yudhishtira his might. Yudhishtira was reduced to such a hopeless stage that he (Yudhishtira) could be killed any time. But Radhey left him and moved towards Arjuna. Arjuna was also proceeding towards Radhey. The two great archers on the earth now faced each other. A spectacular fight started. Devas in heaven were witnessing the duel. Radhey released Nagastra which was sure to kill Arjuna but he was saved by Shri Krishna who lowered the chariot a bit below in the ground and the Astra went above Arjuna's head without causing any harm to him.

Arjuna was saved by Shri Krishna but there was nobody to save Radhey. He tried to invoke Brahamastra but he forgot the incantation. One wheel of the chariot sunk in the ground. Radhey tried his best to lift the wheel and place it on the firm ground but of no avail. He pleaded to Arjuna to be fair and wait till he was able to make the chariot movable. Shri Krishna reminded Radhey about his own behaviour on various occasions. On the advice of Shri Krishna, Arjuna invoked a divine Astra and released an arrow. The arrow cut the head of Radhey and the pride of Duryodhana fell dead.

With the fall of Radhey, Duryodhana lost the spirit of war. His fate was now sealed. He lost everything. He went to battlefield and saw the glowing face of a dead Radhey. Duryodhana could not think anything. He simply ran to Bheeshma and wept before him.

Bheeshma consoled him. On Duryodhana's request, Bheeshma told the entire background of Radhey; "Radheya was Kaunteya not Radhey; He was the son of Kunti and the elder brother of Pandavas. Throughout his life, he searched for his identity and suffered humiliation and bad luck. He knew that he would die but he kept his promise to Duryodhana. He fought against Pandavas, his brothers, to prove his loyalty to Duryodhana." Duryodhana was spellbound. He was boldened by the sacrifice of Radhey (Kaunteya). He was now not afraid of death. He decided to fight with Pandavas and die like a Kshatriya. He saluted dying Bheeshma and came back.

It was now the 18th day of the war. Salya was made the Commander of Kaurvas army. Salya concentrated on Yudhishtira. It was a wholesale slaughter of men and animals. Yudhishtira fought very well. Everybody was surprised to see this form of Yudhishtira. Yudhishtira was determined to kill Salya. Yudhishtira thought for Shri Krishna and threw a javelin on Salya. It was a very terrible weapon. It pierced the chest of Salya and Salya was no more.

Duryodhana, however, continued to fight. He put up a tough fight against Pandavas. Sudarsana, his last surviving brother, and Sakuni were helping Duryodhana. With a sharp arrow, Bhima cut off the head of Sudarsana. Simultaneously, Sakuni was killed by Sahadeva.

Duryodahna was now alone. He was burning with fire from inside for various reasons. He wanted to cool himself so as to think coolly and decide the final course of action. He ran away and hid himself in the nearby Dwaipayana lake. Duryodhana had the unusual power to stay in water for a long time. The only surviving trio of Kauravas namely Aswatthama, Kripa and Kritavarma came to the lake and asked him to come out. On the other side, Pandavas were searching for Duryodhana. A hunter who happened to pass by the lake, informed Pandavas the whereabouts of Duryodhana. They came to the lake accompanied by Shri Krishna. Yudhishtira asked Duryodhana to come out and fight; that there was no point in hiding; that he had to face death. There was no other option for him. Duryodhana came out of the lake.

It was decided that Duryodhana would fight with Bhima in a duel of mace. Balarama also joined. Venue was chosen as Sappmantapanchaka, a holy place, on the advice of Balarama. Both Duryodhana and Bhima saluted Balarama and started the duel. It was a spectacular fight. Duryodhana was avoiding the hits of Bhima by jumping here and there and also high up in the sky. Duryodhana was expert in mace war. It was becoming difficult for Bhima to kill Duryodhana. Shri Krishna gave a hint to Bhima by thumping his thighs. Bhima got a clue and during such jumps Bhima gave a strong blow on his thighs; Duryodhana fell on the ground with broken thighs and could not get up. The king of Hastinapur was on the ground waiting for his death. Balarama was not happy because Bhima violated the rules of Gaddayudh (war of mace) by hitting below the waist. Shri Krishna pacified Balarama stating that Duryodhana was the greatest sinner and he should not mind this wrong doing on the part of Bhima. Seeing the condition of Duryodhana, a one-time king of Hastinapur, Yudhishtira was sad. He addressed Duryodhana, "There was no fault of ours. You had chosen this path. You will, however, reach Heaven. I salute you King of the World."

Pandavas returned to their camp leaving Duryodhana the one time monarch of earth with his last minutes thoughts to himself.

After the death of Duryodhana, Mahabharata war was over. Shri Krishna and Pandavas then assembled at a place in the battlefield. Shri Krishna asked Arjuna to get down the chariot with his Gandeeva bow. Arjuna alighted from the chariot. Shri Krishna then followed Arjuna and too got down from the chariot. As soon as Shri Krishna got down from the chariot, it started burning like a heap of woods. The horses too were burnt alive. The Pandavas were amazed. Shri Krishna clarified "that everything has a purpose in the world; Once the purpose is over, it is not required; so was with the chariot and the horses." On that night of victory, Shri Krishna asked Pandavas to sleep at a different location than in their usual tent.

On the Kauravas side, only three survived the war viz: Aswatthama (son of Dronacharya), Kritverma and Kripa. All the three went and met Duryodhana in the battlefield. They were shocked to see the condition of their king. Aswatthama decided, then and there, to finish the Pandavas, come what may. The trio took leave from Duryodhana and came to a tree to take some rest. Aswatthama witnessed an owl destroying the nests of birds at dead of night and happily enjoying his meals. Aswatthama got a clue and immediately started for his intended prey. He reached the Pandava camp and entered the tents. He first found Dhrishtadyumna (brother of Draupadi) and killed him ruthlessly. Next he overpowered the five sons of Draupadi one by one and finished them too. Subsequently Kripa set the camp on fire. The blazing fire destroyed everything. Pandavas, however, escaped because they slept elsewhere on the advice of Shri Krishna. Aswatthama hurriedly went to Duryodhana and narrated his achievement. Duryodhana beamed with joy and embraced death happily.

Pandavas were greatly shocked on hearing the death of their sons. They located Aswatthama and arrested him. In frustration, Aswatthama released Brahmseersastra (missile) to kill all Pandavas including their any unborn baby. It was a ghastly act. Shri Krishna cursed Aswatthama, "You are the most contemptible of all creatures. I will give back life to Abhimanyu's son from Uttara (who was in the womb of Uttara), however, you are now destined to live for ever; you will wander about this earth alone." He was then stripped off his 'mani' (gem) and let off because he was the son of guru (teacher) Drona and a brahmin as well. From there, the three survivors of Kauravas dispersed. Aswatthama went to the banks of Ganges to the hermitage of *Rishi* Vyasa; Kripa went to Hastinapur and Kritverma went to Dwarka, the capital of Shri Krishna.

Pandavas now proceeded to Hastinapur and met Dhritarashtra and Gandhari. They expressed their helplessness over what had happened. It was a tense moment to face the king and queen whose all the 100 sons had been killed. Nevertheless, Dhritarashtra embraced each one of them pretending a show of affection. Dhritarashtra was extremely angry with Bhima who killed Duryodhana by unfair means. Shri Krishna placed a steel statue of Bhima between Dhritarashtra and Bhima when the blind king was about to embrace Bhima. Such was the pain and anger in the heart of the blind king against Bhima that the metal statue was reduced to powder and Dhritarashtra was drenched in sweat and blood; but Bhima was saved. The king begged pardon for his conduct and thereafter he became calm. He was reconciled to the reality of the death of all his sons, a tragedy for which he was equally responsible.

Dhritarashtra, Gandhari, Kunti, Shri Krishna, all Pandavas, Draupadi and other women of family went to the battlefield to have a last look at their husbands, children and other slain members of the family. The women started weeping bitterly. Gandhari saw all her sons lying dead. She saw dear Duryodhana lying dead, uncrowned and unattended. Suddenly she was overpowered by anger. She turned to Krishna and shouted, "You are witnessing this carnage. You could have averted it. The house of Kauravas has been destroyed because of your indifference. I am cursing you. The entire family of Virsnis, to which you belong, would be destroyed by itself just as our family. The Vrisnis will fight among themselves and kill each other. The women of Vrisnis will weep as these women are weeping." Shri Krishna accepted the curse of Gandhari. He, however, commented that king Dhritarashtra and Duryodhana were to be blamed for this great tragedy and that she should not grieve on the outcome of war which was destined and consequences were known and predicted. Gandhari had no words to counter Shri Krishna.

Kunti was sad over the death of Karna. She now disclosed to Pandavas that Karana was their brother. Pandavas, specially Yudhishtira, was sorry on learning this secret. He was unhappy with Kunti. He cursed all womankind, "From now on, no woman will be able to keep secrets with her." As we know the curse continues till this day; women have been generally found weak in keeping a secret which sometimes generate big issues in the family.

Yudhishtira was crowned as the king of Hastinapur in a ceremonial manner. Immediately thereafter, Dhritarashtra, Shri Krishna, Yudhishtira and others went to battlefield to meet the family's patriarch Bheeshma. Bheeshma taught Yudhishtira the duties of a king; how a kingdom should be governed in a fair and just manner, philosophy of life, etc. Yudhishtira was enlightened; he felt greater confidence in handling the affairs of kingdom, while observing Dharma.

And then Makar Sankranti came, on first day of dark fortnight of the month of Magha. Sun had come in the Makar Rashi. It was the day of final departure of Bheeshma. Shri Krishna, Dhritarashtra, Yudhishtira and other Pandavas went to meet the grand old man of the family. *Rishi* Vyasa and many other *Rishis* had already reached there. Bheeshma worshipped Shri Krishna and sought deliverance from the world. "My Lord, you are the Creator of the world; you are the Supreme Eternal Soul. Permit me to leave this world." Shri Krishna blessed Bheeshma and the great soul got salvation. Last rites of Bheeshma were performed with great honour.

Shri Krishna then left for Dwarka. Yudhishtira performed Aswamedha Yagna and established his supremacy. A baby boy was born from Uttara but it was dead at the time of birth. Shri Krishna revived the baby. He was named as Parikshit. Parikshit was the son of Abhimanyu and grandson of Arjuna.

15 years passed under the rule of Yudhishtira. Dhritarashtra, Gandhari and Kunti went to forest and settled in the ashram of Rishi Vyasa to spend rest of their life. Sanjay accompanied them. One day Yudhishtira and other Pandavas went to forest to meet mother Kunti, etc. There was a happy union of the family. Yudhishtira met Vidura. Vidura was standing under a tree doing penance; he had turned himself in to a mass of bones. When Yudhishtira saw him face to face, Vidura left his own body and went inside the body of Yudhishtira. Vidura was dead. There was a voice from heaven who told that Vidura was incarnation of Dharma-- just as Yudhishtira was---and asked Yudhishtira to leave the body of Vidura as it was. Yudhishtira did as he was told by the Heavenly voice.

One day there was a fire in the forest. Sanjay asked Dhritarashtra, Gandhari and Kunti to run to escape from the fire but they decided to stay and burnt themselves dead in the blazing fire.

Thirty-six years passed since the war happened. Shri Krishna remembered the curse of Gandhari. He too was tired of his worldly existence. His role was over as an Incarnation an earth to restore Dharma. He took all the Vrisnis to a holy place called Prabhaasateertha for the worship of Lord Shiva. The Vrisnis had a great time there and little they knew that it was their last celebration. Because of the curse, they drank heavily, lost control of themselves and started fighting among themselves. Lord Krishna was watching the fight undetached and waiting to see the inevitable. Satyaki cut off the head of Kritverma. Later Satyaki and Pradyumna, the son of Shri Krishna, were killed. As it was destined, all Vrisnis finished themselves in a matter of minutes. All Vrisnis were dead except Sri Krishna, Balarama and Daruka. Shri Krishna then sent Daruka to fetch Arjuna to take away the women and children to Hastinapur.

Balarama also left his body in the presence of Shri Krishna. Shri Krishna now knew that his own time had come. He thought of Yashodha. He remembered Radha. He remembered Arjuna. Shri Krishna then lay down under a tree. A hunter by the name Jara was passing by. He mistook Shri Krishna as a deer. He shot an arrow which pierced Shri Krishna's body. Jara was feeling sorry and extremely guilty. Shri Krishna pardoned him and left for his Dham, Vaikuntha. He, however, blessed the hunter for relieving Him from earthly existence.

Arjuna reached Dwarka only to find Shri Krishna dead. Sea engulfed entire Dwarka in a matter of minutes in the presence of Arjuna. Arjuna collected all the Vrisnis women and children and left for Hastinapur. On the way, some robbers attacked the group with an intention to commit robbery. It is said that Arjuna was ineffective in stopping the robbers; Gandeeva failed him in the absence of Sh. Krishna and robbers had their way.

Arjuna returned to Hastinapur with Vrisnis women and children. He narrated the events of Dwarka to Yudhishtira and others. Yudhishtira was a wise person. He could now sense the future. He consulted the Pandava brothers and decided to leave the earth. Parikshit was made the king of Hastinapur with Yuyutsu (son of Dhritarashtra from another woman, Yuyutsu had joined Pandavas and thus survived the war as his guardian and Kripacharya as his guru.

Pandavas and Draupadi then started for their final journey led by Yudhishtira. They first went to Dwarka and paid their homage to Shri Krishna. They then reached Mount Meru. As they were proceeding to heavens, Draupadi dropped dead. Upon asking by Bhima, Yudhishtira said that "her fault was that she loved Arjuna more than her other husbands. That was the only sin she committed." Sahadeva was next to fall dead; it was because he was proud of his wisdom. Nakula fell a little later; Yudhhishtira explained that he was proud of his beauty. Next Arjuna fell because he had sworn that he would kill all the enemies by himself, thereby insulting other great warriors. At last Bhima also fell dead; Yudhishtira told him that his sin was that he was proud of his strength.

Yudhishtira was now alone with a dog who accompanied them since they left Hastinapura. He was received by Indra with a chariot. Indra asked Yudhishtira to alight from the chariot and to leave the dog there by itself. Yudhishtira, however, insisted that he would not go without the dog since it had been his companion all throughout the journey. Suddenly, the dog turned in to Lord Dharma, his father. He blessed Yudhishtira for showing compassion to the dog at such a critical time.

Lord Dharma asked him to proceed to heaven. All along Yudhishtira was insisting that he would not go to heavens without his brothers and Draupadi and that he would stay in hell in case they too happened to be in hell. Yudhishtira was then taken through a difficult, dark, frightening, dreadful route in which he heard cries of Bhima, Radhey, Draupadi, etc. He insisted the accompanying attendants of Indra that he would prefer to stay with his brothers and other ancestors in that dark place and would not go elsewhere. Suddenly there was a cool breeze; the place turned into a very beautiful area filled with heavenly pleasures. Indra himself appeared before Yudhishtira. He explained to Yudhishtira that the dreadful journey of an hour was to punish him for the one lie he spoke (about the death of Aswatthama) when Drona was to be killed. Yudhishtira was then united with all the brothers, Draupadi, Abhimanyu, Bheeshma, Drona, Satyki, Vidura, etc. in Heaven. Shri Krishna was at the centre of all the Gods.

Even Duryodhana reached heavens which was a great surprise to Yudhishtira. Narda explained to him why Duryodhana reached Heaven. "Duryodhana died fighting. His soul has been cleansed because he died fighting bravely. He was true to his birth. He was a kshatriya and he died like a kshatriya. He was not afraid to die. Moreover, Duryodhana was blessed by Balarama that he would go to heaven. Gandhari's penance also contributed for Duryodhana's ascent to heaven." **Narada concluded that rules of Heaven are different from those of Earth.**

Srimad Bhagavad Gita

Srimad Bhagavad Gita popularly known as "Gita" is a sacred, divine book of Hindus but its philosophy is independent of any religion. For this reason, it is equally popular in Western countries. Gita is a part of Bhishma Parva of Mahabharata having a total of 701 verses. Mahatma Gandhi once went to one of the biggest libraries in London and asked the library in-charge as to which spiritual book was most popular, and the answer was – Srimad Bhagavad Gita. In view of its importance, Gita Jayanti is celebrated in India by its followers on the 11th day–Ekadesi of the bright half of the Margasirsha month of the Hindu almanac.

- Gita and its teachings were told by Shri Krishna to Arjuna in the battlefield of Kurukshetra when the Kaurava and Pandva cousins were facing each other in the bloodiest battle of the world ever fought. When the war was about to begin, Arjuna scanned the army of both sides. He saw Kaurava cousins, friends, relatives, teachers and sons of all of them and millions of others whom he was supposed to kill. Arjuna became despondent. He dropped down his Gandeev Dhanush (Bow) and showed his unwillingness to fight war which involved death of many close persons. It was, therefore, necessary to motivate Arjuna if Pandavas were to win the war. Shri Krishna then taught Arjuna the deeper philosophy of life, what is the real goal of life, the various paths of salvation; Self versus body, the status of mortals in the overall situation of life. Lord Krishna showed his virat swaroop, showing the "maya", entire universe, there by convincing Arjuna that he (Arjuna) was merely an agent of divine will for slaying the Kauravas and that in performing this act, he is not incurring any sin; rather it his duty as a kshatriya, to fight and kill the enemy and by doing so he will attain the heaven. An enlightened Arjuna lifted his Gandeev Dhanusha (bow) and demolished the Kauravas, killed the mighty Bheeshma, Karna, Dronacharya and millions of their warriors and brought victory to the Pandavas in a devastating war which lasted for only 18 days.
- All the teachings of Shri Krishna in the battlefield have been recorded as the Song Celestial or the Bhagavad Gita for the benefit of the entire humanity. Gita is an ocean of wisdom. It is a great spiritual guide. Gita contains the cream of Vedas and teachings of Upanishads. Therefore, its teachings are eternal and universal. They are relevant today as they were, five thousand years ago in that situation of war. It is relevant to individuals, families, kings, kingdoms, nations and the world at large.
- As per Gita, the human birth is very valuable. It is a God given opportunity to get liberated from the repeated cycles of birth and death called 'samsara'. Goal of life should, therefore, be to get liberation from samsara. Gita recognises that people are of different temperaments and hence need different approaches depending upon their inclination to realize God. Accordingly, Gita contains philosophy of Janana Yoga for people of sharp intellect, Bhakti Yoga for emotional people, Karam Yoga for people having zest for work and Raj Yoga for people of contemplation, for getting liberation from the samsara **(~~definite~~)** upon one's spiritual inclination. The salient features of these four paths is given below.

Bhakti Yoga

- Bhakti Yoga or path of devotion is one of the paths to reach the Supreme. It can be adopted by anybody, the weak and the lowly; the illiterate and the ignorant. At the same time it is the easiest path but equally effective as the other paths. There are no fixed rules to follow this path. Initially the aspirants have to use all the techniques, namely knowledge, devotion, action and meditation to train the wandering and impure mind to turn godward. The devotee is required to look upon the world as manifestation of the Supreme. Slowly the mind becomes pure and then rises higher in its spiritual journey to reach Almighty.
- In Bhakti Yoga, the devotee develops a relationship with the Lord, namely that of a sakha bhav (friend), assuming the Lord as parent/mother, Madhurya Bhav (Lover), Santa Bhav (peaceful adoration), Dasya Bhav (attitude of a servant towards the master). Meera Bai looked upon Shri Krishna as her husband, Arjuna looked upon Shri Krishna as a friend, Shri Ramakrishna looked upon God as mother, Vidura had the attitude of a servant to the Lord. Milkmaids of Vrindavan looked upon Shri Krishna in their own way. There is a story in Bhagvata. One milkmaid was locked in her home by her husband. The result was she became totally absorbed in Shri Krishna, in deep meditation and she was later found to have left her body in the state of Samadhi.
- **Most important requirement of Bhakti Yoga is that the devotee should have Shraddha or faith in God as the highest reality till He reveals itself in devotee's consciousness. The devotee constantly remembers God. He sings His name in kirtans, he chants His mantra. He sings God in prayers. He attends religious congregations to hear His glory. In a way he totally surrenders to Him to get His divine grace. Devotion of the devotee reaches to a height that worshipper and the worshipped become one like Radha and Shri Krishna. Meera Bai, a true devotee of Shri Krishna, used to say, "Mere to Girdhar Gopal, doosra na koye."**
- Absolute self-surrender and dedication of all activities to God marks the conduct of the true devotee. Then in the eyes of the devotee, God appears everywhere, in the animate as well as in the inanimate. He is a man; He is a woman; He is the master and He is the servant. Entire universe appears to be Him only. The devotee merges himself with the Divine.

Karam Yoga

- Karam or action can be another way to reach the Almighty. Human mind is continuously at work; it cannot stop working. It does not stop thinking even for a moment. Our thoughts, worries and dreams also come in the category of action. In verse III. 5, Lord Krishna says,
- "No man can ever remain, even for a moment, without performing any action.

  "You must, therefore, perform your prescribed duties, definitely action is superior than inaction. Even plain survival (of body) requires lot of action, we have to arrange money for food clothing, etc.

- In general, we work expecting some results from our actions. Gita says that work done with a sense of doership (i.e., I have done this work), or expecting some results, binds us to the samsara and generates Karmic fruit of action. This is reflected in verse III 9.
- "In this world all actions, unless they are done as an offering to God, become causes of bondage. Therefore work for the sake of God without personal attachment or sense of ego or doership."
- Karam Yoga tells us to act (by thoughts, words and deeds) in such a manner as not to bind us to the samsara. To achieve this, we have to do our actions without ego, in a detached manner and offering all actions to God. Work done without any selfish motive and purely as service to God, makes us rise in spiritual heights. The way to work without any attachment, is not to sit quiet but to surrender the assigned duties and sense of doership to the Supreme. In verse III 19, Lord reiterates,
- "Therefore perform action without attachment, for by working without attachment, a man attains the Supreme."
- In verse IV.18, the lord clarifies as to who is a true Karam Yogi.

  "One who sees inaction in action and action in inaction, is a true Karam yogi."
- **If we give up the idea of doership and also feel that nature does everything not me, this is called inaction in action. Similarly, when we think in our mind that I have done such and such though appearing quiet from outside, that is called action in inaction. The action done by a restless thinking mind also bind us to samsara. The true state of no work is when the work continues through the body and mind but we ourselves are not working. Once we reach the blessed state of non-work, our body might continue to work but every moment we shall be aware of the truth that "I am not doing any work. I am totally separate from the body and senses". The central focus of Karam Yoga, therefore, is on training oneself to be non-working, even while working.**
- Shri Ramkrishna Paramhamsa has given a beautiful example to illustrate the Karam Yoga. He says that we should work like a maid in the house of a rich person. She does so many work for them; she takes care of their children; she is happy when they are happy; she is sad when the family is sad; but in her heart of hearts, she knows that she does not belong to the family and she may have to leave the house any time. Similarly we must also live in the world with the same feelings, fully involved but detached.
- Thus through the practice of Karam Yoga, an aspirant becomes ripe in the knowledge of Brahman. The Self in us gets separated from the mind, intellect, ego, sense organs, and the body and then it lives blissfully established in its true nature Paramatma.

The Yoga of Meditation

- Yoga of Meditation is explained in chapter VI of Gita. According to this Yoga, we can reach God through meditation which is also popularly known as Raj Yoga. However, human mind is very powerful. It is as fast as wind and it is difficult to concentrate the mind to meditate on the Lord.

  Gita suggests that such an aspirant should first resort to action to learn concentration of mind.

- **In verses VI.11 to VI.17, Gita prescribes the techniques for meditation. The aspirant should prepare a firm seat, should hold his body, head, neck erect and fix the gaze at the tip of nose, or any other deity for meditation. The aspirant should eat a moderate diet and he should be in good health. The aspirant should lead a regulated and disciplined life. The aspirant should practice this yoga with a firm conviction and iron determination. He should control the senses through dispassion. Further he should control the wavering mind without the use of force but gradually, by bringing it again and again, to be absorbed in Self. Gradually the practitioner shall attain tranquillity, mind will get assimilated in the Self and will then enjoy the Supreme bliss.**
- **Such a Yogi beholds all beings one with Brahman. Lord Krishna says, "He who sees Me in all beings and sees all beings in Me, he never becomes separated from Me nor I am separated from him", i.e., the Lord dwells in him and he dwells in the Lord.—VI.30**
- Gita in verses VI.40 to VI.45 further says that if a person has not been fully successful in Dhyan Yoga in spite of best efforts, (because of mind's extremely fickle nature) even then, such a person has not lost anything. He gets a good birth in his next incarnation. He will remember his previous efforts of becoming the Yogi by virtue of his samskaras. He will be able to complete the unfinished task and can reach the highest state of a Dhyan Yogi if the meditation practice is continued. The spiritual efforts never go waste; they are carried in next incarnation and give their fruits.

Jnana Yoga (Yoga of Knowledge)

- Jnana Yoga is another path to reach the Supreme by knowing the Self. The ignorance envelopes our wisdom, we identify ourselves with the body and ignore the Self. By knowing the Self through knowledge, we identify ourselves with the divine Brahman and get liberated from samsara cycles of birth and death.
- In the manifested universe, there are ever changing forms covering all beings and dead matter and the unchanging "Consciousness"—Supreme supports them. Disciple of Jnana Yoga must turn away from the illusions of the manifest world and turn inward. Only by turning inward, the illusion of the manifested world can go. A focused mind, gradually trained to contemplate on the Supreme, is required to get the desired benefits.
- Ahm Brahm asmi, "I am the Brahman". Knowing one's divine identity or divine Self through knowledge is the ultimate goal of Jnana Yoga. The devotee takes the help of an enlightened teacher (Guru) to follow this path. He has to practice purity of thoughts, train concentration of mind, develop faith in his guru and have faith in the teachings of scriptures. Then only he can make tangible progress in reaching the highest.
- To begin with, the aspirant is first asked to understand the meaning of "Tat Tvam Asi" which means "You are Divine". The Guru then asks the aspirant to meditate on this true inner Self. The aspirant then contemplates on his divine Self and by "manana" (contemplation) and reasoning, he understands the true meaning of 'Self'. He identifies himself with 'Universal Soul'.

Let us see what Gita says about some other important areas of life.

- **Soul:** Soul occupies a central place in Hinduism; what we see around are beings having the same Self but different shapes and forms–*yoni*–; it is very necessary to understand the nature of Self. According to Gita, soul is eternal. When a person dies, soul does not die, it leaves the body and acquires a new body.
- Soul is the master of intellect. We should purify the soul by following teachings of scriptures, and then following its advice, we will never suffer.
- Since soul is same in all beings, everybody is divine and deserves respect, good treatment and everything which an individual aspires.
- **The Supreme:** Gita says that God or Supreme is everywhere, from in the smallest to biggest; in all living beings to all non-living things. In verse 7.7 to 7.15 the Lord says about himself: there is no other cause of Universe; I am the cause of the Universe. I am the light in Sun and Moon. I am life in all beings. I am the syllable in AUM in all the Vedas, sound in ether and virility in men.
- In verse 9.16, Lord Krishna says that "I am the ritual and the sacrifice. I am the medicine that heals the body, the chant that calms the mind. I am the offering, the fire that consumes the offering and also the one to whom the sacrifice is offered". Continuing further in verse 9.17, Lord says, I am the father of the world, the mother, the dispenser and the grandfather, the purifier and the Vedas. In verse 9.18, Lord Krishna further explains, I am the witness of the good and evil actions done by the Jivas (individuals), I am the abode where all living beings dwell. I am the shelter for the distressed. I am the source of this universe. In verses 10.32 to 10.41, Lord says, "I am the time that never ends. I am the destroyer who brings death. I am the future which decides what would happen. I am all that, which makes a woman beautiful, her appearance, her voice, her qualities. In music, I am the melody. Among seasons, I am the spring, etc. There is no end to what I am", i.e., He is omnipresent, omnipotent and omniscient.
- Since Supreme is everything and everywhere, in verse 9.27 to 9.32 Lord Krishna stresses, "Consecrate all actions to Me; Whatever you eat, whatever you offer in sacrifice, whatever you give and whatever you practice in austerity, do it as an offering to me." Doing all actions in the name of Supreme will purify the soul; Atma then meets Paramatma which is the ultimate aim of human birth. Mind may be trained to do all actions in the name of God and results can be highly rewarding including Moksha.
- Birth after Death--In verse 8.5 and 8.6, the Lord says that whosoever goes from this world remembering Me, finally attains Me; Further whosoever leaves the body, thinking of any being, to that being only does he go; in other words, last thoughts of a person determine his next birth. The most prominent thought of one's life occupies the mind at the time of death. Whatever we have pursued in life, our desires, our cravings, attitude, likes, dislikes, etc. will mould our thoughts at the time of death. Accordingly, one should cultivate pure thoughts in life through Samaskaras, so that satvik thoughts occupy our mind at the last moment of leaving the world, and we get a good birth in next incarnation.

✡✡✡

Chapter 4 : Hindu Vratas & Festivals

Hindus are religious people. They have a large number of festivals spread throughout the year. It is popularly said that in India every day is a festival. Festivals make people feel refreshed from the melancholy of everyday life. Almost all Hindu festivals involve worship of a specific deity, e.g., Goddess Lakshmi is worshipped on Diwali, Lord Krishna is worshipped on Janamashtmi, Hanumana is worshipped on Hanuman Jayanti and so on. Hindu festivals are days of enjoyment. People dress differently, special food is prepared, families or communities meet and celebrate. Diwali, Holi, Janamashtmi are some such festivals of Hindus which depict the festive mood, high spirits among the people and in the overall environment.

On the other side, festivals in India also have a great role in unifying a large number of communities having different language, different temperament, different religious inclinations. A festival like Diwali is celebrated across India by all communities, irrespective of cast, creed, religion, language just like Christmas in Western countries. Lok Manya Tilak mobilized the Indian people in freedom movement through the festival of Ganesh Chaturthi.

Hindus also observe numerous Vratas (fasts) spread throughout the year. Hindus believe that Vratas are a great cleanser of body and mind and increase their will power to face the ups and downs of life. Vratas are also helpful in the spiritual upliftt of the devotee. Again vratas are also associated with some devas. Through vratas, Hindus seek the blessings of gods and goddesses for material and spiritual uplift.

Vratas invariably involve fast and worship of the concerned deity. Hindu scriptures provide methods of worship separately for each vrata. The common items used in worship are milk, honey, rice, mauli, haldi, ghee, earthen lamp, fruits, dry fruits, prasad in the form of sweets/halwa/kheer, Gangajal, Tulsi leaves, incense, flowers, etc.

Some vratas are very stringent like Nirjala Aikadeshi, Karvachauth, Chhath but Hindus observe them with great reverence and bear the stringent requirements happily.

Hindus follow lunar calendar for the purpose of identifying festivals and vratas. It is, therefore, necessary to describe the Hindu calendar months and days. The Hindu calendar has the following twelve months shown with the corresponding months of the English calendar.

No.	Hindu Calendar Months	English Calendar Months
1.	Chaitra	March – April
2.	Vaisakha	April – May
3.	Jayeshtha	May – June
4.	Asadha	June – July
5.	Shravana	July – August
6.	Bhadra	August – September
7.	Asvina	September – October
8.	Kartika	October – November
9.	Margasirsa	November – December
10.	Pausa	December – January
11.	Magh	January – February
12.	Phalguna	February – March

Every Hindu month ends with Puranmasi (Full Moon Day) when moon is seen as complete. Each month is divided in two 'Pakshas'—fortnights: Shukla Paksha or bright fortnight, Krishna Paksha or dark Fortnight. The days of each fortnight are called as:

1. Pratipada 1st day
2. Dvitiya 2nd day
3. Tritya 3rd day
4. Chaturthi 4th day
5. Panchami 5th day
6. Sashthi 6th day
7. Saptami 7th day
8. Ashtmi 8th day
9. Navami 9th day
10. Dashmi 10th day
11. Aikadeshi 11th day
12 Dwadashi 12th day
13. Trayodashi 13th day
14. Chaturdashi 14th day

The days ending in Amavasya are called dark fortnight–Krishna Paksha–and those ending in Puranmasi are called bright fortnight–Shukla Paksha.

Festivals and Vratas of Hindus

Some important festivals and vratas of Hindus are described in this section in order of their occurrence as per the Hindu calendar.

New Year Day

Hindu new year starts from 'Pratipada'—the first day of the dark fortnight of the Chaitra month of Vikrami Samvat (March/April of English calendar). According to Brahma Purana, Lord Brahma created the 'sristi' (universe) on this day and reckoning of time started from sunrise of this day. On this day king Chandragupt Vikramaditya defeated Shanka tribe, hence this was given the name of Vikrami Samwat.

This day is celebrated across India in various forms. This day is among the three and a half days considered to be extremely auspicious, others being Vijyadashmi, Balipratipada, and Akshayatritiya. At this time, new crop is ready and there is celebration among the farming community.

People of Andhra Pradesh celebrate it as 'Yugadi', meaning thereby the commencement of the Yuga. Sindhi people celebrate the birthday of Sri Jhulelal on this day. Kashmiri people celebrate this day as 'Navreh' — New Year day. People of Maharashtra celebrate 'Gudi Parva' on this day. Assemese celebrate Bihu festival on this day.

On this day, Lord Ganesh and Lakshmi are worshipped to seek their blessing for material benefits and a trouble free new year. Lord Brahma is worshipped in a ceremonial way. Other deities, Vishnu, and all the navgrahas are worshipped as per the traditions. The idea is to seek the blessings from the vast universe of gods and goddesses to make coming new year as smooth as possible.

Gangaur Vrata

This vrata is specially kept by married women for the long life of their husbands. Women wear colourful dresses with good make up, wear bangles, bindi, kajal, sindoor (which are considered sacred for a Hindu married woman). Women form a group, listen the katha of Gauri--Parvati and then break the fast later in the day.The vrata is observed between first to third of the bright fortnight of the Chaitra month of Hindu calendar.

Gangaur Vrata is specially celebrated with lot of zeal in Rajasthan. The celebrations last for nearly 18 days. For a newly married girl, it is mandatory to observe fast for all the 18 days. Women and girls worship Gauri -- Parvati, all through the festival. Images of Gauri are decorated with beautiful and colourful dresses and jewellery. A procession is taken out in the village, town and city with women singing, dancing to the tune of a local band. There is a boat procession taken out in Pichola lake in Udaipur. Images of Isar and Gauri are taken around the lake. In Jodhpur thousands of girls dressed in their best attire gather and bring water and durba (grass) in silver or brass pots and assemble singing and dancing at a place called Girdikot. People of nearby villages also assemble and enjoy the festive mood.

Poranik Katha: Shree Khund Puran mentions about the origin of this vrata. Once on the third day of dark fortnight of Chaitra month, Lord Shiva, Parvatiji and Naradji came to a village while roaming. A group of ordinary women welcomed them and worshipped them in a formal manner. Parvati was very happy and blessed them for long life to their Suhag—husbands. Another group of women from well to do families came subsequently and worshipped Parvati and offered good food, etc. Parvati was extremely pleased and this time she blessed them with long life of their Suhags—husbands, by sprinkling her blood on them.

Subsequently Parvati took bath in the river. She worshipped Shiva in the form of a mound of sand. Shiva was extremely pleased and thus blessed her, "A woman who worships me on this day and keeps vrata for you, her husband will live longer and he will ultimately get liberation." *Rishi* Narada, who was accompanying Shiva and Parvati, was also impressed by the actions of Parvatiji. He remarked, "You are most superior among the women. Those women who observe this fast and worship their husbands from inside, Lord Shiva will bless them for long life of their husbands." Since then, this vrata is being observed by women of India for longevity and welfare of their husbands.

Ganesh Chaturthi

This vrata is also called 'Sankashti Ganesh Chaturthi'. Since Lord Ganesh is called as 'Vighan Vinashak' (remover of obstacles), this vrata is considered as an antidote to bail out the devotee from a difficult situation. Ravana got his kingdom back from Bali by the grace of this vrata. Hanumana was blessed by this vrata only and could locate Sita in Lanka through the power of this vrata. Lord Shiva observed this vrata for killing the demon Tripura.

Worshipp of Ganesha on this fastival

This vrata can be done on the Chaturthi of the dark fortnight of any month but Chaturthi of Magh, Shravan, Margshirsha and Bhadrapada are considered more auspicious. In the morning, the devotee takes a 'Sankalp' (vow) that he is observing this vrata for general well-being and to ward off any current problem. Lord Ganesha is invoked to bless the devotee. Lord Ganesha is ceremoniously worshipped in the evening. 'Laddoos'- modaks are offered to the Lord. At night, Moon is worshipped and fast is broken and meals are taken.

Poranik Katha: In Satyug, there was a king of the name Nala. His wife Damayanti was very beautiful. Once king had to pass through extremely bad times. His wealth was stolen by dacoits. His palace was reduced to ashes by a blazing fire. He left the kingdom and went to forest. By bad luck, he was separated from his wife. He had to do petty jobs to survive.

Damayanti was also totally broken. She then met *Rishi* Sharbhang and told him her sad story. *Rishi* then advised her to observe the 'Sankat Chaturthy vrata' in the month of Bhadrapada to ward off her bad times. Damayanti then observed this vrata from the Chaturthi of dark fortnight of Bhadrpada month and continued to observe it every month on this day for seven months. Ultimately, she was united with her husband and her son. King Nala got back his kingdom too. Since then, this vrata is being observed by Hindus to ward off bad times.

Akshya Tritia Vrata

This vrata falls on third day of bright fortnight of Vaisakha month of Hindu calendar. It is said that whatever is done by way of charity, offerings to ancestors on this day, become 'akshya'–inexhaustible. Vishnu Dharmmotra mentions that one vrata of Akshya Tritiya is equivalent to vising all the places of pilgrimage. Offerings to ancestors in the form of "Pind Daana" and "Tarpan" are specially considered auspicious on this day. It is also considered an extremely auspicious day for commencement of any important ceremony like marriage, construction of new house, commencement of new business, etc., and it is believed that success is assured.

Vrata of Aksha Tritiya

Parshuram's birth anniversary falls on this day. Badrinath shrine is opened on this day after winter break. According to Puranas, Treta Yuga in which Lord Rama was born, started from this day.

On this day the devotees observe fast and worship Lord Vishnu, Lakshmi and Shri Krishna. Gram pulse, sugar and Tulsi are offered to deities and distributed as 'prasad' among people. Giving of barley, in charity, is specially considered auspicious on this day.

Poranik Katha: There is a story in Purana that a businessman of the name of Mahodaya was poor. His income was small and he had to feed a large family. He heard about the benefits of vrata of Akshya Tritia. He observed this vrata regularly and did charities as per the scriptures. It is said that he became king of Kushavati city in his next birth; and he enjoyed all the pleasures of world and lived happily thereafter.

Nirjala Aikadeshi Vrata

This vrata is very stringent but equally auspicious for the devotee. It is stringent because it falls on the Aikadeshi of bright fortnight of Jayeshtha month. At this time, summer is at its extreme (temperature is around 45°C in north India) and this vrata prohibits to take even water. The vrata starts before the sunrise and lasts till the sunrise of next day. No food and water is permitted in between these 24 hours.

It is believed that this vrata brings prosperity, health and happiness to the devotee. Charity, dana, havana and worship done on this day has a great effect; the benefits are equated to the charity done in Kurukshetra at the time of solar eclipse.

Next day on twelfth day, the fast is broken with the worship of Lord Vishnu or that of Peepal tree. Brahmins are given food and dakshina in cash and kind.

Poranik Katha: Mahabharata and Padam Puran mentions the following story about the benefits of this vrata. Once Bhima asked *Rishi* Vyasa, "Grandfather, all my brothers, mother Kunti and Draupadi observe fast on all the Aikadesi; I am not able to do because I have a large body and very strong urge for food; Is there any simpler method to get the same benefit?" *Rishi* Vyasa then advised Bhima to observe Nirjala Aikadeshi fast on the 11th day of bright fortnight of Jayeshtha month which will give benefit equal to all 14 Aikadeshis. That is why this Aikadeshi is also called Bhimseni Nirjala Aikadeshi.

Devshayani Aikadeshi

This vrata falls on the Aikadeshi of bright fortnight of Ashvin month of Hindu calendar. It is believed that Lord Vishnu goes to sleep for four months from this day to the Aikadeshi of bright fortnight of the month of Kartika. No important auspicious functions like marriage, shifting to a new house, etc. is celebrated during these four months by Hindus. This day is therefore called Devshayaniand (going to sleep by Devas) and Kartika month Aikadeshi is called as Devauthani (getting up from sleep by Devas) Aikadeshi.

This vrata is basically to remember Lord Vishnu. Water is offered to Surya (Sun) in the morning. Lord Vishnu is worshipped in the evening in a ceremonial way with 'panchamrit', etc. Lord is then laid to rest for sleep in a symbolic way. It is prohibited to take cereal, salt on this day and only one meal is taken in the evening after worship of Lord Vishnu. Devotee is supposed to observe celibacy. Hindu scriptures mention that Lord Vishnu bestows prosperity and happiness to the devotees, who observe this vrata. The devotee gets even 'mukti' (salvation) if this vrata is done regularly and as prescribed by the scriptures.

Poranik Katha: There was a Suryavanshi king by the name Mandhata in Satyayuga. His kingdom was very popular; people were happy and prosperous. It so happened that there was no rain in the kingdom for three years in succession. There was a famine and both cattle and men were dying for want of food and water. The king was at a loss and could not assess why that misfortune had fallen on his kingdom. He set out to find a solution. On the way, he met *Rishi* Angira, son of Brahma. The King consulted the *Rishi* who did not see any particular reason for the cause of famine. He advised the king to observe the vrata of Devshayani Aikadeshi. The king returned to the city. Entire kingdom including the king observed this vrata in a ceremonial manner. The god of rains was pleased and the kingdom got a good rain. Since then, this vrata is observed in India to please rain God in times of poor rains.

Guru Poornima Vrata

Guru Purnima vrata is very auspicious for the Hindus. This vrata is observed by Hindus in honour of the great *Rishi* Ved Vyasa who gave Hindus precious texts like Vedas, Mahabharata and Puranas. Ved Vyasa was born on this day of Poornima of month of Ashvina of Hindu calendar.

Guru (teacher) occupies a central place in Hindu values. “Gu” means darkness and “Ru” means “dispeller”, thus Guru means one who shows the light and provides guidance so that journey of life is smooth. Sant Kabir has given Guru higher status than God in his famous verse.

Guru Govind dono khare, kake lagu paon.

Balihari guru aapne, Govind diyo dikhaye.

(Guru and God are standing together; whom I should give respect by touching the feet; I would bow to the Guru because Guru enables the disciple to realise God.)

Another verse reads —

“Gurur Brahma, gurur Vishnu, gururdevo Maheshwarah,

Guru shakhshat para-Brahm, tasmai shri guruve namah”,

Which means that Guru is equivalent to the Hindu Trinity of Brahman, Vishnu and Mahesh and even the Supreme, hence I salute the Guru.

Guru therefore has an exalted status in Hinduism. Swami Vivekananda adopted Ramkrishna Param Hansa as his Guru. Even Lord Rama adopted Vishwamitra as his Guru. In ancient times, Guru used to be the spiritual guide of the king/emperor and he was consulted on all important matters of the state.

On this day, vrata starts from morning. Respective Guru is worshipped by the Hindus by invoking *Rishi* Vyasa. Guru is given good food, clothing and suitable cash, etc. Guru is formally requested to forget and forgive any inadvertent mistake, bad behaviour done in the past. Brahmins are also fed and given suitable cash and kind in charity.

Poranik Katha: Satyawati was the daughter of a fisherman in Hastinapur in the times of king Shantanu. She was very beautiful. One day she was having her routine round of Ganga and *Rishi* Parasher happened to see her. He was greatly attracted by her beauty. He asked Satyawati to make love with him. Satyawati persuaded the *Rishi* not to insist for that as she was still a virgin and it was not wise to do such acts in full view of others. *Rishi* assured her that nobody will be able to witness their act and also she would get back her virginity. *Rishi* then covered the boat with a curtain of fog and made love with Satyawati. Vyasa was born from this union of Satyawati and *Rishi* Parasher. He was having Jatas (matted hair) and sacred thread since birth. He went to Himalayas immediately after birth. Later he was called Ved Vyasa as he compiled the Vedas in the present form of four Vedas from a single Veda, Rig Veda.

Shankracharya

Adi Shankracharya is considered the incarnation of *Rishi* Vyasa, hence holy people also worship Shankracharya on this day.

Naga Panchmi

Snake worship on Naag Panchmi

"Nagas" i.e. snakes occupy an important place in Hindu scriptures. In fact Puranas mention the existence of a separate 'Loka' (world) of snakes called 'Nagloka'. Snakes have made great contribution in the evolution of 'sristi'. Ocean churning or "Samudramanthana" was done by devas and asuras in which Vasuki, the chief of snakes, had agreed to be used as the rope. Lord Vishnu has adopted Sheshnag as his bed. There is a mention in Varah Puran that Brahma the Creator showered praises on Sheshnag on this day for supporting mother earth when 'sristi' was being created. Since then, this festival is being celebrated as an expression of gratitude towards the snakes by mankind.

The vrata of Nag Panchmi is held on Panchmi of bright fortnight of Shravan month of Hindu calendar as a mark of respect to snakes. The devotee takes full meal one day prior to panchami i.e. on Chaturthi and then observes fast on Panchmi for the full day. Snakes are ceremoniously worshipped by making a symbolic snake from a rope. Some people draw figure of snakes on a wall with chalk and worship them with milk, ghee, water, etc. Snake charmers roam on this day and people give milk to the snakes and cash and kind to the snake charmer. Brahmins are also fed good food and offered suitable cash and kind. It is forbidden to do any digging after sunset on this day, presumably to avoid the snakes getting killed by accident in this process.

Poranik Katha: Hemadri Granth mentions the following story regarding Naga Panchmi.

A family of a farmer used to live in a village. The three infants of a snake got killed when the farmer was ploughing the fields. The mother snake took a revenge and killed both the farmer and son. When the family came to know about the tragedy, the farmer's daughter gave some milk to the mother snake and begged her pardon for the wrong done to her offspring. The mother snake was satisfied and she revived the farmer and son by sucking back the venom. Since then, it has become customary to worship snakes on Naga Panchmi.

Raksha Bandhan

It is a very popular Hindu festival. It falls on the Poornima of bright fortnight of Shravan month of Hindu calendar. Basically it is a festival to seek protection and security. On asking by Yudhishtira, Shri Krishna told him that observance of Raksha Bandhan festival as prescribed by the scriptures, gives protection from ghosts and demons and wards off bad times. Therefore, on this day, worshipping of Gods and Goddesses is done in the morning in a traditional way by offering flowers, mauli (a sacred thread of red colour), vermilion, rice grains, coconut, etc. and their blessings and protection from bad times is sought.

Raksha bandhan

Sister ties Rakhi on the wrist of brother and in return brother makes a promise of taking care of her in all respects. Sisters prepare good food for the brothers and brothers give her gift in cash and kind.

Poranik Katha: Bhavisha Puran mentions the following story about this festival. There was a war among devas and demons which lasted for 12 long years. Ultimately devas were defeated. Devas had to abandon their capital, Amravati and Amravati came under the control of demons. The demons king ordered the devas to forget God and worship him only from then onwards. Indra, the Lord of devas met his guru Brihaspati and requested him to suggest a way out, to get back the lost kingdom. Acharya Brihaspati got Indra to perform the Raksha ceremony. Then the wife of Indra took the raksha (protective) thread from the brahmins on this day, tied it on the wrist of Indra and asked Indra to wage the war with demons again. As Indira was protected by the sacred thread he won the war and got back his kingdom.

In another story, Shri Krishan was once hurt; blood was coming from his finger. Draupadi immediately tore a piece of cloth from her saree and tied it on Shri Krishna's wrist. Shri Krishna repaid the gesture of Draupadi and saved her from humiliation in the Kaurvas assembly when Dussasana tried to disrobe her. Draupadi worshipped Shri Krishna as her brother; hence he always protected her.

Janmashtami

Janamashtami is celebrated as the birthday of Lord Krishna. It falls on the 8th day of dark fortnight of Bhadrapad month of Hindu calendar. The position of stars is Rohini Nakshtra.

Shri Krishna is held in high esteem by Hindus. He is de facto Supreme for them because of his divine deeds for the welfare of mankind and also for helping the individual devotees in times of need. There are innumerable instances which we have covered in detail in Shri Mad Bhagvat Purana. He was a great karamyogi. He guided Pandavas to defeat and eliminate Duryodhana and his notorious team in the Mahabharata war, thereby establishing Dharma. Shri Krishna gave the world a spiritual guide in the form of Gita which is a unique text independent of any religion and leads to spiritual uplift and ultimately God realization. The philosophy of Gita is followed world over for spiritual uplift.

Janmashtami is celebrated throughout India with great faith and enthusiasm. A day-long fast is observed by the devotees which is broken only at midnight, the time when Shri Krishna was born. Temples are decorated richly. Prasada made of curd, butter, Panjiri, dry fruits – is distributed at midnight in the temples after the worship ceremony. Generally temples place an idol of Shri Krishna in the form of a baby in a cradle;

devotees come and pay their respect to the Lord.

On this day, special arrangements are made in the temple at Mathura where Shri Krishna was born and in Dwarka, (in Gujarat) where He ruled. The idol of Shri Krishna is worshipped in these two temples in a ceremonial way as per the scriptures. The ceremony is broadcast to the entire world for the benefit of all. Similarly there are day-long activities at all temples and ISKCON temples across the world.

Janamashtmi celebration

Poranik Katha: Shri Krishna's birth itself speaks of his divinity. King Kansa of Mathura had put Devki, his own sister, and her husband Vasudeva in prison because it was forecast that their 8th child will kill him (Kansa). Cruel Kansa killed all the seven children of Devki immediately after their birth. When Shri Krishna was born as their 8th child at midnight, both Devki and Vasudeva were worried that Kansa would kill this baby too. Baby Krishna himself told Vasudeva, his father, what was to be done. Then with the grace of Lord, all the guards of prison went to sleep and the shackles of Devki and Vasudeva got broken and the gates of prison opened automatically. As guided by baby Krishna, Vasudeva took Him to Nand Baba and Yashodha's house in Gokul and brought back their newborn baby girl in the prison. Thereafter, the gates of the prison closed automatically as if nothing had happened. Next day, when Kansa tried to kill the baby girl, she disappeared immediately and spoke to him from heavens that "O, Kansa, there is no use in my killing, your killer has already been born." Later Shri Krishna killed Kansa and restored kingdom of Mathura to his maternal grandfather Ugrasen.

Dussehra

Dussehra is also a major festival of Hindus. It starts from first nine days of bright fortnight of Asvina month culminating in Dashmi on tenth day. Nine days are Navratras when Hindus observe fast. Dussehra is celebrated to mark the victory of Lord Rama over Ravana on tenth day. Demon king Ravana took away Sita, consort of Rama, when they were in exile. Shri Rama raided Lanka, killed Ravana and released Sita. Because of triumph of Rama over Ravana on this day, this festival is also called Vijaya Dashmi- 'vijay' meaning

Burning of effigies of Ravana

triumph. Ravana had ten heads and he was defeated, hence it is called 'Dussehra' - "Dus (ten) 'hara' (defeat).

Lord Rama was an incarnation of Vishnu. He was manifestation of truth, dharma, and wisdom. This festival, therefore, represents the triumph of Dharma over Adharma, wisdom over ignorance, truth over lie and goodness over evil. For this reason, the time of appearance of stars on the Dashami day of bright fortnight of Ashvin month is considered auspicious for getting success in war or in important matters of state.

Theatrical shows (called Ram Leela) lasting ten days are held in open in cities and villages across India depicting the lifestory of Lord Rama based on Ramayana. The effigies of Ravana, his brother Kumbhakarna and his son Meghnatha who were his key persons and who were killed in the battle are burnt at all these Ram-leela venues on Dussehra amidst applause from public.

In Bengal, the festival is celebrated as Durga Puja with great fun and involvement of people rich and poor alike. Highly attractive idols of Goddess Durga are erected at various places in the city, villages, workplaces. Worshipping of Goddess is done in a traditional manner at each of these venues and lots of cultural programmes are held which include dances, music show. The idols of Goddess are finally immersed in the river/sea on Dashami day.

In the state of Tamil Nadu, the festival is celebrated in a mixed way. First three days are dedicated to the worship of Lakshmi, the Goddess of wealth; next three days are dedicated to the worship of Saraswati, the Goddess of arts and Learnings and next three days are dedicated to the worship of Durga, the Goddess of Shakti. People traditionally exchange gifts and sweets of coconuts as part of celebrations. Vijaya dashmi is also considered auspicious for the commencement of education of children in arts and dance in southern Indian states.

There are some other important events on Dussehra which make it auspicious. It is said Pandavas married Draupadi on this day; Mahabharta war was also started on this day; It is also said that Arjuna removed his Gandeev bow from Sami tree on this day and defeated the Kauravas - Duryodhana, Karna and others --when they tried to take away the cows of king Virata during one year of hiding of Pandavas in Virat kingdom. Therefore Sami tree is also worshipped on this day.

Sharad Poornima

As the name suggests, this vrata of Sharad Poornima is observed on the Poornima of bright fortnight of the month of Ashvina of Hindu calendar. Women observe this fast for the welfare of their children.

Moon is at its best on the night of Sharad Poornima; it is very near to earth on this night and moonlight is very pleasing. Kheer (a milk product), curd, milk, Rabri (again a milk product), etc. are kept outside in moonlight. It is supposed to be very tasty and auspicious to eat these items next day.

On this day, worship of chosen deity, and of Kartikya, son of Lord Shankra, is recommended. A jug of water and a glass full of wheat are kept on a small stand. A 'Swastika' sign is made with vermilion powder, a small amount of money (dakshina) is kept. The relevant katha of vrata is read and listened to by all the devotees. The glass full of wheat and money is given to a lady brahmin and water is offered to the Moon. Special pooja ceremony are held in the temples on this day. At night sweetened cow milk is kept exposed to moonlight. Later at midnight, it is offered to deities and distributed as Prasad. Night-long devotional songs (keertan) is also performed.

Poranik Katha: Once Radha asked Murli (Bansuri) the reason that she is so close to Krishna. Murli said – "Radha, I was born in a lonely place. My youth was going waste. One day a gentleman came and drilled several holes in to me and threw me in a small corner of his house. I was in terrible agony. Luckily, from there Krishna picked me stealthily and he started blowing in me at my birth place on the night of Sharad Poornima. A very sweet music emerged from me. All the people of Vraja rushed to that place. I was hilarious from inside. Shri Krishna then celebrated Raas Lila with the Gopis on that great night. This is how I became dear to Shri Krishna."

Shri Krishna has nominated the night of Sharad Poornima for Raas as the Moon and the whole environment are at their best.

Navratra Vrata

Navratras are very very auspicious days for Hindus. All important programmes like marriage, commencement of a big project, entry to a new house start of business etc are done during these days. Navratras are observed twice in a year. First nine days of bright fortnight of Chaitra month are called Vasantik Navratras and first nine days of bright fortnight of Asvin month are called as Shardiya Navratras. The Shardiya Navratras are considered more auspicious. These days the weather is fine, mood is good and prevailing environment is festive.

Devi Puran mentions that Navratra vratas bestow great achievements, give success in all types of businesses, and bestow all types of rewards like wealth, kingdom, relief from the enemies, etc. Lord Rama worshipped Shakti before attacking Lanka. Even Lord Shiva observes these vratas.

The nine forms of Devi namely Shailputri, Brahmcharini, Chandraghanta, Kooshmanda, Sakandmata, Katyayani, Kalyatri, Mahagauri and Siddhidatri are worshipped during Navratravratas. The respect of girl child is the most important aspect of these vratas. She is worshipped as the embodiment of Devi Parvati. Tantra texts mention that Goddess Durga is most pleased with the respect and honour given to the girl child than by any other methods of worshipping. Hindu scriptures mention that worshipping a girl child bestows supreme blessings on the person and bestows good health, happiness, wealth, freedom from diseases, marital happiness, etc.

Navratra vratas start by establishing the image of Devi the previous day. Next day, 'sankalp' (vow) is taken to observe the vratas with the worship of Ganesha, etc. An earthen lamp is kept lit all the nine days of Navratras. Recitation of Devimahatmaya is done regularly on nine days. On the last day, 'havana', worship of girl child, etc. is done and the vratas are concluded. Image of Devi and other items of pooja are immersed in the river. The devotee is supposed to observe celibacy during these days. Dussehra follows on the 10th day after Shardiya Navatrai Day. The 1st day of Vasants Navaratris marks the beginning Hindu New Year (Vikrami Samvata). The Navratras culminate in Rama Navami (Birthday of Lord Rama).

Durga ji and her worshipping

Poranik Katha—Markendya Purana mentions about the origin of Navratra vratas. On the advice of their guru Shukracharya, demons worshipped Brahmaji very intensely. Brahma was greatly pleased with their devotion. He blessed the demons that no man, animal and even an enemy will be able to kill them. On getting this blessing from Brahma, a demon of the name Mahishasur started torturing the devas. Devas were frightened. Lord Indra rushed to Brahmaji and sought his help to curb the menace of Mahishasur. On the advice of Brahma, all devas and goddesses created a Devi (female) having their combined power. She fought with Mahishasur for nine days and finally killed him on tenth day. All these nine days, devas, goddesses and people on earth worshipped that Devi (Shakti). Worshipping of Shakti in the form of girl child, started since then.

Similarly Parvatiji adopted nine forms and destroyed many demons backed by the power and weapons of devas. This happened in the Navratras of Chaitra month and these Navratras vratas are observed to revive those events.

Karva Chauth Vrata

This vrata falls on the Chaturthi (fourth day) of dark fortnight of Kartik month of Hindu calendar. This vrata is very important for the Hindu women as its observance is prescribed for the longevity of their husbands. This vrata is very stringent as even taking of water is prohibited in day-long fast which is broken at night after sighting the moon which generally appears after 8.30 PM only.

This vrata starts early in the morning. Woman takes a 'sankalp' (vow) that she is observing the vrata for the welfare of her husband, children and that of the family. In the evening they listen, generally in a group, to the prescribed katha (story). A utensil containing rice, urad (lentil), items which represent "Suhag"—bangles, vermilion, mirror, comb, ribbon, etc. and some money is offered to a respectable woman or to the mother in law. Good food is prepared for the family. At night when moon is sighted, fast is broken and food is served to husband and family.

Poranik Katha: Vamana Purana mentions following katha in connection with this varta.

Moon sighting on Karva Chauth Vrata

Shri Krishna narrated this story to Draupadi when she asked for a way out from bad luck being faced by the Pandavas. "There was a wise brahmin in Indraprastha by the name Ved Sharma. He had seven sons and one daughter of name Veeravati. Veeravati was married to a brahmin boy in a nearby village. On the day of Chaturthi of dark fortnight of Kartik, Veeravati observed the Karvachauth Vrata with her sisters–in–law. Since the vrata was very stringent, Veeravati became unconscious without food and water for a long time. The brothers became worried. They artificially showed Moon to Veeravati and she broke her fast. After some days, however, her husband died. Veeravati was highly disturbed internally and got depressed. On one night Indrani, wife of Lord Indra, was moving in the village, Veeravati asked Indrani the cause of her tragedy. Indrani told her that she broke the Karva Chaturthi fast before the prescribed time, hence she was having a bad time. Veeravati then observed the Karvachauth Vrata as laid down in the scriptures. Indrani was pleased and her husband was revived and Veeravati led a happy married life thereafter."

It is believed that a woman who observes this vrata regularly by following the procedure laid down in the scriptures, gets health, wealth and happiness in life.

Ahoi Ashtami Vrata

This vrata is observed on the Ashtami of dark fortnight of Kartik month of Hindu calendar. This vrata is kept by Hindu women for the welfare of their sons. An image of Syahu Mata and her children is made on the wall, nowadays picture of Syahu Mata printed on paper is available. A day-long fast is kept. Food is prepared in the evening, Syahu Mata is worshipped. Following katha is read by the women and the fast is broken.

Ahoi Poojan

Poranik Katha: There was a family of a rich person having seven sons and one daughter. All were married. One day the daughters-in-law and the daughter went to the fields. While digging, the daughter hit the child of Syahu and he died. Syahu cursed and made the womb of the daughter ineffective for giving birth to children. Daughter requested her sisters-in-law to accept the curse instead of her but none of them agreed. The youngest daughter in law was more considerate and she agreed to help the daughter.

Because of the curse, the newly born sons of the youngest daughter in law started dying. It happened seven successive time. She was now worried. She consulted the astrologers, they suggested to worship mother cow. The daughter-in-law started worshipping the cow.

Mother cow was greatly pleased with her service. A pleased cow asked what was her problem. She narrated the story, how 'Syahu' was unhappy with her. Cow took her to Syahu Mata. Syahu Mata deployed her for taking care of her own children. Syahu Mata was greatly happy with her service and temperament. She asked her the cause of her unhappiness. Daughter in law narrated the story. Syahu Mata blessed her and told that her children will not die from then onwards. Syahu Mata then sent the daughter in law home with lots of gifts. When the daughter in law came back home, she found all her seven sons alive again. That was the day of vrata of Ahoi. She also observed vrata of Ahoi with other ladies of the family and continued and lived a happy life thereafter.

Dhan Teras Vrata

It is part of Deepawali festival. It announces the coming of Deepawali. It falls two days before Diwali, on thirteenth day of dark fortnight of Kartika month. On this day, Lord Dhanvantri appeared with the vessel containing nectar (when ocean was being churned) which was later given to the Devas to achieve immortality. Lord Dhanvantri was incarnation of Vishnu and is said to be the father of the Ayurveda system of medicine. He is, therefore, worshipped on this day to ask for the blessing of long and healthy life.

Yama, Lord of death, is also worshipped on this day. A lamp made of wheat flour is placed at the main entrance of the house. The lamp is lit at night with four wicks and Yamraja is worshipped ceremoniously with rice, water, flower, incense, vermilion and gur, etc.

Traditionally purchasing utensils, specially of silver, on this day is also considered auspicious.

Poranik Katha: Once Lord of death "Yamraja" asked his staff (Yamdoots), "Did you ever feel sad and compassionate while taking life from a person?" The yamdoots replied, "No Sir, never, we execute your orders and do not spare anybody". Yamraja was not satisfied. He persisted, the Yamdoots then opened up. They narrated the following incident.

"There was a king by the name Hemraj. His wife gave birth to a son; however, to his dismay, astrologers predicted that the child would die within four days of his marriage. The king became very very alert. He arranged a cave near the Yamuna river and made arrangements for the son to live there, always away from the sight of girls. As bad luck would have it, one day the boy saw the beautiful daughter of another King Hansa when she was walking on the bank of the River Yamuna. The boy married her in the manner of Gandharva Vivah (a sort of love marriage). As was forecast, that son of King Hemraj died on fourth day after marriage. His newly wed wife. It was a heart rending scene." Yamraja too felt sorry after listening to the story.

One of the Yamdoots, then asked, "Sir, is there a way out by which such untimely deaths can be avoided?" Yamraja replied, "Yes, there is way out. If a person does the lamp and poojan ceremony properly on the day of Dhan Teras, fear of such untimely death is eliminated." Since then, people observe this vrata and worship Yamraja and observe the lamp ceremony.

Deepawali

Deepawali

The festival of Lights, Deepawali, is the most colourful festival of Hindus. It is celebrated by people of all communities with great fervour and joy. This festival is Christmas of India. On this day, Lord Rama returned to Ayodhya with Sitaji after killing demon king Ravana of Lanka. The people of Ayodhya were extremely happy by the return of Rama and they welcomed Him by lighting lamps of ghee in all the houses and streets. Lord Rama was made the king of Ayodhya on this day. His rule was an ideal rule and popularly called 'Ramarajya'. Since then Deepawali is being celebrated every year as a festival of lights on the Amavashya of Kartik month of Hindu calendar.

Further, on this day, Lord Vishnu got released Goddess Lakshmi and other gods from the prison of demon Bali and also got back his (Vishnu) wealth due to the mercy of Lakshmi; hence goddess Lakshmi is worshipped on this day. Brahm Purana mentions that on the night of Deepawali, Goddess Lakshmi moves from house to house; it is therefore, customary in India to keep the home clean and lighted in the hope that Goddess Lakshmi will visit their home and bless with her favour.

Since Deepawali is associated with wealth, traditional Hindu shopkeepers start their new accounts from Diwali only. It is also said that Lord Shankara and Parvati gambled on this day; therefore, the custom of gambling on the night of Deepawali continues till date. People hope that if they win in gambling on this day, they would be blessed with wealth in the coming days.

Diwali is celebrated on Amavashya of Kartika. There are lights and lights in all households, streets, bazaars, govt. buildings and all over. Candles, earthen lamps, tiny electric lamps are lit, giving the environment, a great festive look. Lots of shopping is done by the people. The markets, shopping plaza are full with new items of all types.

New clothes are worn by the people. Women specially the newlyweds, wear colourful dresses. Every corner of the house is lit with candles and lamps. Lord Ganesha and Lakshmi, the Goddess of wealth, are worshipped at night at the auspicious time—Muhurat. After the pooja, sweets are distributed among the people. Later fire crackers are burnt, creating great festive mood but at the same time noise and pollution are also caused.

Next day of Diwali, there is Govardhan Pooja when people worship mount Govardhan whom Lord Krishna worshipped once to protect the people of Vraja from incessant rains. This is followed by Bhaiya Dooj when sisters visit their brothers, apply Tilak on the forehead and pray for their welfare. In a nutshell, there are a lot of celebration for nearly a fortnight at the time of Deepawali as we witness the celebration of Christmas by the western countries.

Govardhan Pooja/Annkoota

This is an important festival of Hindus and has got special significance for the people of Vraja. Earlier Lord Indra was worshipped on this day but Govardhan/Annkoot is being worshipped in the present form since the time of Shri Krishna. This festival is basically celebrated for seeking blessings for welfare of cattle and for a good harvest. This vrata also bestows material benefits to the devotees.

This festival is celebrated on the first day of bright fortnight of Kartik month of Hindu calendar. A replica of Govardhan mount is made either from cow-dung or out of Annkoot--cooked rice and other cooked food at the entrance of house. Image of Shri Krishna is placed in between. A variety of food is prepared. Worshipping of Annkoot and Govardhan in the presence of images of Shri Krishna, cows, Gopis, Indra, Varun, etc is done and prasad of curd mixed with sugar is distributed. The priest is given food and gift in the form of cash and kind.

Poranik Katha: In a congregation of *Rishis*, some *Rishi* asked "What is Govardhan? What is Annakoot? What is the purpose of worshipping Annakoot and Govardhan on the first day of dark fortnight of Kartika month?" The chief *Rishi* then narrated the following story:

"Once Shri Krishna was out with his cowherds and he reached near Govardhan mountain. He saw that lots of Gopis had assembled there with large variety of delicious food. They were in a jubilant mood. They were singing and dancing. On asking, they told Shri Krishna that this is being done to please Lord Indira so that he gives plenty and timely rainfall required for the survival of Vraja, its people, its cattle wealth and other beings. Shri Krishna said "you should worship Govardhan mountain instead of Indra; Govardhan mount is more powerful than Indra; Govardhan only brings us rains."

There was lot of discussion between Shri Krishna and people of Vraja. Finally they agreed to what Shri Krishna was suggesting and they started worshipping mountain Govardhan.

Rishi Narada came to know of this development. He informed Lord Indra that people of Vraja were worshipping Govardhan mountain in place of Indra. Indra was furious. He ordered that clouds should pour in a torrential manner over Vraja to appear as if dooms day had arrived. Accordingly there was torrential rain in Vraja. People got frightened and they rushed to Shri Krishna for help and protection. Shri Krishna told them to collect near Govardhan mount, then Shri Krishna lifted the entire Govardhan on his little finger. People of Vraja were asked to collect under Govardhan with their cattle and other belongings. The rains lasted for seven days. Later Lord Indira came to know that the decision of worshipping Govardhan was taken by none other than Shri Krishna. He felt sorry; he begged pardon from Shri Krishna. And normal life was restored in Vraja. Since then, it is customary to worship Govardhan and Annakoot."

Bhaiya Dooj

Bhaiya Dooj/Yam Dwitiya

This festival falls on second day after Diwali, on the second day of bright fortnight of the month of Kartika. On this day, Goddess Yamuna and her brother Yama, the Lord of Death, had met after a long time; Yamuna served him good food and sought welfare and long life of the brother. Skand Purana mentions that taking bath in Yamuna river and worshipping Yama on this day bestows material prosperity and longevity in life.

This festival is a symbol of love and respect between brothers and sisters. Sisters apply tilak of vermilion on brother's forehead and pray for his welfare. He is served good food; the brother in turn gives her cash, gifts, jewellery etc. Married sisters come to brothers' houses or brothers go to sisters' places depending upon the circumstances. If brother is away, tilak material is symbolically sent to him by post. Yama is worshipped by sister for the longevity of the brother.

Poranik Katha: Goddess Yamuna river and Yama, the Lord of Death, were the children of Surya and were born as twins. Yama used to live in Yamaloka and Yamuna in Golok. One day Yama remembered his sister Yamuna; he reached Golok and met her. Yamuna was extremely pleased. She gave a warm welcome to her brother and served him good food. Yama asked her for a boon. Yamuna asked to give a boon "whosoever takes a dip in my water, shall not go to Yamaloka." Yama said that it will not be possible to grant because that means that virtually nobody shall go to Yamaloka and He (Yama) will lose his significance. Seeing Yama as disturbed, Yamuna then modified her request and asked "whosoever takes a bath in Yamuna at Vishram ghat in Mathura and takes food at the place of his sister, shall not go to "Yama Loka"; Yamaloka means a place where punishment is given to the dead by Yama as per their 'karmas'. This wish of Yamuna was granted by Yama. Since then "Bhai Dooj" is celebrated as a symbol of love between brother and sister."

Chhath Parv

This festival is celebrated as the day of Surya (Sun). Sun has occupied a central place in Hindu society since Vedic times. Sun is the dispeller of darkness and sustains life in the universe. However, over a period of time, this festival became more popular in Bihar and eastern parts of UP. In fact nowadays Chhath Prava is the biggest festival of Bihar. People of Bihar origin celebrate Chhath festival at their respective place of living with the same fervour and zeal.

There are a few legends why this festival has got its origin in Bihar and areas around. It is believed that Lord Rama and Sita observed fast on this day and worshipped Sun God on the banks of Saryu river when they were returning after completing their 14 years of exile and killing of Ravana etc. and broke the fast next day on Saptami. Sun God blessed Lord Rama and Sita. Since then, this festival is being celebrated in the form of worship of Sun in this region.

The festival falls on sixth day of bright fortnight of the month of Kartika; however, celebrations start from fifth day after Deepawali called 'Kharna' –beginning of vrata; "Kheer" a milk and rice product made from gur, is eaten and distributed among the people as 'prasadam'. Eating and distribution of kheer is considered auspicious on this day. Next day, on Chhath, a twenty-four hour fast is observed. People come to the riverside and Sun God is worshipped in the evening at sunset standing in river water or pond. Prasad is distributed at the pooja venue. Vessels containing lit lamps, candles are floated in water at night which presents a very beautiful sight. Celebrations continue till late night with folk dance and music praising Sun God. Nothing is taken throughout the day, not even water. Next day, just before Sun rises, devotees again go to river side and offer prayers to rising Sun. After that only fast is broken with prasada or offering which typically includes grape fruits, whole coconut, bananas, 'puris'— a cake of wheat flour deep fried in oil, etc. The Prasad and offerings are shared with friends, relatives, etc.

Chhath Prava

Poranik Katha: Sri Devi Bhagvad Purana mentions the following story about this festival.

King Priyavat, son of *Rishi* Manu, got a baby boy after lot of delay and that too -- born dead. The queen mother lost her consciousness when she heard that it was a dead baby. King Priyavat also became emotional and he attempted to give up his life at the venue of cremation of the infant. Shashthi Devi then appeared.

She told the king that "My name is Devasena and I am known as Shashthi Devi in the Universe. I understand your agony; you worship me in the prescribed manner and also ask the people of kingdom to do the same." She then picked up the dead infant and it regained life then and there. King Priyavat was greatly pleased. The king returned home and immediately performed the worship of the Devi in the entire kingdom as per the tradition. That day happened to be sixth day of bright fortnight of Kartik month since then vrat of Shashthi Devi is observed on this day.

Dev Uthavni Aikadeshi

It is said that Lord Vishnu wakes up from sleep on this day of Aikadeshi of bright fortnight of the month of Kartika after four months of sleep. Among Hindus, all auspicious functions are started from this day onwards.

It is believed that this vrata is highly auspicious and brings immense benefits to the devotee. By observing this vrata, the devotes get immense benefits like virtuous sons, name and fame, salvation. It is also believed that whosoever observes this vrata and keeps awakened all through the night, he and his ancestors get liberation 'mukti'. One night of awakening dissolves all the sins of the devotees.

Lord Vishnu

It is further believed this vrata is so auspicious that mere narration and listening to the katha of this vrata blesses both the storyteller and the listener and brings immense luck and material happiness to them.

This vrata is for Lord Vishnu; He is ceremoniously worshipped by the devotee. Cereals are not taken, only fruits are permitted. At some places, new crop of sugarcane is also worshipped.

Poranik Katha: In ancient times, there was a king, in whose kingdom all people used to observe the vrata of Dev Uthavni Aikadeshi. People used to take only fruits to break the fast. Everybody was happy in the kingdom. Once God decided to put the king to test. God adopted the disguise of a very beautiful woman and sat on the way. When the king happened to pass that way, he saw the beautiful woman. He was greatly attracted by her beauty. He proposed to marry her. She agreed with a condition that entire kingdom will be under her control and whatever she would cook, the king would be duty bound to eat the same; the king reluctantly agreed.

When Aikadeshi came, the queen ordered cereals can also be cooked as on other days and at home she arranged a non-vegetarian meal for the king. When the king sat to eat, he said that being Aikadeshi, he would take only fruit as a meal. The queen reminded the king the vow taken before the marriage and said, "In case you do not take this meal, I would behead the elder prince." The elder queen was equally virtuous. She advised the king to stick to the Dharma of vrata.

Meanwhile the elder son arrived. He was also equally virtuous; he was prepared to get beheaded than to go against the rules of vrata. Lord Vishnu was greatly impressed by the gesture of king and his family. He presented himself and asked the king for a boon.

The king desired that Lord should liberate him. Immediately a divine chariot appeared and took the king to the heavens.

Tulsi Vivah (Marriage)

Tulsi Vivha is an important Hindu festival. This event is celebrated on the Aikadeshi of bright fortnight of Kartik month. Tulsi is related to Lord Vishnu. Vishnu married Tulsi; hence there is divinity attached to it. Tulsi is, therefore, also called Vishnu Priya. Tulsi is always a part of offerings to Vishnu. Every evening lighting a lamp and keeping it near the Tulsi plant is considered auspicious and devotee gets the blessings of Lord Vishnu.

Tulsi is also supposed to be dispeller of grief and poverty. It is believed by Hindus that giving Tulsi and honey to a person nearing his death gives 'mukti' to the soul. It is also believed that offering Tulsi to Lord Krishna – an incarnation of Vishnu- gives salvation to the devotee. In all religious ceremonies like vrata, havan, poojan, etc offering of Tulsi is a must to please Hindu gods and goddesses.

The Tulsi marriage is celebrated decorating an idol of Vishnu with new clothes and jewellery, and taking it to 'Tulsichorra' with great pomp and show. Dance, music and folk songs are part of celebrations. Marriage is then solemnised ceremoniously, thereafter the vrata is broken. Some women take 108 rounds of Tulsi, offer rich food to Tulsi and then break the fast. Some people perform the celebrations and festivities for a longer time from Aikadeshi to Poornima and then marriage is solemnised on Poornima.

Poranik Katha: Padam Puran mentions the following story about Tulsi Vivah.

There was a demon by the name Jalandhar. He was terrorizing the people. His wife Vrinda was however, a 'Pativrata'—pure and faithful to husband. This demon was invincible mainly because of the sacredness and purity of Vrinda. All the devas and *Rishis* went to Vishnu and prayed to get rid of the demon. Lord Vishnu decided to spoil the purity of Vrinda so that demon Jalandhar would also lose his power and get killed.

Vishnu managed to drop a dead body in Vrinda's house. Vrinda was shocked and she embraced that body assuming it as her husband Jalandhar. The demon was however fighting with Indra in heaven at that time. But by now Vrinda had lost her purity with the result Jallandhar was defeated and got killed in the fight with Indra. When Vrinda came to know the truth, she was highly repentant. She felt bad and burnt herself at the funeral pyre of her husband. Parvati then planted Tulsi, Amla and Malti plants and put Vrinda's ashes in them. Lord Vishnu adopted Tulsi assuming her as Vrinda. Lord Vishnu then told Tulsi that "You are dearer to me than Lakshmi. Because of your purity, you will always remain with me; whosoever celebrates marriage between me and you, shall get salvation." Since then, Hindu women have been celebrating Tulsi Vivah to seek the blessings of Lord Vishnu.

Ganga Snan (Kartik Poornima)

The day of full moon of bright fortnight of Kartik month –Kartika Poornima is very auspicious for the Hindus. Lord Vishnu took the incarnation of Matsya (fish) on this day and saved all forms of life including vegetation, animals, birds, mankind etc. from the Dissolution (Pralaya) that was forecast. Lord Shiva killed demon Tripura on this day. On this day, Parvati acquired the power of all the devas, in the form of Durga for the purpose of killing the demon Mahishasur. On this day, people take a dip in Ganges early in the morning and listen to the Katha of Lord Satyanarain; in the evening, earthen lamps are lit near Tulsi plant, Peepal tree. Lit earthen lamps are also offered to Ma – Ganga. People also do charities and give donations both in cash and kind to brahmins and poor people.

Poranik Katha: It is said that Lord Shiva killed demon by the name Tripura on this day. Demon Tripura did 'tapasya' for one lakh years. All beings and devas were afraid of him. They sent a celestial beauty to disturb his devotion but could not succeed.

Ultimately Brahma himself went and asked Tripura for a boon. On his asking, Brahma blessed him that he would not be killed by any man or deva. Equipped with this blessing, Tripura started torturing the people in a bigger way. A plan was hatched by the devas to eliminate the demon. Devas somehow managed to incite Tripura to attack Mount Kailash -- abode of Shiva. There was a tough fight between Shiva and Tripura. The fight was joined by Brahma and Vishnu and ultimately Tripura was killed by Shiva, since then, this day has become very sacred for Hindus.

Makar Sankranti

It is a very important festival for Hindus. This festival falls on the first day of dark fortnight of the month of Magh of Hindu calendar. The Sun moves from Dhanur Rashi to Makar Rashi on this day. Sun now begins its journey northwards and enters in 'Uttarayanam'. This festival generally falls on 14th of January.

Makar Sankranti festival

Bheeshma, grandfather of Kauravas, was blessed with "Ichhamrityu" – he could choose the day of his death. Bheeshma was deeply wounded in the Mahabharata; arrows pierced his body but he waited for twenty six days to give up his earthly existence on Makar Sankranti. It is believed that a person gets Mukti- liberation—when he happens to die when Sun is in Makar Rashi. Brahand Puran mentions that Yasodha got Shri Krishna as her son because she did vrata on this day.

This day is celebrated all over India by all communities in some form or the other. It is celebrated as Pongal in southern India, Lohri in Punjab, Khichri in eastern UP and Bihar. Ganga Sagar in West Bengal hosts a huge fair on this day. The famous Kumbh mela is held at Allahabad, Ujjain, Nasik and Haridwar on this day.

Taking bath in Ganga is considered highly auspicious on this day. Lakhs of people from all over India reach Allahabad/ Haridwar/Varanasi and Ganga Sagar to take a dip in Ganges. However, some people go to Ajmer to take a dip in Pushkar Lake and some go to Kurukshetra to take a dip in Brahmkund. Giving 'Til' or items of Til like 'gajjak', 'rewari' etc. are considered highly auspicious on this day. Charity of any kind in the form of cash, blankets, clothes, khichri (a combination of rice, dal) etc. brings immense benefits to the devotees. Hence people do all of charities on this day for spiritual and material benefits.

Poranik Katha: Once Guru Gorakh Nath was out with his students. The number of students were large and the quantity of raw food items like rice, lentils, salt etc. were limited. He mixed all the items and named it 'Khichri'. It turned out to be tasty and everybody enjoyed it. Since then it is customary to prepare Khichri—mixture of all possible items-- on the day of Makar Sankranti.

Mahashivratri Vrata

Maha Shivratri calebrations

It is a very important Hindu Vrata associated with Lord Shiva, one of the Hindu Trinity. Mahashivratri festival falls every year on the 14th day of dark fortnight of the Phalguna month of Hindu calendar, February/March of Gregorian calendar. It is said that Lord Shiva was born as Rudra from the eyes of Brahma on this day in the beginning of "Srishti"– Creation.

Following are some other stories associated with this festival.

Once Parvati asked Shiva as to which vrata was best in giving maximum benefit to the devotees, Lord Shiva himself revealed about this auspicious day.

Secondly, on this day, Shiva appeared in the form of Linga of fire before Lord Vishnu and Brahma when both the Lords fought for show of strength and Lord Shiva showed that none is stronger; Worshipping of Shiva in the form of Linga started from then onwards.

Third myth is that the marriage of Lord Shiva and Adi Shakti was celebrated on this day.

Another myth is that Lord Shiva drank the halahala poison- which emerged from the milky ocean – when it was being churned by devas and danavas (gods and demons) and thus saved the world from destruction.

Though it is a very major festival, it is celebrated with great austerity and solemnity. Fast is the essence of this festival. All Shiva temples are well decorated. Devotees of Shiva, specially the women, throng in hundreds from morning and offer their offering to the Lord. Offering of leaves of bilva (bael) tree specially a branch having three leaves (which are associated with three eyes of Shiva), milk, flowers, fruits are considered highly auspicious. It is said that this vrata destroys sins and leads to salvation of the devotee and at the same time gives him material pleasures of life. This vrata is therefore considered very very auspicious for the devotees.

Priests perform rituals like Abhishek, Rudra Mahayagna and archanas with flowers in all the temples. Lord Shiva is associated with Bhang, Dhatura (intoxicating substances), it is therefore considered auspicious to take bhang on this day. It is also considered auspicious to take bath in the Ganga on this day.

This festival is celebrated for 16 days by Kashmiri pundits in a big way. Marriage of Shiva and Parvati is a special feature of celebration by the Hindus of Kashmir.

Poranik Katha: There is a story in Ling Purana concerning this vrata. A hunter got transformed and gave up his profession and adopted humane approach when accidently he observed the fast of Shivratri and attended the various religious ceremonies carried for the Lord while he happened to be in a Shiva temple on the eve of Mahashivratri. Ultimately the hunter was liberated from 'samsara' by the grace of lord shiva.

Holi

Holi Fire poojan

Festival of Holi is a colourful festival of Hindus and marks the fall of winter. It is a very ancient festival and falls on the Pooranmasi of the month of Phalguna of Hindu calendar. Holi fire is arranged to commemorate the triumph of Prahlad, who was a devotee of Vishnu, over Holika who was burnt alive in the fire intended to kill Prahlad. Prahlad was the son of Hiranyakashipu, a demon king. Hiranyakashipu gave orders to his people to worship him only and not the Almighty God. Prahlad his son, was the devotee of Lord Vishnu. Hiranyakashipu tried all methods to kill Prahlad as Prahlad did not give up the worshipping of Lord Vishnu but every time he was saved by the Almighty. Finally the king asked his sister Holika to burn Prahlad alive in the fire (Holika had the blessings that fire would not harm her). She sat in the fire with Prahlad but instead she was burnt alive and Prahlad came out unhurt. Since then Hindus celebrate this festival to commemorate the triumph of good over evil by burning a symbolic fire made from wood, dry branches of tree, cowdung cakes, etc. At this time of year, new crop of wheat, gram and barley is also ready. Branches of new crop of wheat, barley and gram containing seeds are roasted in the sacred Holi fire and given to everybody present.

As per another myth, Lord Shiva opened his third eye and reduced Kamadeva (the god of love) to ashes on this day. It is further said Shri Krishna killed demoness Pootna on this day. Shri Krishna did the Ras Leela with the Gopis of Vrindavan on the night of this day and next day He played colourful Holi in Vraja.

Rishi Manu was also born on the full moon night of Phalguna. This day is also celebrated as the birthday of Sri Krishna Chaitnaya mostly in Bengal, Puri in Odisa, Mathura in UP.

Dhuledi is celebrated on the day after Holi. People meet and play with colours and water, eat sweets (gunjiya) and dance with loud music. Old enemity, if any, is forgotten and friendship is revived. Colourful 'Gulal' (coloured powder) mixed with sandalwood powder is applied by the people among each other. Children use 'pichkaris'(water pipes) and throw colourful water on each other. The festival is greatly enjoyed by the newlyweds when relatives of both sides gather, play with colours and dine together. One special attraction of Dhuledi is drinking 'Thandai' (a tasty drink) with 'Bhang' (an intoxicating substance) mixed in it. An interesting feature of Dhuledi is that it is free for all to apply gulal, throw water, even sometime muddy water, dance, play loud music, cut jokes or any other nonsense one may feel like; everything is excused; the spirits are very high, equivalent to which are not seen in any other festival.

Satya Narain Bhagwan Vrata

This vrata is observed to remind and put in to practice the truth contained in the phrase "The Truth is God". Truth means not only speech but encompasses all actions which protect the Dharma and bring goodness to living beings. God is greatly pleased with the good conduct and noble deeds done by a person following the path of truth; such a person enjoys material benefits and also gets liberated from 'samsara'. Such a person becomes pure in thoughts, words and deeds and following the path of righteousness, he enjoys God's bliss.

Once *Rishi* Narada asked Lord Vishnu the way out for getting relief from sufferings by beings on earth. Lord Vishnu himself recommended to observe Sri Satyanarain Vrata which not only gives relief from sufferings but bestows material benefits as well as 'mukti' (liberation) from 'samsara' from repeated cycles of births and deaths.

Mundaka Upanishad mentions that "Satyamev jayate, nanritam" meaning there by Truth always triumphs, not the 'astaya'.

This vrata is generally observed on Poornimasi, Amavasya or Aikadeshi days; however, it is also undertaken on important occasions like marriage, grah pravesh (entry to a new house), etc. After taking bath, etc in the morning, Sun is worshipped and devotee takes a 'sanklap' (vow) to observe the vrata of Sri Satya Narain for getting God's blessing on the family. All the five Lokpals, Navgrahs etc are ceremoniously worshipped. Devotee does the 'japa'— meditation of Lord Vishnu throughout the day. Later in the day, vrat 'katha' (story) is listened to, generally in a group, prasad is distributed and fast is broken.

Poranik Katha: Following story is mentioned in Sri Skanda Puran regarding this vrata.

A poor Brahmin of named Shatanand used to live in Kashipur. He had no income of his own and was surviving on begging. Lord Vishnu was greatly moved by his poor condition. Vishnu appeared before him as an old man and told him about the manner in which the Sri Satyanarain Vrata is performed and its benefits. Shatanand decided to observe this vrata. Next day he set out for begging with the intention that he would observe Satyanarain Vrata. That day he got alms in good quantity. He was happy and excited. In the evening, he did the poojan of Satya Deva, listened to the prescribed katha and broke the fast. Slowly his fortune turned and he became well off in a short time. He continued to observe this vrata as long as he lived. Ultimately he was liberated from 'samsara' also.

✡✡✡

Chapter 5 : Hindu Gods and Goddesses

Volumes have been written about Gods since the very beginning of Hindu Society Vedic period. Prima facie, all Hindu Gods appear to be different and bestow their blessings in their own way, however, Hinduism believes that all gods are forms of one Absolute Brahman.

- Every Hindu worships a deity say Lord Rama, Shri Krishna, Vishnu, Shiva, Durga, Parvati, Hanumana etc depending upon his religious inclination. A Hindu places great faith on his chosen deity and believes (what Lord Krishna says in Gita) that Supreme Lord will respond to the devotee in whatever form they worship Him and in whatever way they approach Him.
- Hindus can be divided in three main groups so far as their religious leanings are concerned viz: 'Saivas' who worship Lord Shiva, 'Vaishnavas' who worship Vishnu and 'Saktas' who worship 'Shakti'.
- Brahma, Vishnu and Mahesh form the Hindu Trinity. Hindus believe that Brahma created the 'Srishti', (universe), Vishnu preserves the 'Srishti' and Shiva is responsible for its destruction. This has been a continuous cycle since time immemorial, which has no beginning and which has no end. Trinity also represent the three Gunas – Rajoguna, Satavguna, and Tamoguna respectively of which all being are made.

Brahma (Creator of Universe)

- Brahma is the source of entire Creation. He is selfborn–Svayambhu, and entire universe has come out of Him. He is, therefore, called Prajapati since all creatures are his progeny. Saraswati is His consort.
- The icon of Brahma is shown as having four heads. These face in the four directions. It is believed that four heads also represent the four Vedas, four Yugas and four Varnas. His icon also has four arms; One hand holds a Aksamala [rosary] which represents Time i.e. he controls Time; One arm holds a Kamandlu (water pot) which represents Causal Water meaning that entire Creation has come from Him. Other arms hold Kusha grass, Sruk (a Ladle) and Sruva (spoon) items used in the sacrifice,

Brahma

an activity central to Hinduism; He holds a Pustak (book) which represents that he is the bestower of knowledge of arts and science and wisdom. His one hand is shown as providing Abhay (protection) and other as Vardan (boon). Hamsa (swan) is His carrier. Hamsa is known for its wisdom and power of discrimination. It is said that Hamsa has the rare quality that it can separate milk from water.

Vishnu (Sustainer and Protector of Universe)

- Lord Vishnu is the Lord of sustenance & protection of the entire creation. He is popularly called Naraina. Vishnu is always depicted as Nilameghasyama–of a dark blue hue resembling a rain-bearing cloud. His image is generally shown as having four arms, holding Sankha (conch), Chakra (discus), Gada (mace), Padma (lotus) and wearing a necklace having the gem Kastubha. He wears a garland called Vaijayanti.
- Vishnu's abode is Vaikuntha — the highest Loka which a liberated soul goes to. His another abode is Ksheersagara — Ocean of Milk where He is shown reclining on Ananta or Shesha (king of snakes having thousand heads). The ocean represents Causal Water from which the Universe has sprung. Ananta is assumed to support the world on its hoods. Hindus believe that Lord Vishnu comes as an incarnation on earth whenever there is predominance of Adharma over Dharma; He thus restores order in the working of 'Shristi' for the welfare of all beings. Lord Rama and Lord Krishna have been very popular incarnation of Vishnu.

Vishnu

- Lord Venkatesha of Triputi is a very famous temple of Vishnu in southern India in the state of Andhra PradeShri Lord Venkatesha is the richest God in India. Thousands throng here daily and do charity by a huge amount both in cash and kind. He is also called as Balaji of Tirupati and Lord of Hills.
- The famous Jagannath temple at Puri is also a Vaishnava temple. It houses the images of Shri Krishna, Balarama and Subhdra (Shri Krishna's sister). These images are carved out of special logs of wood.
- Lord Vishnu and his consort Rukmini are worshipped in the famous temple at Pandharpur in Maharashtra. Here the deity is called as Vitthala.
- Shrirangam temple in Tamil Nadu is also a famous temple of Vishnu. The original deity of Vishnu is believed to have been given by Lord Rama to Vibhishana when he was going back to Lanka after Shri Rama became the king of Ayodhya. Here Vishnu is shown as lying on the serpent bed in Yoga posture.
- Similarly Vardaraja temple at Kancheepuram in Tamil Nadu is a famous Vishnu temple.
- You will find all Vishnu temples as having the image of Garuda, the divine bird and vehicle of Lord Visnu. Image of Garuda is depicted as having conch, wheel, mace and

most important the nectar pot. It is said that Garuda brought nectar from Indra's heaven and that is why Vishnu chose Garuda as his vehicle.

- The idol of Hanumana, the great devotee of Lord Rama, is also found in the Vishnu temples. Hanumana is generally shown sitting as if praying and seeking the blessings of the Lord Rama. His other images are in three poses; one, carrying a Gada (mace) as a symbol of strength; two, carrying entire mountain on his palm while bringing Sanjivani herb to revive Lakshmana and third, showing Lord Rama and Sita in his heart with chest split open. Hindus do japa/chanting of Hanuman Chalisa –verses containing the glories of Hanumana. In difficult times, Hindus worship Hanumana to seek his blessings and to provide necessary protection and strength.
- Lord Vishnu is worshipped as Salagrama which is a blackish, rounded and polished stone with a hole containing the fossils of tiny molluscs. Salagramas are found in several varieties which represent various aspects of Lord Vishnu.

Mahesha (Shiva) (Destroyer of Universe)

- Shiva is the third pillar of Hindu Trinity. He is responsible for the dissolution of the universe. He is associated with death, destruction and dissolution. Lord Shiva is worshipped both in the form of an image as well as in Linga form. Linga form, however, is more popular.
- Lord Shiva is shown having four arms, two arms holding Damru (drum) and Trishula (trident); other two are in Abhya (protection) and Vardan (blessing) Mudra (poses). He has three eyes, third eye being in the middle of two eyebrows. It is said that the third eye is responsible for the death and dissolution. Holy Ganges flows from his matted hairs. He uses tiger and elephant skin as his robes. There are serpents all over His body. He also wears a necklace of skulls. Parvati is his consort. Lord Ganesha and Kumara are his sons. Nandi, the bull, is his vehicle. Mount Kailash in Himalayas is his abode.

Shiva and Parvati

- The three eyes of Shiva represent the Sun, Moon and Fire. The wind and sky represent his hair; that is why, he is called Vyomakesa. The tiger skin symbolizes that he has complete control over desires which are as strong as the lion. The necklace of skulls and ashes of funeral pyre over his body, indicate that he is the lord of death and destruction. Shiva holds trident in his hand which represents three Gunas from which universe has evolved, and that Shiva is the supreme ruler. Shiva is often shown in a meditating pose which represents that he is the Lord of Yoga. Hindu calendar is based on waxing and waning of moon. Shiva wears Moon as diadem which represents that He exercises control over Time. Coiled snakes all over his body represent that he has control over death. Damaru represents all words spoken or written i.e., he is the master of arts, science, religion etc. Since Ganga flows from his head, it gives Him a symbol of purity.

- There are many mythological stories about the various aspects of Shiva. When ocean was being churned, the poison appeared to threaten the lives of everybody. Shiva drank the poison thereby saving all the beings.
- In another story, it is said that that there was an argument between Brahma and Vishnu as to who is superior between the two. Shiva then appeared as a huge pillar (linga) and asked both the lords to find its ends; none of them could find thereby humbling their pride.
- Parvati was the daughter of Daksha, son of Brahma. Once Daksha organised a yajna but did not invite Shiva and Parvati. Parvati went to her father's place on her own uninvited . Daksha humiliated her openly in the presence of all the invited guests. Parvati could not bear the humiliation and committed suicide. On getting the news of demise of Parvati, Shiva was extremely annoyed and He destroyed the yajna of Daksha.
- Shiva destroyed the pride of Ganga by locking her in his matted hair. After a lot of apologies from Ganga and prayers from Bhagiratha, he let Ganga flow out from his head.
- Lord Shiva is widely worshipped in the form of 'Shivalinga' in Hindu temples. Shivalinga is made from stones. It represents Hindu Trinity; Brahma is represented by lowest part which is square in shape; Vishnu is represented by middle part which is octagonal in shape, these two parts representing Brahma and Vishnu are embedded inside the pedestal, the cylindrical part which is projected outside called Rudrabhaga is the one which is worshipped. Shiva means auspicious and Linga means symbol; hence 'Shivalinga represents Lord of Universe who is auspicious.
- Lord Shiva is the master of dance. All the108 known forms of dancing have emerged from him. "Nataraja" is His most popular form of dance. Philosophically Shiva's dance indicates a continuous process of creation, preservation and destruction.
- **Lord Shiva is a universal teacher and is called 'Daksinamurti'.** He is called Daksinamurti since he taught the knowledge of Atma (Self) - to the sages at Himalaya in a sitting pose facing Dakshin (South).
- **Shiva is also shown in Ardhanarisvara (half man and half woman) form.** In this form Parvati is shown as his left half which represents that a woman is an equal partner in the entire set up of the 'Shristi' (Universe).
- **Nandi, the elegant and calm bull, adores all temples of Lord Shiva and is the carrier of the Lord.**

Ganapati

Ganapati, Ganesha is a highly respected Hindu deity. He is invariably worshipped before starting any auspicious or important ceremony/function so that everything goes smoothly since he is lord of all those powers which obstructs, restricts, hinders and prevents an action. **He is called 'vighanvinashak' – destroyer of obstacles.**

Ganapati is having a human body and an elephant's head. The story of Ganapati getting an elephant's head is well known. Parvati prepared a child out of scurf from her body, gave life to it and asked him to stand as guard at the entrance of her house. One day Shiva came to meet Parvati; however, child guard would not permit him to enter. Shiva felt bad. It became a show of strength between the two and ultimately Shiva had to behead the child. Parvati was extremely angry and was inconsolable from grief. The head of the child was nowhere to be found. Ultimately, the head of an elephant was brought and child was given life. **To make up for his mistake, Shiva appointed his new son as the head of his retinue—'Ganas' and he was called 'Ganapati.'**

Ganapati

Ganapati is considered to represent the identity of individual 'Soul' with the 'Universal Soul'. **Elephant head represents the cosmic Soul, his human body represents the individual Soul and complete Ganapati represents that two are same. He has two tusks out of which one tusk of the elephant is broken. This broken tusk was used by Ganesha as a pen for writing Mahabharata which was dictated by Ved Vyasa.** His body is of red colour. He has four arms. One of the arms is in the form of Abhay (protection) and another in the pose of Vardan (blessing) form. The belly is quite bulging but looks graceful. His Shaktis Ridhi and Sidhi are generally shown sitting on his lap. He is wearing a sacred thread which could be represented by a snake. One leg is bent and one leg is resting on a seat. A mouse is his vehicle which is generally shown enjoying the modaks (laddos).

- Ganapati is worshipped in many forms, to quote a few;
- 'Balaganapati' as a child
- 'Tarunganapati' as a youth
- 'ShaktiGanapati' with his Shaktis' Lakshmi, Ridhi, Sidhi and Pushti etc.
- 'Nrttaganapati' in a dancing pose. Ganapati is also said to be master of music and dance.
- **'Varasiddhi Vinayaka' is used in the famous Ganesh Chaturthi festival.**
- Ganapati is also worshipped as a female deity and in the form of his Yantra.

Hindu Goddesses

In Hinduism, each of the Trinity have their consort which represents His Shakti—power behind. eg Sarasvati is the divine consort of Brahma, Lakshmi that of Vishnu and Parvati that of Shiva. Radha is the Shakti of Shri Krishna. We will describe these Goddesses very briefly.

Saraswati

Saraswati is consort of Brahma and hence she is the mother of entire Creation. Various names have been given to her representing her various aspects. e.g. Sharda (the giver

Saraswati

of essence), Brahmi (wife of Brahma) and Mahavidya (knowledge supreme). She is the knowledge-personified all inclusive viz arts, science, medical and all skills etc.

In her image, she is shown as pure white representing purity and dispeller of ignorance. **She holds a book representing that she is custodian of knowledge.** She holds a Vina (flute) representing that she is the controller of arts. She holds a rosary-which is a symbol of spiritual knowledge etc. Swan is her vehicle, same as of Brahma. 'Swan' is the symbol of wisdom and discrimination between right and wrong.

In all events involving books, music, dance, mother Saraswati is invariably worshipped by Hindus by chanting Aarti, verses and mantras.

Lakshmi

Lakshmi

Lakshmi is the Goddess of wealth and naturally is the most sought after Goddess. She is the consort of Vishnu. When Vishnu incarnated as Rama and Krishna, she appeared as Sita and Rukmini as his consort. Lakshmi is associated with lotus. She holds lotuses in her hands and hence also called as Kamala or Padma. She is shown in various colours like dark, golden yellow, white and pink. Dark colour represents that she is consort of Vishnu-the dark God, golden yellow colour shows her as the Goddess of wealth and white colour represents her purest form from which the universe has evolved. Her four hands represent that she has the power to fulfil the four pursuits of humans viz Dharama, Artha, Karma and Moksha. Her carrier is an "owl".

Sita

Ram Sita

Sita She is the daughter of mother Earth. King Janaka of Mithila got her while ploughing the fields. She is an Avtar of Lakshmi, consort of Shri Vishnu. In Ramayana she is the ideal wife of Rama, the Avtar of Vishnu who chose the sufferings of exile than the comforts of palace. She was a 'pativrata' and proved her purity on several occasions. In fire test, Goddess Agni herself vouched for her purity. Her image is always worshipped in conjunction with Shri Rama.

Radha

Radha is the 'Shakti' –power behind Shri Krishna. Being the Shakti of Shri Krishna and Shri Krishna being the de facto Supreme Lord of Hindus, Radha occupies an exalted position among Hindu Goddesses. She is widely worshipped with Shri Krishna as well as an independent goddess. Brahmhavaivarta Purana, mentions that Radha took birth from left side of Shri Krishna. Devi Bhagvat Purana mentions that Lord Vishnu took her help in the creation of 'Shristi'. There are songs, bhajans in which she is shown as having intense selfless love for Shri Krishna and both having a divine connection. Shri Krishna remembered her at the time of His Death (when he was to leave His earthly existence) at Prabhaasateertha near Dwarka. She is inseparable from Shri Krishna and therefore, invariably worshipped in images with Shri Krishna.

Lord Krishna and Radha

Parvati

Parvati

Parvati is the Sakti (power) and consort of Shiva. According to the Tantric Shastras, Shiva and His Shakti – Parvati are responsible for the Creation; She is therefore known as Mother of all Creations.

Parvati is a symbol of power and Shakti (strength). Hindus believe that most of the Hindu Goddesses are variations of Parvati and represent various divine roles played by Parvati in running the 'Shristi'. She is addressed by many names like Haimavati, Girija, Daksayani, Sarvani, Aparna, Uma, Gauri, Amba, Ambika, Annapurna, Kameshwari, Katyayari, etc.

The following Goddesses find important place in Hindu society.

Durga

Durga is the most widely known aspect of Parvati –'Shakti'. In fact word Durga has become synonymous with power and strength. An entire Purana, Devibhagavatam, is totally dedicated to her. Devimahatmyam is another text which is similar to Devibhagavatam. Devimahatmyam is also called 'Durgasaptasati' or 'Chandi'. This is a highly respected text and personifies Devi as the ultimate Shakti, controller of Time and bestower of all attributes in the beings.

Durga

Devimahatmyam describes her as responsible for the creation, sustenance and dissolution of universe.

The text describes her role in killing the powerful demon Mahisasur. When Mahishasur was at the peak of his nuisance, devas approached the Trinity Brahma, Vishnu and Mahesh for relief. The three Lords discussed the issue. Goddess Durga was then created from the combined wrath of Brahma, Vishnu and Mahesh plus the energy of all gods and goddesses. She was given the duplicate of weapons of all the devas. Equipped with that enormous power & riding on the lion, she fought with demon Mashisasur and killed him; She is therefore also called "Mahisasuramardini'.

In her manifestations of Kaushiki Durga, she destroyed extremely powerful and dangerous demons Sumbha, Nishumbha, Chanda, Munda, Raktabeeja etc.

In her most popular form, Durga is shown as having four arms, wielding bow, arrow, discus, trident, riding on a lion and demon Mahisasur under her feet. She is dressed in rich red colour adorned with heavy ornaments. That animal instincts should be subjugated is the message given by Goddess Durga when riding upon the ferocious animal lion as her carrier.

Kali

Kali derives its name from 'Kala'— Time which is destroyer of everything, howsoever mighty it is. That is why she is shown as producing terror in the mind and controller of death and destruction. In her image, she is standing on the body of none other than Shiva; she is completely naked and she wears an apron of human hands only. She wears a garland of 50 human skulls; her hair are completely dishevelled (which give her the name Muktakeshi). She has three eyes and four hands; in one hand she is holding a freshly severed head from which blood is dropping, another hand is holding a chopper — a slaughtering weapon, her face is red and tongue is protruding; yet at the same time she is a mother and gives boon and Abhay (protection) from her other two hands.

Kali

She is shown as trampling over the body of Shiva with a protruding tongue. There is a mythological story about this picture. Once Kali destroyed many demons. Accordingly she started dancing in a terrific way out of sheer joy. As a result, entire universe was trembling. Gods approached Shiva to control her. Shiva lay on the floor among the corpses of demons to absorb the shocks but in her excitement she trampled Shiva under her feet. However, immediately she realized her mistake and in awe her tongue came out.

She is also called Chamunda, the killer of demons Chanda and Munda. Seeing in philosophical manner, Kali represents energy and energy cannot be separated from source; hence she is shown with Shiva under her feet. (She being the Shakti/energy of Shiva).

Lalita

While Durga and Kali represent the power of Parvati, Lalita is personification of her beauty and femininity. Lalita is generally shown as slightly red in colour and extraordinarily beautiful. She has four hands, holding a bow of sugarcane, arrows, the goad (Ankusha) and the noose (Pasa). These are indicative that she controls our minds and sense organs.

There are various forms in which Lalita is worshipped viz Chanting her name thousands times as contained in 'Lalitasahasranaama', chanting her three hundred names as contained in 'Trishati'. Lalita is widely worshipped in the form of her Yantra – 'Shreechakra'.

There are three modes of worshipping Hindu deities viz in image, second by the recitation of mantras and third worshipping his or her Yantra. Yantra is a geometrical figure. When the Yantra is installed and worshipped properly, the deity is supposed to reside there in the Yantra and bless the devotee. 'Shreechakra' is the Yantra of Lalita. It is a complicated geometrical figure of forty-three triangles, concentric circles, lotus petals surrounded by squares etc. There is a dot in the centre of diagram which represents Shiva and Shakti. The 'Shreechakra' represents the continuous creation and evolution process of the universe.

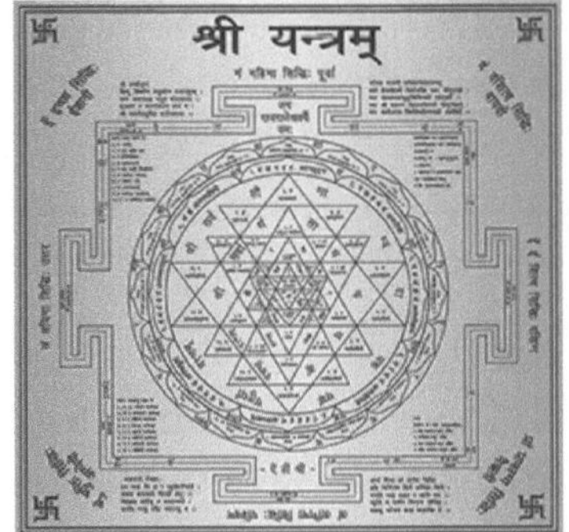

Yantra

Navagrahas

Hindus believe that Navagrahas (planets) influence the life of individuals. Navagrahas constitute nine planets. There is a deity corresponding to each of the Navagrahas. The Navagrahas are

(i) Ravi/Surya (Sun)
(ii) Soma or Chandra (Moon)
(iii) Mangla (Mars)
(iv) Budh (Mercury)
(v) Brihaspati (Jupiter)
(vi) Sukra (Venus)
(vii) Sani (Satrun)
(viii) Rahu
(ix) Ketu

Navagrahas

It would be seen that days of the week have been given based on the planets. Sani, Rahu and Ketu are believed to exert a negative influence on humans and hence they are invariably placated by worshipping.

Navagrahas deities are always installed in Shiva temples in south India. In northern India, they are installed in the doors of temples itself or in a separate niche to keep away the evil spirits.

Hindu Temples

Temple is a sacred place for Hindus where images of gods and goddesses are installed for the purpose of worshipping. All Hindus have a temple made of wood, marble etc in their houses. In addition temples are constructed in each locality for community worship. In India, even offices, factories, hospitals have temples as a Hindu loves to be in the company of God all the time. Proximity to Gods not only provides him the security but it also keeps him reminding that there is a supreme authority who is controlling the life around.

A Hindu temple

Huge temples dedicated to a deity or temples housing gods and goddesses have being constructed by Hindus since ancient times.

Most of the Hindu temples have the images of Lord Rama and Sita; Lord Krishna and Radha; Lord Shiva and Parvati; Goddess Durga, Goddess Lakshmi, Lord Ganesha and Lord Hanumana etc. The images are made from a variety of material like clay, wood, stone, silver and gold etc. These deities are dressed in rich colours and are clad with ornaments etc. Big temples like Birla Mandir, Akshardham have different separate temples for different deities in the same complex.

There is an elaborate and highly technical procedure for construction of a Hindu temple. The builder, architect, the financier, the Acharya etc have to be person of purity and well versed in Hinduism and its philosophy. After construction of the temple, the image of various deities are installed in a ceremonial manner. Thereafter the regular devotees are permitted to worship in the temple. Hindu temples generally have the following provisions:

(I) Hindu temples are also categorised in three categories. viz Shiva, Vaishnava and Shakta and accordingly house the deities. The images could be in standing position, sitting or meditating posture and 'Sayana' (sleeping) pose. Generally image of Vishnu is seen in 'sayana' posture.

(II) A dome called "shikhara" (height) meant to represent mythological mountain Meru, most sacred of all mountains. It also symbolises the spiritual height to which the devotee wishes to rise.

(III) Inner Chamber is called "garbha-griha" (Sanctum Sanctorum), here the idols of various Gods are kept. Only temple priest are allowed to go to the grabha-griha. This chamber resembles a cave. Images of Gods are generally dressed with colourful dresses and decorated with ornaments as prescribed by the scriptures.

(IV) Audience hall. Here the devotees perform worship or do japa or meditation etc.

(V) Comparatively bigger Hindu temples have a walkway around the walls of garbha-griha for going around the deities in a clockwise direction as a mark of respect to the gods and goddesses.

(VI) Normally a big metallic bell hangs at the entrance or in the middle of the audience hall of the temple. The devotees ring this bell once or twice to seek the blessings of Gods.

Images of Gods, Goddesses, scenes from the epics and mythological literature, religious symbols, verses from Gita, Ramayana, Mahabharata, Bhagvatam and other scriptures are generally carved, painted inside and outside walls of the temples.

All Hindu temples have a priest who performs worship rituals on behalf of the devotee. Priests are holy people well acquainted with rites, rituals associated with worshipping. Priests are also responsible for the proper upkeep of temple. Priest also gives a ceremonial bath to the deities. "Prasada" in the form of sweets, coconut etc. is given to the devotees by the priest. On festive occasions, elaborate arrangements are made in the Hindu temples, to facilitate worshipping by a large number of devotees. "Kirtans" (devotional singing) are also held in the Hindu temples regularly and/or on various auspicious days.

Chapter 6: Hindu Rites, Rituals, Customs and Traditions

We have seen that life of a Hindu is governed by the teachings contained in the scriptures. These teachings have been handed over from generations to generations for thousands of years. In additions, religious discourses, satsangs, melas, old system of education in ashrams of *Rishis*, Gurukuls have facilitated the continuity of the Hindu philosophical thoughts, beliefs, traditions and customs.

- Hinduism is not a religion in conventional sense of the term. There is no single person responsible for its philosophy. Thousands of *Rishis*, thinkers for thousands of years, have influenced its philosophy and wisdom. Vedas, Upanishads, Mahabharata, Bhagavad Gita are unique texts and relevant for all times to come. Puranas contain the wisdom of Vedas, Upanishads, Gita and Mahabharata, in a manner which can be understood by the common man. Therefore the so-called common man of India is equally philosophical because of his exposure to Puranas. The women of India have contributed immensely in continuing the treasure house of ancient wisdom.
- The Hindu wisdom contained in Vedas and Puranas are also reflected in the various rites, rituals, ceremonies, which Hindus observe in their daily pursuit. There is a philosophy behind these age old traditions, beliefs, customs etc. There is a prescribed procedure in all these rites, rituals, customs and traditions. Some Hindus observe these with modifications, necessitated by circumstances, convictions. Hindu religion has always assimilated such changes without disturbing the basics. The list is big, however, some of the important Hindu beliefs, rites and rituals are given below.

AUM

Hindus consider AUM a very sacred symbol. Its chanting is considered very very sacred. It is believed that its three letters stand for Hindu Trinity Brahma, Vishnu and Mahesh Chandogya Upanishad explains the spiritual importance and benefits of chanting AUM. According to this Upanishad, 'Omkara' or Syllable AUM is also called "Udgitha", one who meditates on Udgitha- syllable AUM,

AUM

looking upon it as Supreme, gets all his desires fulfilled. AUM is therefore considered the essence of Vedas. All Vedic mantras are chanted by beginning with AUM. Hindus do *(japa)* of AUM as a daily spiritual practice.

Lord Ganesha

☛ Lord Ganesha is worshipped on all important occasions.

Lord Ganesha is invariably worshipped by Hindus before the start of any important occasion like marriage, construction of a new house, Grah Pravesh (entry to a new house), start of a new business, etc. It is believed that Lord Ganesha removes any likely obstacles and hence ensures the successful completion of the event. Ganesha is generally prayed by the following mantra

"Vakratund mahakaya Gazanann, Suryakoti samprabh
Nirvighan kuru mum deva, subh karyeshu sarvada"

There is a story in Shiv Purana about the glory of Ganesha. All Gods went to Lord Shiva and asked Him, who is the superior most among them. Shiva said that whosoever would make three rounds of world and returned to Mount Kailash first, would be considered most superior. All the gods started to make rounds of the world. Ganesha did not go anywhere. He simply went around the parents, Lord Shiva and Parvatiji, three times and presented himself to Shiva. He was greatly pleased with his understanding and ingenuity. Lord Shiva blessed Ganesha and declared that whosoever offers prayers to him before starting a ceremony will not face any obstacles. Since then Hindus have been offering prayers to Ganesha before any auspicious occasion.

In another story as to who is superior between the two sons Kartikeya or Ganesha, Kartikeya went around the globe and visited many places of pilgrimage. Ganesha simply went around the parents and argued before mother Parvati that devotion of parents is far superior to visiting holy places. Parvati was greatly pleased. She blessed Ganesha that he will be revered on auspicious occasions and first offering will be made to him.

Navagrahs

Hindus believe that Navagrahs influence the life of individuals. The position of planets at the time of birth is used to forecast the fate of individuals in the journey of life. Entire astrology is based on the analysis of events and happenings as the planets move in the universe. There are nine planets, viz Surya (Sun), Chandrama (Moon), Mangal (Mars), Budh (Mercury), Brahspati (Jupiter), Shukra (Venus), Shani (Satrun), Rahu and Ketu. Their daily movements have been documented with remarkable precision in ancient Hindu books of astrology. According to Hindu beliefs, each of the planets exert an influence on the life of individuals. Astrologers have developed techniques to predict bad times, remedies are prescribed to ward of the bad effects of each of the planets. Expert astrologers are, therefore, generally consulted by the Hindus for remedial measures to handle bad phases in life.

Shalgrams

Shalgrams are very auspicious for Hindus. Shalgrams are black, smooth, shining stones in the shape of eggs and are found on the banks of river Gandki in Nepal. Hindu scriptures mention that Lord Vishnu resides in Shalgrams. In Padampurana, it is mentioned that Shalgram is the symbol of Vishnu and those who offer prayers to it are blessed with peace and prosperity and are led to salvation. That is why Shalgrams are considered sacred by Hindus.

Vishvakarma Pooja

Hindus worship Vishvakarma at their respective workplace. Vishvakarma is the engineer among gods; therefore in all establishments using machinery, blessings of Vishvakarma are invariably sought to avoid accidents and to ensure proper functioning of the machinery. Vishvakarma stands for builder of universe. It is believed that Vishvakarma built Puspaka Vimana, Sudarshan Chakra, Trident for Shiva, a beautiful castle for Kubera at Lanka, thunderbolt for Indra and many ornaments and weapons for the gods. Vishvakarma's son Nala helped Lord Rama a build bridge across the ocean at Rameshwaram in a remarkably short time; Time was running out and fast completion of the bridge helped Rama to quickly attack Ravana and recover Sitaji.

It is customary to worship Vishvakarma the day after Diwali. Plant and machinery, tools, equipment are formally worshipped by the artisans to seek his blessings.

Difference Between English Calendar and Hindu Calender

Throughout the world, Gregorian calendar is generally used. This calendar is based on solar year of 365 days. Hindus have their own calendar based on Solar-Lunar systems. Every Hindu month starts after 29 ½ days i.e. after every Purnima – Full Moon. Twelve Lunar months make 354 days, the difference of eleven days between the two calendars is made up by adding one additional month called Adhik-Mas every three years.

The twelve months of Hindu calendar are Chaitra, Vaishakha, Jayeshtha, Ashadha, Shravana, Bhadrapada, Ashvin, Kartik, Margashirsha, Poush, Magha and Falguna. First day of Hindu calendar i.e. Pratipada, of month Chaitra generally falls around 20th of March. Date of various Hindu festivals, vratas and other auspicious days are fixed based on the Hindu calendar e.g. Diwali is invariably celebrated on the Amavasya of Kartik month. You will find that every year the dates of festivals based on English calendar change but the day of as per the Hindu calendar is always the same.

Worship of a Peepal Tree

Peepal tree is considered a sacred tree by Hindus. This tree always finds a place in a temple complex. It is said that Vishnu resides in the roots of a Peepal tree, Krishna resides in the trunk and Narayan reside in its branches, Lord Hari in the leaves and all Gods in the fruit.

Peepal is, therefore, considered an extremely divine tree by Hindus. In verse 10/26 of Bhagavad Gita, Lord Krishna says

"Amongst trees, I am the Peepal tree".

Peepal tree is worshipped by Hindus by watering it, lighting a lamp and circumambulation while praying. People also tie a thread around the trunk of Peepal tree for fulfilling a wish Cutting a Peepal tree is generally avoided; in case it is unavoidable, it is done in a formal manner under the guidance of a priest.

Peepal tree has a unique feature as it converts carbon dioxide in to oxygen round the clock unlike most of plants and trees which release carbon dioxide at night. Further the shade of Peepal tree is cool during summer and warm during winter. The leaves of Peepal tree are used to make buntings on special auspicious occasions.

Worship of a Peepal

Tulsi a Sacred Plant

Tulsi

Tulsi finds a prominent place in Hindu belief system. It is considered a very sacred plant. According to Hindu scriptures, the Hindu Trinity–Brahma, Vishnu and Mahesh--reside where Tulsi is planted, respected and cared for. It is therefore, customary to light a lamp and offer prayers to Tulsi in the evening by Hindus.

Tulsi leaves are put in the water used for pooja, havan, etc. Tulsi and Ganga water is put by Hindus in the mouth of a dying person with the belief that soul is liberated.

In addition, Tulsi has great medicinal values. It is widely used in Ayurvedic system of medicines. Tulsi leaves and ginger is very commonly used for making tea in India (specially in winter and rainy season) as an antidote against flu, common cold and cough, etc.

Cow Worship

- Cow is considered a holy animal by Hindus. It occupies a special place in the Hindu value and belief system.
- The sacredness of cow finds mention in Hindu scriptures. Mahrishi Chavan preferred a

cow than getting a kingdom. It is believed that almost all gods and goddesses reside in cow. Atharva Veda mentions that cow is mother of Rudras; that she is the sister of Surya. In Bhagvad Gita, Shri Krishna says that amongst cows, I am 'Kamdhenu'. Mahabharata mentions that donation of cow protects the donor from the darkness of hell and the donor is bestowed with peace and happiness. Giving a cow in charity is therefore, very common among Hindus.

Cow

- Cow's milk, ghee, even urine are prescribed for treatment by Ayurvedic physicians. Its milk is very useful for patient.
- Hindus prepare first 'chapati' (roti) for the cow every day which is considered to bestow bliss on the family. In India there are exclusive shelters for caring for cows called 'Gaushalas.' Lots of donation are given by the Hindus to these Gaushalas for the proper upkeep of cows.

Conch Shell

- Hindus consider a Conch Shell auspicious. A conch is an important part of a worship ceremony of Hindus. It is considered auspicious to blow a conch before and after prayers daily/ on auspicious occasions. A majority of conch shells open on left side--formed anticlockwise.

Blowing a conch in a pooja ceremony

- Many Hindu scriptures mention that right opening clockwise shells are highly auspicious. It provides for peace, prosperity and general well-being and fulfils all desires. Brahmvaivartpuram describes that right side conch is divine like Chandrama (Moon) and Surya (Sun); further Ganga,Vishnu and Brahma reside in this conch; also all pilgrimage places reside in this shell. According to Maharishi Pulstya, Vishwamitra, Markendya, right side conch shell attracts Goddess Lakshmi and makes the owner prosperous. It helps in getting rid of poverty, bad loans etc. Hindu guru Shankarachya has greatly emphasised to keep right side conch shell at home as it motivates to perform noble deeds.

Rosary

- Hindus use rosary for prayers. A rosary is an important item of prayers for Hindus. It facilitates to count the mantras or timing in respect of prayers. It has 108 beads and a bigger bead called Someru after the name of a sacred mountain. Rosary is made from any Rudraksh (seeds of tree Elaeocarpusganitrus) Tulsi, Vaijyanti, pearls, glass beads or even precious stones. Rosary facilitates concentration of mind during prayers. While doing japa by using rosary, it is believed that Someru should not be crossed rather the counting should be done in reverse direction when Someru is reached.

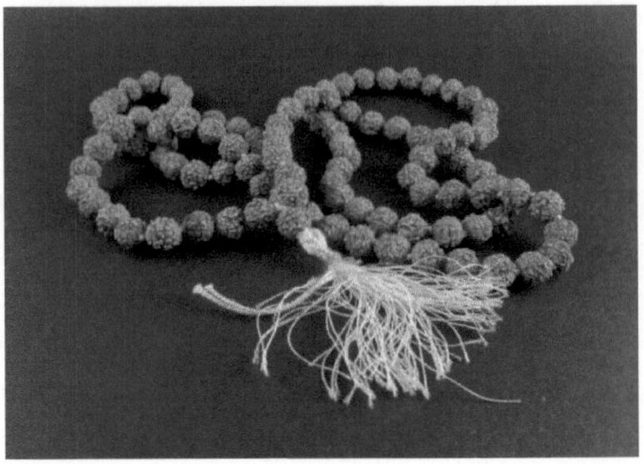

Rosary

- There are various explanations for having 108 beads in the rosary. One of the explanations is that universe is divided in to 12 segments, each segment represents a zodiac sign. As per Hindu texts, there are 9 planets which have a bearing on our lives; Hence no.12×9 = 108 represents our universe. A Hindu religious personality is respected by prefixing Shri 108 Swamy xxxx or Shri 108 Maha Mandelshwar xxxx ;thus 108 is a sacred no. for Hindus.
- Hindu texts like Shivpuran, Bhagvatam speak very highly of the benefits of Rudraksh Rosary. According to these texts, wearing a Rudraksh Rosary of 108 beads brings immense spiritual and material benefits to the wearer. In addition, it provides lots of medicinal benefits like control of blood pressure, vanishing of imaginary fears, balance of the flow of biles, etc; Similarly a rosary of Tulsi helps in preventing cough and cold, headache, skin disease and blood disorders etc.

Kalava, Tilak, Coconut, Lamp (Diya)

Hindus tie a red thread called Kalava around the wrist, apply Tilak, use coconut etc. in all pooja ceremonies. Kalava is tied on the right wrist for men and left wrist of the women. It is said kalava invokes the blessings of Brahma, Vishnu and Mahesh and their consort Saraswati, Lakshmi and Durgaji respectively. It thus provides wisdom, prosperity, strength and well-being of the devotee.

Kalava

- **Tilak:** Hindus have a tradition to apply Tilak on their forehead on every important occasion, ceremony. Tilak is considered auspicious. It brings good omen for the recipient. Tilak is a symbol of purity and sacredness. Sisters apply Tilak on the forehead of brothers, on the occasion of festivals of Raksha Bandhan and Bhai Dooj. Whenever there is religious ceremony say a Katha or a Havana, Tilak and Kalava is invariably applied.

Generally sandalwood, kumkum (vermilion) is used for applying Tilak. Tilak is applied at the centre of forehead because entire body is controlled from this point. It is said that Shiva's third eye is located here. Soul also resides at this point. Generally ring finger (next to little finger) and thumb is used to apply Tilak.

- **Coconut in Ceremonies:** Coconut is also invariably used in all Hindu ceremonies. It is considered auspicious which brings good fortune. It is believed that Hindu Trinity Brahma, Vishnu and Mahesh reside in coconut. Coconut is also known as Kalpavrishka which fulfils the desires. Coconut is considered the favourite fruit of Shiva; three eyes of coconut are symbolic of three eyes of Shiva.
- **Lamp:** A lamp is invariably lighted in all religious ceremonies of Hindus. Lamp is considered a symbol of God which dispels darkness and brings wisdom and prosperity. In 'Arti' of deities, lamp is used seeking light and immortality. In many temples of Hindus, lamp is lit continuously as an offering to God with the belief that God is present as long as lamp is lit. When Badrinath temple is closed for six months during winter season, lot of oil (ghee) is arranged so that a lamp continues to be lit for those six months.

A Priest/Brahmin

All religious activities are done with the help of a Priest/Brahmin by a Hindu. Brahmins are supposed to be the custodians of wisdom contained in Hindu scriptures. In Vedic times they used to impart this knowledge to the ordinary people to facilitate them to lead a life based on Dharma. In the times of kingship, a head priest was invariably the part of royal court; he used to guide the king to rule by adhering to moral values. Guru Vashishtha was the guide to King Dashratha in Ayodhya. All Hindu scriptures including Vedas, Mahabharata, Gita and Puranas have spoken highly about brahmins and their role in the society.

In modern times also Brahmins continue to play this role. In Hindu families, all religious festivals, Shraddha for the ancestors, marriage rituals, Naamkaran Sanskar, etc involving ceremonies/rituals are invariably performed by brahmins and priests only.

Yantras

Hindus use Yantras in religious ceremonies. A yantra of a God, Goddess etc is a geometrical shape. Made on a plate/ various metals. These shapes could be triangle, square, rectangle, circular, conical, eight-sided etc. It is believed that Gods and Goddesses reside in these Yantras. Praying to the Yantra, therefore, pleases the respective God and goddess; they bless the devotee and fulfil his desires.

Shri Yantra

- Yantras, however, have to be used only after Pran Pratistha—infusion of life--in a ceremonial way. The best occasion to establish Shri Yantra are Diwali, Dussehra, Akshay Triteya and other such auspicious days.

- Of all the Yantras, Shri Yantra, is believed to be very very effective. This Yantra is of Goddess Bhagwati Mahatripur Sundri. This Yantra is considered as the Kamdhenu-celestial cow of Kaliyuga which grants everything. In Vedas, it is mentioned that 33 crores gods and goddesses reside in Shri Yantra. It is believed that Lakshmi is pleased by the daily prayer of Shri Yantra and devotee is blessed with prosperity and happiness.

Bell Ringing at Temple

Hindus ring a bell when they enter a temple. It is customary by Hindus to ring the temple bell when they enter and leave the temple. It is basically to make the deities know that a devotee is seeking their blessings. Temple bells are also rung at the time of evening prayers so as to announce that evening Arti has commenced and devotees can join the same at their respective place or by coming to the temple.

Devotee ringing bell at the temple

In 'Skandpurana' there is a mention that ringing of temple bell, absolves the sins of the devotee.

Chaturmas

Hindus do not perform auspicious functions during Chaturmas. The period of four months between the Aikadeshi of bright fortnight of the month of Assadha to the Aikadeshi of bright fortnight of the Kartika month of the Hindu calendar is called 'Chaturmasa' meaning four months. All important functions like wedding, moving to a new house, construction of a new building, start of business etc. are postponed during these four months. It is believed that Gods and Goddesses are at rest during this period. Hindu religious texts refer this period as 'Yognindra' when Lord Vishnu is in deep meditation.

Even otherwise these four months include rainy season; weather is quite disturbed and unreliable, the spirits are low and there is an onset of various type of diseases and hence not suitable for any auspicious ceremony like marriage.

Hindu Marriage Customs

- Hindu marriages are very very colourful. It is a celebration for nearly a month, if not longer. Marriage being a very important event in life, Hindus observe lots of formal ceremonies which are considered a must for the marriage to be valid and complete. Some important rites and rituals concerning Hindu marriages are described below.
- Horoscopes of both girl and boy are matched before accepting a marriage proposal to ensure that there would be compatibility between the boy and girl.
- A religious ceremony is performed, either Sunder Kand of Ramayana or a Havana or Devi Jagaran. Ganesh Pooja is invariably held before the actual marriage celebrations start. In cities, ladies' Sangeet is organised on a large scale in which ladies, young boys and girls dance to the tune of music. A grand dinner is given to the invited guests.

- On the day of marriage, Mangal Snan is taken by both the boy and girl. A paste of sandalwood and turmeric is prepared and applied on their body to make them look attractive. Bride also adorns her body with mehandi applied by women.
- Bride is given a good make-up and is adorned with costly dress and jewellery so that she looks beautiful as the eyes of entire gathering of hundreds are set on the bride. There is a marriage procession (barat) from the bridegroom side which goes to the bride's place at the appointed time and place. A band of musicians is generally engaged to lead the procession. Elderly men and women, boys and girls, friends, ladies dressed in their best, reach the marriage venue singing, dancing to the tune of music. The barat is given a warm welcome by the bride's family. It is received at the gates of marriage venue in a formal manner. The barat enters the venue in high spirits where a grand feast is awaiting them.
- Now a series of important ceremonies commence.
- The first ceremony is 'Jaymala'—in which both boy and girl garland each other in full view of all guests gathered at the venue.
- Actual marriage is solemnized in a mandap specially erected for the purpose and where sacred fire is lit. All important people of both sides collect there at the auspicious time called "Muhurat".
- Here one important ceremony is when both bride and groom exchange vows to be life partners in true spirits so that their married life goes smoothly. The priest reads the vow and bride and groom accept them. They take the vows separately. The acceptance of vows binds the couple morally for observance in their actual life.
- The husband vows that he would remain faithful to wife, shall take full care of the her by way of health, money and clothing; shall consult her on all important matters; shall be respectful and courteous to her etc.
- Bride takes vows that she would merge her personality with that of the husband; will treat his relatives with respect; will perform the household work efficiently; shall manage the household with economy; shall resolve the differences, if any, amicably etc.
- Another important ceremony is of seven Pheras – seven rounds –which the bride and groom take round the sacred fire among chanting of mantras by the priests. These seven rounds are considered very sacred and are a must for a Hindu marriage to be declared legal and binding.
- Saptpadi, meaning "Seven Steps" is next important ceremony. Here the bride an d groom walk in unison –seven steps among chanting of mantras. "Saptpadi" is symbolic that the marrying couple has to walk together in their journey of life.
- When these two important ceremonies are completed, bride is asked to sit on the left side of the groom. In Hinduism a woman is called

Hindu Marriage Phere

Vamangi–one who is on the left side. This is also reflected in other Hindu rites .e.g. Mauli (kalava) is tied on the right hand of man but on the left hand of a woman. Similarly palmist reads the right hand of a man but reads left hand of a woman. Ayurvedic physicians feel the pulse of right hand of a man but of left hand of a woman. In Devi Bhagavat, it is mentioned that

- "Of his own will, God divided in to two parts; from the left portion a woman emerged and from the right portion, a man emerged", therefore the place of a woman is on the left of man.
- A Hindu married woman always applies Sindur (vermilion) in the middle line of her hair as a symbol of being married. For the first time, Sindur is applied by the groom when seven rounds and 'Saptpadi' have been completed and bride and groom have changed seats as mentioned above. This ceremony is also called 'Sumangalikriya' meaning an auspicious ceremony. Vermilion also enhances the beauty and looks of a Hindu woman.
- All married Hindu woman wear a "Mangalsutra" which means an auspicious thread. This thread is having black beads interspersed with beads of gold. It is customary for the husband to give 'Mangalsutra' to wife after the marriage. Mangalsutra is a symbol of love, faith and trust and is considered to be highly auspicious.
- After the marriage ceremony, bride goes to groom's family. She is given a solemn and tearful farewell by her parents and other members of the family. She is received by the mother of groom in a formal manner by performing Aarti, etc.

Namkaran and Mundan

Namkaran and Mundan ceremonies are important for Hindus. Namkaran ceremony of the newborn baby is done on tenth day by performing purification Havana. Some communities however, do it after 100 days and some do it after one year. The priest suggests the possible names based on the planets position at the time of birth. Hindus believe that names convey a lot about the personality of a person and hence they prefer to give auspicious names like Aditya, Varuna i.e. words whose meaning are divine, cheerful, powerful.

Mundan ceremony/ namkaran ceremony

- Similarly Mundan or Chudakaram ceremony—removing the hair of the new born-- is considered important by the Hindus. It is generally done within one year of birth. Since the hair grow inside the womb which is a divine act, first time they are removed at a place of pilgrimage and immersed in the river.

Swastika — A Divine Symbol

Hindus use Swastika on auspicious occasions. Swastika consisting of a cross with arms bent at right angles is considered an auspicious symbol and is used on all important occasions and ceremonies in Hindu families. Another name given to Swastika is Satiya, which is symbolic of Sudarshan Chakra.

Swastika

It is believed that eight arms of Swastika are symbolic of earth, fire, water, air, sky, mind, emotions and feelings. Its four main arms represent four directions, four Vedas, four Varnas, four Ashrams of life, four basic pursuits of life (Dharam, Artha, Kama and Moksha). It is believed that they also represent the four faces and four arms of Brahma; It is also believed to represent Lakshmi, the Goddess of wealth and Consort of Vishnu. In other words Swastika symbolises the entire Creation; hence it is a divine symbol for Hindus.

Char Dham Yatra

Char Dham

- Hindus aspire for the Char Dham Yatra. Char Dhams are four places of pilgrimage which are considered auspicious and all Hindus aspire to visit these four divine places at least once in their life time. It is believed that Char Dham Yatra bestows boon to get liberation from 'samsara'— cycles of births and death. These four shrines are Jagannath Puri in East, Dwarka on the west coast, Badrinath in deep Himalayas in North and Rameshwaram in the south.
- Jagannath Puri is in the State of Orrisa. 'Jagannath' means Master of Universe i.e. Lord Vishnu. The temple houses the deity of Lord Krishna who was an incarnation of Vishnu. In addition, it houses the deity of Balarama and Shubhadra. The idols are made of sandalwood.
- Dwarka is a great pilgrimage centre, being associated with Lord Krishna. Shri Krishna made Dwarka as the capital after he left Mathura. An idol of Lord Krishna adores the temple. Puranas mention that it is a divine place and those who visit this pilgrimage, get salvation, even insects, birds, animals, who live here, are absolved from their sins.
- Rameshwaram is situated in southern India. Out of the twelve Jyotirlingas, one is at Rameshwaram. It is believed that 'darshana'—visit of this Jyotirlingam gives salvation to the devotee. It is considered a sacred shrine as Lord Rama offered his prayers to Lord Shiva before attacking Lanka to secure victory over Ravan. Dhanushkodi temple here houses the idols of Lord Rama, Sita, Lakshmana, Hanumana and Vibhishana.
- The fourth Dham is at Badrinath in Himalayas in Uttranchal state of India. It is situated deep in the Himalayan range at 10,000 feet above sea level. Here the principal deity is of Lord Vishnu which is made of shaligram stone. Hindus believe that visit to Badrinath shrine gives salvation to the devotee; one also becomes free from grief and worry in

his daily life. There is a cave nearby; it is believed that *Rishi* Vyasa wrote Puranas in this cave.

Kumbh Melas

Kumbh Mela

Kumbh Melas are held every 3 years at four different places in India. It is a congregation of millions of men and women, old and young, boys and girls, saints and fakirs, rich and poor irrespective of their cast, creed and religion and assembled with a common purpose of getting blessings from gods and goddesses. The places of Kumbh Melas are Haridwar on the banks of River Ganges, Allahabad (Prayag) where Ganga, Yamuna and Saraswati meet, Ujjain on the banks of Shipra and at Nasik on the banks of Godavari. People take a dip in the holy river amidst chanting of mantras. Religious discourses, devotional songs and music etc. are held at the venue for spiritual uplift. It is believed that visit to Kumbh Melas absolve the sins and bless salvation to the devotees.

It is believed that when pot containing the nectar received during churning of ocean was being carried, it was rested at these four places where the Kumbh Melas are presently held.

Funeral Rites and Ceremonies for Ancestors

- Hindus cremate their deadand mourn the loss in an elaborate manner.
- When a person is near his end in a Hindu family, it is customary to call all close persons of the family by his side. It is also customary to ensure that the dying soul breathes his last on mother Earth. Efforts are also made to put holy Ganga water in his mouth before he breathes his last.
- Hindus cremate their dead. Hindus believe to cremate the dead as early as possible so that soul is released as early as possible for the body. The dead body is given a bath and wrapped in new clothes. The body is then taken to the cremation ground. Last rites are performed by the eldest son or a male member of the family. Hindus prefer that last rites of the dead person be performed by his son. Manusmirti says that "Pu" symbolizes hell and 'tra' one who protects; Put together "Putra" (son) means one who protects from hell; that is why birth of a son is cherished by a Hindu family. When Pandu was cursed in the forest, one of his worries was that he would not have a son for performing his last rites.
- Next day, the ash and bones called 'Phools' are collected from the cremation ground. Hindus prefer to immerse these 'phools' in the Ganges; it is believed that Ganga gives happiness to the soul in the after life.

- A mourning period of 10 to 13 days after death is kept so that family comes to terms with the loss of its member. After this period, brahmins are fed with food and are given 'dakshina' in the form of cash and kind. It is believed that feeding the brahmins provides contentment and happiness to the departed soul.
- 'Pinddaan' is done by Hindus to satisfy and make the soul of the deceased and ancestors peaceful. Pind means 'body' and daan means 'giving'. Symbolically body is given to the soul in the form of balls. The balls are made of a mixture of wheat, rice flour mixed with sesame seed, milk and honey. Seven balls are made from 100 grammes of flour. It is believed that first Pinddaan was performed by Brahma at Gaya. Since then, it is customary to perform pinddaan at Gaya. Kurmpuran mentions that ancestors of a person are pleased when the family members visit Gaya and if Pinddaan is also performed, it gives those souls salvation and peace. Again it is customary that Pinddaan is performed by the son or a male member of the family.

Pinddaan

Shraddha–Hindus observe the dark fortnight of Ashvin month of Hindu calendar as the period of Shraddha. During this period the ancestors of the family are remembered; Brahmins are fed with good food and small Dakshina in cash and kind are given to them. It is believed that food and items given to Brahmins, during this period, goes directly to the ancestors.

There is a mention in Puranas that when Shraddha is performed, ancestors bless the performer with peace, prosperity, fame, salvation etc.

- Tarpan – Hindus perform 'Tarpan' meaning "offering of water" to the deceased. Milk, rice, sesame seeds, sandalwood and flowers are also added while offering Tarpan. Tarpan is performed with the chanting of mantras. Manusmirti describes Tarpan as PitraYagya – a Yagya which is dedicated to the memory of forefathers. Tarpan is done on the death anniversary of the deceased. The ancestors are contented by 'Tarpan' and the performer is blessed.
- In a nutshell, Hindus respect their ancestors; always remember them on important occasions and observe lots of ceremonies to make them contented in their heavenly abode and in turn they bless the bereaved family.

Chapter 7: Hindu Aartis

Aarti

Aarti is one of the forms of worshipping the deity/God by Hindus. It is regularly done in Hindu temples at dusk. Aarti is also done at the conclusion of a ceremony say a Pooja, a Havana (Yagya). In Aarti a lamp of oil or ghee duly lighted is moved around the deity in the prescribed manner with the chants of mantras or the verse for the specific deity, simultaneously bell is also rung. It is believed that Aarti compensates for any deficiency, if committed, in the main ceremony. Text of Aartis of a few Hindu deities is given in this section.

Aarti being performed in a temple

आरती श्री जगदीश जी

ऊँ जय जगदीश हरे, स्वामी जय जगदीश हरे।
भक्तजनों के संकट, क्षण में दूर करे।।
जो ध्यावै फल पावै, दु:ख विनसै मन का।
सुख-सम्पत्ति घर आवे, कष्ट मिटै तन का।।
मात-पिता तुम मेरे, शरण गहूँ मैं किसकी।
तुम बिन और न दूजा, आस करूँ जिसकी।।
तुम पूरण परमात्मा, तुम अन्तर्यामी।
पारब्रह्म परमेश्वर, तुम सबके स्वामी।।
तुम करुणा के सागर, तुम पालन-कर्ता।
मैं मूरख खल कामी, कृपा करो भर्ता।।
तुम हो एक अगोचर, सबके प्राणपती।
किस बिधि मिलू दयामय! तुमको मैं कुमती।।
दीनबन्धु दु:ख हर्ता, तुम ठाकुर मेरे।
अपने हाथ बढ़ाओ द्वार पड़ा तेरे।।
विषय विकार मिटाओ, पाप हरो देवा।
श्रद्धा भक्ति बढ़ाओ, सन्तन की सेवा।।
तन, मन धन सब है तेरा, स्वामी सब कुछ है तेरा।
तेरा तुझको अर्पण, क्या लागे मेरा।।
श्री जगदीश जी की आरती, जो कोइ नर गावे।
कहत शिवानंद स्वामी, सुख सम्पत्ति पावे।।

आरती श्री शंकर जी

जय शिव ओंकारा, ओम जय शिव ओंकारा।
ब्रह्म, विष्ण, सदाशिव, अर्द्धांगी धारा।।
एकानन चतुरानन पंचानन राजे।
हंसानन गरुड़ासन वृषवाहन साजे।।
दो भुज चार चतुर्भुज दसभुज अति सोहे।
त्रिगुण रूप निरखते त्रिभुवन जन मोहे।।
अक्षमाला बनमाला मुण्डमाला धारी।
त्रिपुरी कंसारी कर माला धारी।।
श्वेताम्बर पीताम्बर बाघम्बर अंगे।
सनकादिक ब्रह्मदिक भूतादिक संगे।।
कर के मध्य कमण्डल चक्र त्रिशूलधारी।
सुखकारी दुखहारी जगपालन कारी।।
ब्रह्मा विष्णु सदाशिव जानत अविवेका।
प्रणवाक्षर में शोभित ये तीनों एका।।
लक्ष्मी वर सावित्री पार्वती संगे।
अर्द्धांगी गायत्री, सिर सोहे गंगा।।
पर्वत सोहैं पार्वती, शंकर कैलासा।
भांग धतूर का भोजन, भस्मी में वासा।।
जटा में गंग बहत है, गल मुण्डन माला।।
शेष नाग लिटावत, ओढ़त मृगछाला।।
काशी में विश्वनाथ विराजे, नन्दो बह्मचारी।
नित उठ दर्शन पावत, महिमा अति भारी।।
त्रिगुण शिवजी की आरती जो कोई नर गावे।
कहत शिवानन्द स्वामी सुख सम्पत्ति पावे।।

आरती श्री सत्यनारायणजी की

ओम जय लक्ष्मी रमणा, स्वामी जय लक्ष्मी रमणा।
सत्यनारायण स्वामी, जन-पातक-हरणा।।
रत्न जड़ित सिंहासन, अद्भुत छबि राजे।
नारद करत निराजन, घंटा ध्वनि बाजे।।
प्रकट भये कलि कारण, द्विज को दरस दियो।
बूढ़ो ब्राह्मण बनकर, कंचन महल कियो।
दुर्बल भील कराल, जिनपर कृपा करी।
चन्द्रचूड़ एक राजा, जिनकी बिपति हरी।।
वैश्य मनोरथ पायो, श्रद्ध तज दीन्हीं।
सो फल भोग्यो प्रभुजी, फिर अस्तुति कीन्हीं।।
भाव-भक्ति के कारण, छिन-छिन रूप धरयो।
श्रद्धा धारण कीनी, तिनको काज सरयो।।
ग्वाल-बाल संग राजा, वन में भक्ति करी।
मनवांछित फल दीन्हों, दीनदयालु हरी।।
चढ़त प्रसाद सवायो, कदली फल मेवा।
धूप-दीप-तुलसी से, राजी सत्यदेवा।।
सत्यनारायण की आरति, जो कोई नर गावे।
कहत शिवानन्द स्वामी सुख सम्पत्ति पावै।।

आरती श्री बजरंगबली जी की

आरती कीजै हनुमान लला की, दुष्ट दलन रघुनाथ कला की।
जाके बल से बिरिवर कांपे, रोग-दोष जाके निकट न झांपे।
अंजनि पुत्र महा-बल दाई, संतन के प्रभु सदा सहाई।
दे बीरा रघुनाथ पठाये, लंका जारि सीय सुधि लाये।
लंका सो कोट समुद्र सी खाई, जात पवनसुत बार न लाई।
लंका जारि असुर संहारे, सियारामजी के काज संवारे।
लक्ष्मण मूर्छित पड़े सकारे, आनि सजीवन प्रान उबारे।
पैठि पताल तोरि जम-मारे, दहिने भुजा संतजन तारे।
सुर नर मुनि आरती उतारे, जय जय जय हनुमान उचारे।
कंचन थार कपूर लौ छाई, आरति करत अंजना माई।
जो हनुमान जी की आरति गावै, बसि वैकुंठ परम पद पावै।
आरती कीजै हनुमान कला की, दुष्ट दलन रघुनाथ कला की।
लंक विध्वंश किन्हीं रघुराई, तुलसीदास प्रभु कीर्ति गाई।

आरती श्री दुर्गा जी

जय अम्बे गौरी मैया, जय श्यामा गौरी।
तुमको निशिदिन ध्यावत, हरि ब्रह्मा शिवरी।
मांग सिंदूर विराजत, टीको मृगमद को।
उज्ज्वल से दोउ नैना, चन्द्र बदन नीको।
कनक समान कलेवर, रक्ताम्बर राजै।
रक्त पुष्प गलमाला कंठन पर साजै।
केहरि वाहन राजत, खड्ग खप्पर धारी।
सुर-नर मुनिजन सेवत, तिनके दुःखहारी।
कानन कुण्डल शोभित, नासाग्रे मोती।
कोटिक चन्द्र दिवाकर, सम राजत ज्योति।
शुम्भ निशुम्भ विदारे, महिषासुर घाती।
धूम्र विलोचन नैना निशिदिन मदमाती।
चण्ड मुण्ड संहारे शोणित बीज हरे।
मधु कैटभ दोउ मारे सुर भय हीन करे।
ब्रह्मणी रुद्राणी तुम कमला रानी।
आगम-निगम-बखानी, तुम कमला रानी।
चौंसठ योगिनी गावत, नृत्य करत भैरूं।
बाजत ताल मृदंगा, अरु बाजत डमरू।
तुम ही जग की माता, तुम ही हो भरता।
भक्तन की दुःख हर्ता, सुख सम्मत्ति करता।
भुजा चार अति शोभित, खड्ग खप्पर धारी।
मनवांछित फल पवत, सेवत नर-नारी।
कंचन थाल विराजत अगर कपूर बाती।
श्री मालकेतु में राजत कोटि रतन ज्योति।
माँ अम्बे जी की आरती जो कोई नर गावै।
कहत शिवानंद सुख-सम्पत्ति पावै।

आरती श्री लक्ष्मीजी की

ओउम् जय लक्ष्मी माता, मैया जय लक्ष्मी माता।
तुमको निसिदिन सेवत, हर-विष्णु-धाता।।
उमा, रमा, ब्रह्मणी, तुम ही जग-माता।
सूर्य-चन्द्रमा ध्यावत, नारद ऋषि गाता।।
दुर्गा रूप निरंजनि, सुख-सम्पत्ति दाता।
जो कोई तुमको ध्यावत, ऋद्धि-सिद्धि-धनपाता।।
तुम पाताल-निवासिनि, तुम ही शुभदाता।
कर्म-प्रभाव-प्रकाशिनि, भवनिधि की त्राता।।
जिस घर में तुम रहतीं, तहँ सब सद्गुण आता।
सब सम्भव हो जाता, मन नहिं घबराता।।
तुम बिन यज्ञ न होते, वस्त्र न हो पाता।
खान-पान का वैभव, सब तुमसे आता।।
शुभ-गुण-मंदिर सुन्दर, क्षीरोदधि-जाता।
रत्न चतुर्दश तुम बिन, कोई नहिं पाता।।
महालक्ष्मी जी की आरती, जो कोई नर गाता।
उर आनन्द समाता, पाप उतर जाता।।

आरती कुंजबिहारी की

आरती कंजबिहारी की। श्री गिरधर कृष्णमुरारी की।
गले में बैजयन्ती माला, बजावै मुरली मधुर बाला।।
श्रवन में कुण्डल झलकाला, नंद के आनन्द नन्दलाला।।
गगन सम अंग कांति काली, राधिका चमक रही आली।।
लतन में ठाढ़े बनमाली। भ्रमर सी अलक।।
कस्तूरी तिलक, चन्द्र सी झलक। ललित छबि स्यामा प्यारी की।।
श्री गिरधर कृष्णमुरारी की...
कनकमय मोर-मुकुछ बिलसै, देवता दरसन कों तरसै।।
गगन सों सुमन रासि बरसै, बजे मुरचंग।।
मधुर मिरदंग, ग्वालिनी संग, अतुल रति गोप कुमारी की।
श्री गिरधर कृष्णमुरारी की...
जहां ते प्रगट भई गंगा, सकल-मल-हारिणि श्रीगंगा।
स्मरन ते होत मोह-भंगा, बसी सिव सीस जटाके बीच।।
हरै अघ कीच, चरन छबि श्रीबनवारी की।।
श्री गिरधर कृष्णमुरारी की...
चमकती उज्ज्वल तट रेनू, बज रही बृन्दाबन बेनू।।
चहूं दिसि गोपि ग्वाल धेनू, हंसत मृदु मंद चांदनी चंद।।
कटत भव-फन्द, टेर सुनु दीन दुखारी की...।।
श्री गिरधर कृष्णमुरारी की...
आरती कुंजबिहारी की। श्री गिरधर कृष्णमुरारी की।।

आरती श्री सांई बाबा की

आरती श्री सांई गुरुवर की। परमानन्द सदा सुरवर की।।
जा की कृपा विपुल सुखकारी। दुःख, शोक, संकट, भयहारी।।
शिरडी में अवतार रचाया। चमत्कार से तत्व दिखाया।।
कितने भक्त चरण पर आये। वे सुख शांति चिरंतन पाये।।
भाव धरे जो मन में जैसा। पावत अनुभव वो ही वैसा।।
सांई नाम सदा जो गावे। सो फल जग में शाश्वत पावे।।
गुरुवासर करि पूजा-सेवा। उस पर कृपा करत गुरुदेवा।।
राम, कृष्ण, हनुमान रूप में, दे दर्शन, जानत जो मन में।।
विविध धर्म के सेवक आते। दर्शन कर इच्छित फल पाते।।
जै बोलो सांई बाबा की। जै बोलो अवधूत गुरु की।।
'सांईदास' आरती जो गावै। घर में बसि सुख, मंगल पावै।।

आरती शनि देव जी की

जय जय श्री शनिदेव भक्तन हितकारी।
सूरज के पुत्र प्रभु छाया महतारी।।
श्याम अंक वक्र दृष्ट चतुर्भुजा धारी।
नीलाम्बर धार नाथ गज की अवसारी।।
क्रीट मुकुट शीश सहज दिपत है लिलारी।
मुक्तन की माल गले शोभित बलिहारी।।
मोदक मिशन पान चढ़त हैं सुपारी।
लोहा तिल तेल उड़द महिषी अति प्यारी।।
देव दनुज ऋषि मुनि सुरत नर नारी।
विश्वनाथ धरत ध्यान शरण हैं तुम्हारी।।

Chapter 8: Hindu Prayers

Prayer is an integral part of a Hindu's daily routine. He remembers God when he gets up in the morning and also at the time of going to bed. All his achievements are attributed to the blessings of God. Prayers are done either as chanting of mantras or mentally by Japa. In prayers a Hindu attempts to communicate with God. He seeks God's mercy for his own welfare and of others around him. He considers God as omnipresent, omnipotent and omniscient. He believes that once God is pleased, everything else follows automatically. Therefore a Hindu makes all efforts to be in constant touch with God and please Him through vratas, worships and prayers. Pandavas chose Shri Krishna instead of his army in Mahabharata war and secured victory in that terrible war. "Sudama", the poor friend of Shri Krishna, got wealth by the blessings of Lord.

A Hindu addresses God in various forms in his prayers as father, mother, friend, master, Guru (teacher). A few common mantras used by Hindus in praise of God and to seek His blessings are given in this section for the benefit of the readers.

✡✡✡

Chapter 9: Hindu Teerathsthans (Places of Pilgrimage)

Hindus have innumerable Teerathsthans (places of pilgrimage). The word Teertha is derived from Sanskrit which means to 'get rid of sins'. So a place which helps to get rid of sins is considered to be a 'Teeratha' or place of pilgrimage. Hindu scriptures mention a large number of places, temples, rivers as places of pilgrimage and advise the Hindus to visit as many as possible in life time so that karmic sins (arising from actions) are dissolved. All Hindus rich and poor alike, aspire to visit these places to seek the blessings of Gods.

Hindu Teeraths have been classified in various categories depending upon their sacredness, beliefs, representing the gods/goddesses etc. Some popular places of pilgrimage are described here.

Char Dham

Char Dham are at the four corners of India and are among the most ancient Hindu Teerthsthans. These are Badrinath in North, Jagannath Puri in East, Dwarka in West and Sri Rameshwaram in Southern India.

Badrinath

Badrinath Dham is the abode of Lord Vishnu as Badri Narayana. It is situated in the Himalayas in Garhwal region of the state of Uttrakhand. It is said here the statue of Lord Badrinath is a self-manifested form of 2 feet high black Shaligramsila (rock).

Badrinath Dham

- Lord Badrinath is sitting in a meditating posture. Deities of Uddhva, Nara and Narayana, Sage Narada, Ganesha and Kuber (the Lord of wealth) are also there. Garuda, the carrier of Lord, is also kneeling in front of Lord Badrinath. There is a separate temple of Goddess Lakshmi adjoining this temple.

- Since the temple of Badrinath is situated deep in the midst of Himalayas, it remains inaccessible during winter. The temple remains closed for six months in winter period from November to April. It is believed that *Rishi* Narada does the worshipping here during those six months. The temple priests shift to Joshimath and priests do the worshipping at Narasimha Temple. Narashimha Temple has the deities of Lord Narasimha (man-lion form of Vishnu). It is believed that this deity is also self-manifested from a Shaligram Shila (stone). Deities of Rama, Sita, Hanumana, Garuda, Kuber, Uddhva, Badri Vishal and Lakshmi are there in front and side of the Lord.

Jagannath Puri

The Temple of Jagannath (Shri Krishna) is in the city of Puri in Orissa State, 60 kilometers from the capital city of Bhubaneshwar. The temple houses the images of Lord Krishna, Lord Balarama and Shubhadra (sister of Shri Krishna). This temple was built around 12th century AD. There are nearly thirty different temples surrounding the main temple.

Jagannath Puri

- The most famous festival at Puri is the 'Rath Yatra'. This is celebrated from Ashad Shukla Dwitiya (second day of bright fortnight of Ashadha month of Hindu calendar, generally during the months of June). **The festival commemorates Lord Jagannath's annual visit to Gundicha Mata's Temple through the Danda—Grand Avenue of Puri.** The deities of Lord Jagannath, Balrama and Subhadra are taken out in three huge chariots to Gundicha Temple and these remain there for nine days. Then the idols return to Jagannath Temple. The procession stops at Mausimaa (Aunt's) temple for a meal of sweat Kheer, the favourite cuisine of Lord Jagannath. Lakhs of devotees line up the route to pull the chariots and thus get the blessings of the Lord. The programme is telecast and broadcast throughout India and world.

Dwarka Dham

- Shri Krishna made Dwarka as His capital when he left Mathura. This city is believed to be 5000 years old. It was the most spectacular city of its times having palaces for each of the 16000 queens of Shri Krishna. It is said that when Shri Krishna left his earthly existence, Dwarka was engulfed by the roaring sea within minutes. Presently only a small portion of Dwarka is left which is called 'Bet Dwarka'. Bet Dwarka is in the form of an island in the Arabian Sea, nearly 30 kms from main Dwarka city.
- Dwarkadheesh Temple of Shri Krishna is in Bet Dwarka. This temple was rebuilt

in 16th century. Jagat Mandir or Nija Mandir forms the sanctum of the temple. The main deity of Shri Krishna is in the form of four armed form of Vishnu called Trivikrama. There is temple of Lord Balarama to its right and temple of Praduyamna, Aniruddha, the son and the grandson respectively of Shri Krishna, are to its left.

Dwarka Dham

- In addition there are temples of Vishnu, Kusheshwara Mahadeva, Devaki (mother of Shri Krishna); Radha, Jambvati, Satyabhama and Rukmini, etc.

Rameshwaram Dham

- Rameshwaram is in southern India having the famous Shiva Temple called Ramanathaswamy Temple. The temple was built in 12th century and covers an area of 15 acres. There are two Shivalingams installed in this temple, one is called Ramalingam and another one adjacent to it is called Vishwalingam. It is said that Ramalingam was installed when Shri Rama came back after killing Ravana. Vishwalingam was brought by Hanumana from mount Kailash--the abode of Shiva. Among the two Lingams, Vishwalingam is worshipped first.

Rameshwaram Dham

- There is a shrine of Goddess Parvati to the left of Ramalingam. A huge statue of Nandi, the carrier of Shiva, adorns the temple. The temple houses many bathing tanks, where pilgrims take bath before entering the main temple.
- In addition there is Kothandaramaswamy Temple having idols of Sri Rama, Sita, Lakshmna, Hanumana and Vibhishana. It is said that Vibhishana, met Sh Rama at this site when he was thrown out of Lanka by Ravana for showing his persistent inclination towards Shri Rama.

The Himalayan Char Dham

Himalayan region is a sacred place for Hindus. Badrinath, which we have already discussed, is among the Himalayan Chhar Dhams. The other three Himalayan dhams are the shrines of Yamunotri, Gangotri and Kedarnath. These four form a pilgrimage quadrilateral in Himalayan region.

Yamunotri Dham

Yamunotri is the source of Yamuna river in the Himalayas. The actual source of Yamuna is Saptarishi Kund.The size of this kund is nearly half a kilometer in diameter.

Yamunotri

- Yamunotri temple is built at the base of Kalinda Prabat (mountain). The deity of Goddess Yamuna is carved from a black stone in the temple.
- Yamuna is said to be the daughter of Surya and sister of Lord Yama, the God of Death. It is said that Yama had visited his sister Yamuna on the day of Bhai Dooj; since then Bhai Dooj festival is celebrated on second day after Diwali.

Gangotri Dham

Gangotri

Ganga is a sacred river for billions of Hindus and is being worshipped by them since ancient times. The water of Ganga is stored at home by all Hindus. It is customary to put Ganga water (Gangajal) in the mouth of a person nearing death. Gangotri, the source of Ganga is, therefore, equally sacred for Hindus.

- The source of Ganga is Gaumukh glacier. This glacier appears like the face of a cow, hence named Gaumukh. The water of Ganga comes with a great force from this glacier and forms a very lively stream.
- At this shrine, there is Gangotri temple dedicated to the Goddess Ganga.
- Ganga is also called Bhagirathi. Bhagiratha was the great grandson of King Sagar. Kapil Muni had killed the 60000 sons of Sagar because they had disturbed the *Rishi* while he was doing meditation. Bhagiratha then did the worshipping of Ganga. Ganga Goddess was pleased and agreed to come to earth to revive the 60000 sons of Sagar. It is said that Lord Shiva had agreed to adopt Ganga on his head to absorb the shock before she came to earth. That is why Ganga is seen emanating from the head of Lord Shiva.

Kedarnath Dham

Kedarnath is only 42 kilometers from Badrinath. Kedareshwra (Lord Shiva) is the presiding deity at Kedarnath shrine and temple. It is said that worshipping of Lord Shiva is going on at this place from the time of Pandavas when they had gone to Lord Shiva to seek his blessings to absolve them from the sins of Kurukshetra war.

Kedarnath

- On way to Kedarnath is Gauri Kund where Parvati is said to have done her penance to please Lord Shiva to marry her. There is a temple dedicated to Parvati. It is customary to go to Gauri Temple after taking bath in the sulphur springs flowing nearby.

Holy Cities of Hindus

Cities of Ayodhya, Mathura, Haridwar, Varanasi, Kanchipuram, Ujjain and Dwarka are God's abode from ancient times and are considered holy by the Hindus. Hindus regularly visit these cities to seek the blessings of the Lords.

Ayodhya

The city of Ayodhya is on the banks of River Saryu in the state of Uttar Pradesh. Ayodhya is synonymous with Lord Rama. There are nearly 100 temples which tell the stories and events relating to Lord Rama.

Rama Janmabhoomi is the birth place of Lord Rama. Now there is a Temple of Rama here. There is a temple at Hanuman Garhi dedicated to Hanumana.

- Nandigram is nearly 20 kilometers away from Ayodhya. It is believed that Bharata ruled Ayodhya from here (when Shri Rama was in exile for 14 years) by placing Rama's sandals on the throne.
- Rama Ghat, Sita Kund and Brahm Kund are popular bathing place in Ayodhya.
- Dashratha Teeratha is nearly 12 kilometers away from Rama Ghat. Last rites of King Dashratha were performed here.
- Hindus owe a lot to Saint Tulsidas. He wrote Ramayana in 'Brajbhasha' – local language and named it 'Ramcharitmanas'. Ramacharitmanas is a holy text of Hindus and famous for its teachings. It has been given the status of fifth Veda. Tulsi Samarak Bhawan has been built in Ayodhya in memory of this learned saint. Ramayana recitation, religious discourses, Satsangs, etc. are held in this bhavan regularly.

Mathura

Mathura is a household name among Hindus. Mathura is the birthplace of Shri Krishna. Shri Krishna was born in the prison of Mathura where his parents Devki and Vasudeva were imprisoned by the cruel king Kansa.

- Keshva Deo Temple is the main temple in Mathura. The deities of Lord Krishna and Radha adore this temple. The deities of Lord Rama, Sita, Lakshmna and Hanumana and those of Lord Jagannath, Balarama, Subhadra are also installed in the temple around and in front of main deities.
- Other important temple in Mathura is Shri Dwarkadheesh Temple. This temple was built in 1814.

Lord Krishna

- **Vrindavan** is 12 kilometers from Mathura. Vrindavan was the Raas Leela bhoomi of Shri Krishna. He enacted many leelas (acts) here including the famous Rass Leela with gopis.
- Vrindavan is also full of temples glorifying Shri Krishna and Radha. Some important temples in Vrindavan are:
  - (i) Banke Bihari Temple—This is the most popular temple in Vrindavan. This temple was constructed in 1864 by Haridas Swami.
  - (ii) Radha Raman Temple—This temple was established by Gopal Bhatta Goswami. The deity of Radha and Raman was self-manifested here on full moon day of the month of Vaishkha in 1542.
  - (iii) Radha Damodar Temple—This temple has the deity of Radha and Damodar. It was built by Jiva Goswami.
  - (iv) Madan Mohan Temple—This temple was built in 1580.
- Seva Kunj — It is believed that Sh Krishna created a Kund in this Kunj (garden) to quell the thirst of a gopy by the name Latika. It is also believed that Shri Krishna still massage the feet of Radha here and adorn her hair with flowers; no one is ,therefore, allowed in the Kunj at night.
- 'Parikarma' (going around) of Vrindavan is considered spiritually beneficial by the Hindus. Devotees do the Parikarma of Vrindavana on foot, vehicle, Palki; depending upon their capacity to walk. It takes two and a half hours to complete the Parikarma on foot.
- Mount Govardhana (Giri Raj) is also sacred. It is 20 kms from Vrindavan. Its revolution *(parikarma)* is also considered sacred and auspicious.

Haridwar

- Haridwar means gateway to Hari—Lord Vishnu. It is among the holiest places of Hindus. Tens of thousands of Hindus come to Haridwar for a holy dip in the Ganges. It is considered auspicious to bathe in Ganga at Haridwar on days like Makar Sankranti, Maha Kumbh. It is also considered auspicious to immerse the remains of dead (phools) in Ganges at Haridwar.

Har Ki Pauri

- 'Har ki Pauri' Ghat–Feet of Lord Vishnu is the main spot for bathing in the Ganges in Haridwar. There is temple of Goddess Ganga here where Aarti of Goddess Ganga is recited daily in the evening and it is attended by hundreds of pilgrims.
- Mansa Devi Temple, Chandi Devi, Anjana Devi, Narayana-shila, Maya Devi and Bhairava, Dakesheshwara Mahadev Shilva are other famous temples of Haridwar. Kushavarta Ghat, Gau Ghat and Gauri Kund are some other important bathing ghats in Haridwar.
- **Rishikesh** is the twin town of Haridwar, ideally suited for spiritual practices. It is nearly 24 kilometers from Haridwar. There are many lush green ashrams and meditation places in Rishikesh.
- Triveni Ghat is the main bathing ghat in RishikeShri At this place, Ganga, Yamuna and Saraswati rivers flow together. 'Pinda shradha' or offerings to the ancestors are also done here.
- Lakshmna Jhoola is a swinging bridge which swings when people walk over it and is a pilgrims' delight. Lakshman Temple is there at one end of the bridge.
- Bharat, Shatrughana, Balaji, Chandramouleshwara and Neelkantha Mahadev Temple are some other popular temples in Rishikesh.

Varanasi

Varanasi, also called Kashi, is the ancient holy city of India. The city is on the banks of the Ganges. There are nearly 23000 temples and 81 bathing ghats in Varanasi. Vishwanath Temple (Lord Shiva) is the most popular temple of Varanasi. Thousands of devotees come here daily from all corners of the country to seek the blessings of Lord Shiva. In this temple, Shivalingam is placed on a golden altar. The temple was built by Rani Ahilyabai Holker of Indore in 1776.

Varanasi

Other important temples are Bindu Madhava Temple, Adi Keshava, Durga Devi and Sankat Mochan (Ganesha) Temple.

Among the ghats, Dashashwamedha and Manikarnika Ghat are considered as holiest of all the ghats.

Ujjain

- City of Ujjain is in the state of Madhya Pradesh. Ujjain is famous for its Mahakaleshwar Temple. Mahakaleshwar is an ancient temple which also finds mention in Puranic texts. Lord Shiva is considered as the presiding deity of Ujjain. This is also one of the 12 Jyotirlingams. The celebrated Sanskrit poet Kalidasa was inspired by this temple for his various famous writings.

Ujjain

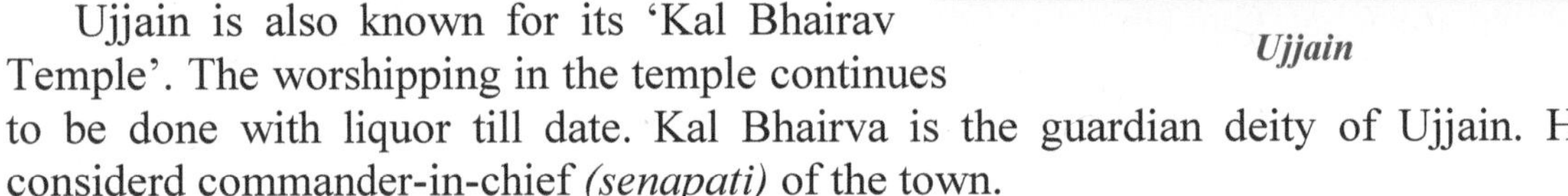

Ujjain is also known for its 'Kal Bhairav Temple'. The worshipping in the temple continues to be done with liquor till date. Kal Bhairva is the guardian deity of Ujjain. He is considerd commander-in-chief *(senapati)* of the town.

Kanchipuram

- Kanchipuram is famous for its temples. At one time there used to be nearly thousand temples in this city; however, now nearly one hundred are remaining. The city is about 70 kilometers from capital city of Chennai.

  Some famous temples of Kanchipuram are –

Kanchipuram

- Varadaraja Temple: This Vishnu Temple was built by Vijaynagara kings in 12th century and covers an area of 23 acres. Lord Varadaraja (Vishnu) is in a standing pose here. The pillars, temple walls, depict many avatars of Vishnu and stories from Ramayana and Mahabharata. 'Brahmotsav' festival is celebrated in this temple every year on a very big scale.
- Vaikuntha Perumal, Ashtabhujam Perumal, Pandava Dootha Perumal, Sri Deepa Praksha, Sri Yathok-takari, Sri Pavalavannar, etc. are other famous Vishnu temples in Kanchipuram. Lord Vishnu is shown in different forms in these temples. For example— in Ashtabhujam Temple, Vishnu is shown as having eight arms; In Yathoktakari temple,Vishnu ji is shown in lying posture.
- Sri Ekambareshwara and Kailashnatha Temples are other very popular Shiva temples in Kanchipuram. Ekambareshwara Temple has nearly 1000 pillars. It has the rare distinction that there is no right angle in this temple. There is a 3500 years old mango tree; each leaf of this tree is different in shape and fruit of each branch has a different taste.

Holy Yatras (Journeys)

☛ Hindus take up arduous journeys to visit sacred and holy places. Such visits involving arduous journeys have become popular as 'Yatras'. We shall be covering some important Yatras being undertaken by Hindus in their quest for Truth and Mukti from 'samsara' — from repeated births and deaths.

Kailash Mansarovar Yatra: This is the most difficult Yatra which involves climbing the Himalayas. Mount Kailash is the abode of Lord Shiva and Mansarovar is a lake atop Mount Kailash The lake is believed to have been built by Brahma, the Creator.

Mount Kailash is considered a sacred place in Jainism and Buddhism too. Pilgrims across the world, therefore, visit this shrine braving freezing cold and hostile terrain of Himalayas. The Yatra to Mount Kailash is undertaken after reaching Nepal or Tibet. The path around Mount Kailash is nearly 52 kms. Lord Shiva is the only God who lives on the earth on Mount Kailash.

Amarnath Yatra: Visit to holy shrine of Shiva at Amarnath Cave is called Amarnath Yatra. The Amarnath Cave is at a height of 13700 feet above the sea level in Himalayan region in the state of Jammu and Kashmir. The cave is open for pilgrims for a small period in summer time otherwise it remains closed due to ice and extremely low temperature.

- Lord Shiva is worshipped here in the form of a Lingam naturally formed from water trickling from above. It is believed that in this cave, Lord Shiva narrated to Parvati the secrets of immortality and creation of Universe.
- Amarnath Yatra is undertaken from Pahalgam from where the shrine is nearly 45 kilometers and this distance is covered on foot.

Vaishno Devi Yatra

- Vaishno Devi shrine is in Jammu and Kashmir state in Trikuta Mountains of Himalayas. It is comparatively an easier journey, nevertheless it involves travelling by foot or ponies etc. of nearly 13 kilometers. Of late, this shrine has become very popular.

The shrine consists of three natural Pindis of Goddess Saraswati, Lakshmi and Kali. They represent the Creation, Preservation and Dissolution aspects respectively of Adi Shakti. Holy Ganga washes the feet of these Goddesses- symbol of Hindu Trinity.

For visiting Vaishno Devi shrine, one has to reach Katra in Jammu city from where we can go to Vaishno Devi Shrine on foot or animal back. Presently very good arrangement of food, travel, has been made by the state government to make the pilgrimage comfortable and enjoyable.

Alandi Pandharpur Yatra

- Alandi Pandharpur is an important pilgrimage place, situated on the banks of river Bhima in Maharashtra. It is famous for its Vitthal Temple. Vitthal is one of names of Sh Krishna. The temple of Vitthal is nearly 2000 years old. Here the idols of Vitthal and Rukmini are in black sandstone and look very attractive.

- The worshipping of Vitthal at Pandharpur was started by Sant Gyaneshwar and later it spread among masses by the initiative of Sants Namdeo, Tukaram and Ekanath.

Thousands of devotees called 'Varis' start their journey on foot/vehicle, etc. from various corners of the country and reach Pandharpur one day prior to Ashadhi Ekadeshi of the month of July. Some of the 'varis' even travel on foot for two months to reach Pandaharpur on the fixed day. The 'padukas' of the above founder saints are still carried in palanquins by the 'varis' to offer to the lord on behalf of these saints in a symbolic way.

Next day, in the early morning devotees take a bath in river Bhima and proceed to Vitthal temple for the darshan of the Lord. The yatra and worshipping of Vitthal in this manner is going on for more than one thousand years.

Panch Kedar Yatras

- Panch Kedar Yatra consists of visiting the five Shiva Temples in Himalayas in a sequence. These places are Kedarnath, Madhyamaheshwar, Tunganath, Kalpeshwar and Rudranath. The yatra of Panch Kedars is among the most arduous pilgrimages as these temples are situated in Himalayas at a height ranging from 7200 feet (Kalpeshwar) to 12000 feet (Tunganath) above sea level. The mountains are snow-clad for most part of the year. These temples are open from May to September only. The Panch Kedar Yatra starts from Kedarnath and ends at Rudranath.

(i) There is a popular legend about the origin and worshipping of Shiva at these temples. It is said that Pandavas were sorry for the death and destruction in Kurukshetra war. They wanted to nullify its karmic effects by worshipping Lord Shiva –the Lord of Death and Dissolution. They went in search of Shiva who was avoiding them as He was not happy with the methods chosen by Pandavas to secure victory in the war. Shiva hid himself in this Garhwal region in the form of a bull. As usual, Bhima was restless. He found the bull and caught hold of it. Shiva bull immediately disappeared, however, appeared in parts at these five places. Pandavas built temples at these five places and worshipped Lord Shiva. Some part of the bull representing Lord Shiva is worshipped at each of these temples since then.

(ii) In Kedarnath, hump of bull is worshipped, In Madhyamaheshwar, 'naval' or middle part of bull is worshipped; In Tungnath, 'bahu' or arm of bull is worshipped, In Kalpeshwar, Jata or 'matted hair' of head of bull are worshipped. In Rudranath; 'mukh' or face of bull Shiva is self-manifested and is worshipped.

(iii) It is also believed that 'forehead' of the bull appeared at the famous site of Pashupatinath temple in Nepal.

Holy Rivers

Some rivers are considered sacred by the Hindus. It is customary for Hindus to take bath at least once in their lifetime in each of these rivers.

Ganga

Ganga is a holiest among holy rivers for Hindus. It enjoys high esteem in Hindu mind. Its sacredness finds mention in all Hindu scriptures i.e. Vedas and Puranas. Ganga water is always available in all Hindu households which is used in all important religious ceremonies.

Ganga is a Goddess and its descent to earth, we have already covered under Gangotri –one of the Himalyan Char Dham.

Ganga travels nearly 1600 kms through the cities of Haridwar, Kanpur, Allahabad, Varanasi, Patna and finally merges in the sea at Bay of Bengal.

Yamuna

According to legends, Yamuna is the daughter of Surya, the Sun God and sister of Lord of Death 'Yama'. Being the sister of Yama, it is believed that taking bath in Yamuna frees the mind from the fear of death.

The source of Yamuna is Himalayas. Several small streams merge in Yamuna en route its journey of 200 kilometers through Himalays. It passes through the Shivalik Range in Himachal Pradesh and Uttrakhand, through Poanta Saheb, a famous Sikh shrine, through Hathni Kund in Haryana and finally merges with Ganga at Sangam in Allahabad.

Saraswati

Saraswati is an ancient river and finds mention in Rig Veda. Rig Veda describes it as Ambitame, Naditame and Devitame—the best of mothers, the best of rivers and best of Goddesses. It has nurtured the civilization on its route since ancient times.

However, modern research is of the opinion that Saraswati River has disappeared due to geological reasons spread over a few hundred years. The main reasons are said to be loss of important tributaries due to changes in river course, climate changes, seepage of water through earth faults, obstruction to the river flow by the shifting of sand dunes river, etc. Earth faults were created by seismic activities in whole of north-west of India. Yamuna and Sutlej rivers were important tributaries of Saraswati but these also changed in the course of time.

Hindus, true to their spiritual values however, believe that Saraswati flows underground and meets Ganga and Yamuna at Sangam in Prayag—Allahabad. Hindus also consider auspicious to take a dip at Sangam—confluence point of these three rivers.

Narmada

It is also a highly sacred river for Hindus. Narmada is believed to have been originated from the sweat of Lord Shiva. She is, therefore, considered the daughter of Shiva. The worship of Lord Shiva is quite common in areas along the route of Narmada.

The source of Narmada is Amarkantak Hills in the state of Madhya Pradesh. From there it flows through Satpura and Vindhiya mountain ranges (in the state of M P), then through the state of Maharashtra and finally it merges in Arabian sea in Bharuch District of Gujarat.

Holy Sarovars

Some sacred Hindu Sarovars (lakes) are mentioned below. Hindus also like to visit these Sarovars and take a dip in their holy water to absolve their sins.

Lake Mansarovar

Lake Mansarovar

We have already mentioned that this lake is atop Mount Kailash. It is believed that this lake was created by Lord Brahma. Taking a dip in lake is considered highly auspicious and is said to cleanse the body and mind and absolves the soul from sins.

Lake Pushkar

Pushkar Lake is 11 kms from the Ajmer city of Rajasthan and is considered among most sacred places of Hindus. It has 52 bathing ghats out of which, ghats of Varaha, Brahma and Gau are important ones. At Varah Ghat, Lord Vishnu is said to have been appeared in His Varah Avtar. Lord Rama is said to have taken bath in Pushkar Lake. There are five famous temples at Pushkar Lake devoted to Brahma, Savitri,Varaha, Badri Narayan and Shiva Atmeswari.

Lake Pushkar

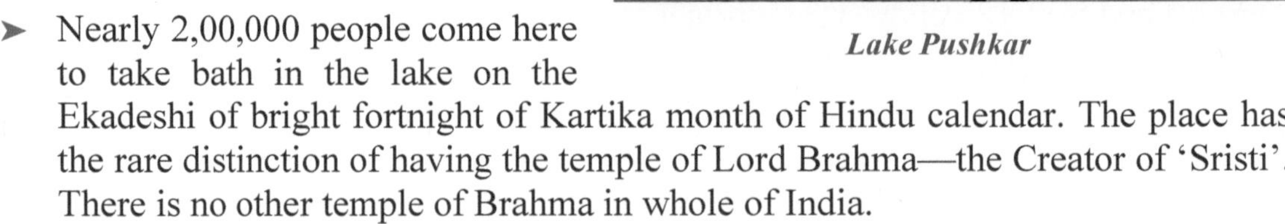

- Nearly 2,00,000 people come here to take bath in the lake on the Ekadeshi of bright fortnight of Kartika month of Hindu calendar. The place has the rare distinction of having the temple of Lord Brahma—the Creator of 'Sristi'. There is no other temple of Brahma in whole of India.

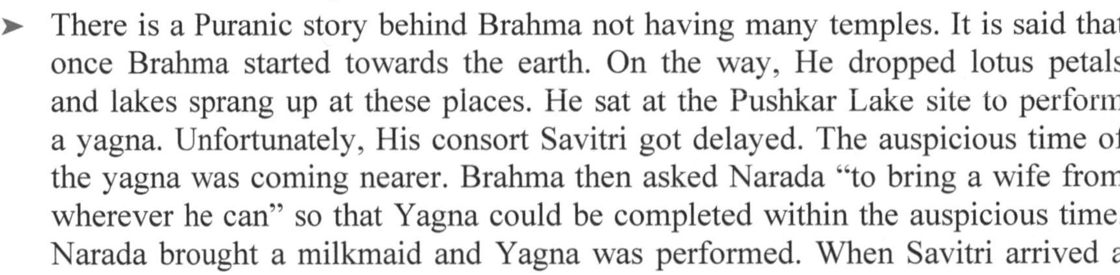

- There is a Puranic story behind Brahma not having many temples. It is said that once Brahma started towards the earth. On the way, He dropped lotus petals and lakes sprang up at these places. He sat at the Pushkar Lake site to perform a yagna. Unfortunately, His consort Savitri got delayed. The auspicious time of the yagna was coming nearer. Brahma then asked Narada "to bring a wife from wherever he can" so that Yagna could be completed within the auspicious time. Narada brought a milkmaid and Yagna was performed. When Savitri arrived a little later, she was greatly annoyed. She cursed Brahma that He would not be worshipped except at Pushkar and that too only once in a year. She then went to Ratnagiri hill and immolated herself. There is a temple of Savitri at Ratnagiri hill in Ajmer.

Bindu Sarovar

It is located near the Lingaraja Temple in the city of Bhubaneshwar in Orissa State. It is believed that this sarovar was built by Lord Shiva by bringing waters from all the holy places.

Bindu Sarovar

- Lingraja Temple is situated near Bindu Sarovar. This temple houses Hari Hara Lingam which is half Shiva and half Vishnu. The deity is also called Tribhuvaneshwra—the Lord of three Worlds. Temples of Mukteshwara, Parashurameshwara, Brahmeshwara, all Shiva temples add to the sacredness of the place.

Narayan Sarovar

It is in Akshardham Temple complex in Ahmedabad in Gujrat. Narayana refers to Lord Vishnu. The Sarovar is believed to be having the sacred water of 151 rivers and lakes including that of Lake Mansarovar. The complex houses the temples of Lakshmi Narayan, Dwarkanath, Adinarayan etc which add to the sacredness of the place.

Narayan Sarovar

Pampa Sarovar

It is in the State of Kerala. The famous Sabrimala Ayyappa Temple is located at a distance of four kilometers from this Sarovar. Devotees take a bath in the Sarovar then proceed to Sabrimala Ayyappa Temple for worship. Ayyappa is said to be the son of Lord Shiva and

Mohini –the female form of Vishnu. He is therefore called Hariharaputra, the son (putra) of Vishnu (Hari) and Hara (Shiva).

Pampa Sarovar

Shakti Peethas

- Shakti Peethas are places of worship consecrated to Goddess Shakti or Sati. She is the female principal of Hinduism and the main deity of the Shakti sect. The Goddess Shakti is the complete incarnation of Adi Shakti. She manifests herself in three forms namely as Durga, the Goddess of strength; Mahakali as the Goddess of destruction of evil and Goddess Gowri, the goddess of benevolence.
- As per the legends, following is the story behind Shakti Peethas.

Sati was the daughter of Daksh (son of Brahma). She married Shiva against her father's wishes. Once Daksha performed a Yagna. Out of anger, he did not invite Shiva to the Yagna. Sati was angry with her father's attitude. She invited herself to the Yagna though Shiva tried to persuade her not to go as an uninvited guest. Daksha misbehaved with Sati and also said humiliating words about Shiva in the open assembly of guests. Sati could not bear the open insult to her and Shiva, she invoked her yogic powers and immolated herself.

On hearing this development, Lord Shiva was extremely angry. He not only destroyed the Yagya of Daksha but beheaded Daksha. (Later Shiva gave life to Daksha by replacing the head of a male goat at the request of all the gods and Brahma.) Shiva then picked up the remains of Sati's body and started doing the Tandava-the celestial dance of destruction across the entire Creation. The other gods then approached Vishnu to stop the destruction. Vishnu used Sudarshana Chakra which cut through the corpse of Sati. The various parts of Sati's body fell at several sites. **These sites are known as Shakti Peethas where Shakti is worshipped in the form of part which fell at that site.**

- There are nearly 51 Shakti Peethas where the Sati's parts fell and Sati is worshipped, however, we will describe briefly seven important Shakti Peethas.

- Mahalakshmi Shakti temple at Kohlapur is a popular Shaktipeetha. It is said that Sati's eyes fell here while her body remains were being carried by Shiva. The statue of Mahalakshmi is believed to be 5000-6000 years old. The goddess has four hands; her crown has a cobra hood and Shiva-ling with a Yoni around. It is said that this place is liked by both Lord Vishnu and his consort Lakshmi; hence this is also called as 'avimuktashetra'.
- **Ambaji — Gujarat:** Ambika Devi Shakti Peetha is a popular shrine of Gujarat. It is located at Arasur near Mount Abu in Aravalli Hills. It is said that left breast of Sati had fallen at Ambaji. Shakti is worshipped here in the form of 'Yantra'. A large mela on the the Pooranmasi of the month of Bhadra month (around July) is held at Ambaji Temple every year.
- **Mangala Gauri:** Mangla Gauri Temple in Gaya Bihar dates back to 1459 A.D. built on the top of Mangala Gauri Hill. It is said that breast of Sati fell here. In addition, there are temples of Maa Kali, Lord Ganesha, Lord Shiva and Lord Hanumana in the same complex which add to the sacredness of the place.
- **Kumari—Kanniyakumari:** Kanniyakumari Temple is in a town of same name in Tamil Nadu state. It is said that Shakti's back fell here. Legends say that Goddess killed demon Banasura at this site. There is a beautiful image of Goddess Kanniyakumari in black stone in the temple. Navratra and Vaishakha festival is celebrated here with great pomp and show.
- **Kalighat (West Bengal):** Kalighat is on the banks of River Hoogly in Kolkata. It is a highly respected shrine of the state of Bengal. Sati's toes of right foot are said to have fallen here. Maa Kali is worshipped here as a form of Sati. She is regarded as the destroyer and at the same time is considered as the protector and blissful to the devotees. Shri Ramakrishna Paramhamsa, the guru of Shri Vivekananda, was a great worshipper of Maa Kali. Dakshineshwar Kali Temple in Belur Math across the river is a living testimony of the legacy of Shri Rama Krishna Paramhansa, a divine soul and a great worshipper of Goddess Kali
- **Bhavani Shaki Peetha—Maharashtra:** Bhavani Shakti Peetha Temple is in Taljipura, near Sholapur in Maharashtra. Sati's right arm is believed to have fallen at this place. It is said that Demon Matunga was terrorising devas and humans and Goddess Bhavani destroyed demon Matunga at this site. The image of Goddess is in granite stone of 3 feet high having eight hands. Readers may recall that the great Maratha ruler Shivaji was an ardent worshipper of Maa Bhavani.
- **Kamakhya Shakti Peetha—Assam**: Kamaakhya temple is an important Shakti shrine in India and is located in Kamagiri Guwahati in the state of Assam. It is said that 'Yoni' of Sati fell here, accordingly the goddess is worshipped here in the form of Yoni, sculptured on a stone. The Yoni is kept moist by a natural spring. Durga Pooja is celebrated here with great fun and fervour during Navratras in September/October.

Jyotirlingams

Lord Shiva is worshipped in the form of 'Lingam' at twelve places which are famous as 'Jyotirlingams'. Shiva Purana mentions that Lord Shiva resides at these 12 Jyotirlingams. Generally all these temples have the idol of Nandi, Parvati, Ganesha and Kartikeya, all members of Shiva Parivar in the same complex. These 12 Jyotirlingams are :

Somnath

Somnath Shiva Temple is in the Gujarat state of India. Historically Somnath is well known among Indian masses because this temple had lots of gold and temple was raided several times by King Mahmud of Ghazni to take away the gold. This temple has been built several times because of these incidents.

Somnath Temple

Mallikarjuna

Mallikarjuna Jyotirlingam Shiva Temple near Vijayawada is in the state of Andhra Pradesh The temple was built by king Hari Hara in 1404. The Lingam was originally worshipped by Jasmine, Mallika, flowers, hence the name Mallikarjuna Temple.

Mahakaleshwar

Mahakaleshwar Jyotirlingam Temple is in Ujjain in Madhya Pradesh. This Lingam at Mahakal is believed to be 'Swayambhu'—born itself.

Mahakaleshwar

Omkareshwar

Omkareshwar Jyotirlingam is in Omkareshwar Jyotirlingam Temple on Mandhata or Shivapuri Island, at the confluence of Narmada and Kaveri rivers. The island also houses Gauri Somnath Temple having a large Shivalingam and a huge statue of Nandi in front of temple.

Kashi Vishwanath

Kashi Vishwanath Jyotirlingam Temple is in Varanasi in the State of Uttar PradeShri It was built by Ahilyabai Holker, the queen of Indore in 18th century.

Baidyanath

Baidyanath Jyotirlingam Temple is in Deoghar in the State of Jharkhand. Lord Shiva presides here as a Vaidya— the physician. There are temples of Sri Parvati, Ganesha, Kal Bhairva, Lakshminarayan etc. in the same complex.

Kashi Vishwanath temple

Kedareshwar

Kedareshwar Jyotirlingam Temple is at Kedarnath in the Himalayas. We have discussed this temple under 'Panch Kedars' in this section. There are also deities of Parvati and Ganesha outside the temple. Idols of Lord Krishna, five Pandavas and Draupadi are also there in the same complex.

Nageshwar

Nageshwar Jyotirlingam Temple is located between Dwarka and Bet Dwarka islands in Gujarat. Outside the temple, there is a huge three storey high statue of Shiva in a meditating pause.

Ghrishneshwar

Ghrishneshwar Jyotirlingam Temple is located in Aurangabad in the State of Maharashtra. Shiva Purana mentions that Lord Shiva was greatly pleased with the worship of a staunch female devotee named 'Ghrishna', He himself manifested in the form of a Lingam at this place and Lord also named it as Ghrishneshwar after her name.

Triambakeshwar

Triambakeshwar Jyotirlingam Temple is nearly 30 kms away from Nasik in Maharashtra. 'Tri' means three and 'ambak' means eye; so triambaka means the 'three eyed one'—the Lord Shiva. This temple has three 'lingams' in the shape of eyes. The Triambak town is an ancient religious place. A special 'Pooja' called 'Narayan Bali' is done here. This place is also famous for its Gurukuls—the ancient Vedic schools.

Triambakeshwar

Rameshwar

At Rameshwar in Tamil Nadu state is Ramanathaswamy Jyotirlingam Temple. Rameshwar is one of the Char Dhams of India which we have already discussed.

Bhimashankar

Bhimashankar Jyotirlingam Temple is in Pune in Maharashtra on the bank of river Bhima. Blessed by Shiva because of his penance, demon Tripurasura started terrorising devas and other people. Parvati then entered the body of Shiva and Shiva-Parvati then killed Tripuarasura on the Poornmasi of Kartik month of Hindu calendar.

Sri Venkateshwra Temple

The Venkateshwara Temple is located on a hill in Trimala in Tirupti in the state of Andhra Pradesh. He is also called the Lord of Seven hills. The deity here is full figure of Lord Venkateshwara also popularly called Balaji. It is believed that the deity represents the preservation and destruction attributes of both Lord Vishnu and Lord Shiva.

This is a very ancient temple. Every day thousands of devotees visit this temple. 'Brahmo-tsavam' festival is celebrated here on a very large scale in the month of September. Anointing the idol with camphor and offering the hair to deity is an important mode of worship here.

Sri Venkateshwra Temple

Guruvayur Temple

Guruvayur Temple is in the state of Kerala. This shrine has been given the status of Dakshina Dwarka — Dwarka of South. It houses the deity of Mahavishnu. It is a very popular and sacred temple.

Guruvayur Temple

Hindu Fairs (Melas)

Fairs are another events of celebration among Hindus. They are the traditional ways of socializing, entertainment and shopping. The environment in fairs is one of gaiety, enthusiasm, fun and excitement. Rural people throng in thousands in these fairs and dance and make marry. Women in colourful dresses greatly add to the attraction of the mela. A large number of traders set up shops in these fairs and earn lots of money. Fairs like Kumbh Mela, Pushkar Mela draw huge crowd from every nook and corner of the country and also from abroad. Some popular Hindu fairs are described below.

Kumbh Mela

Kumbh Mela is immensely popular among Hindus. It is a congregation of lakh of people of all categories, religion including from Europe to get the divine experience. It is said that when ocean was being churned, Dhanvantri, the divine physician, appeared with the Amrit Kalash (pot containing the elixir of life) that could bestow immortality. Naturally there was a fight between demons and devtas to get the amrit. Dhanvantri changed himself to a snook and flew to heavens with the pot. The journey lasted for twelve days and Dhanvantri stayed at four places during that journey. These four places were Prayag, Nasik, Ujjain and Haridwar. Adi Shankracharya, the Hindu's spiritual Guru, introduced Kumbh Melas at these four places since 7 AD.

Kumbh Mela

Kumbh Mela is held every three years by rotation at these four places, on the banks of Godavari in Nasik, the Shipra in Ujjain, the Ganges in Haridwar and Sangam (the confluence of Ganges, Yamuna and Saraswati) in Prayag now Allahabad. These melas have kept the Indian people united and spiritually enlightened.

It is believed that the holy bath in the river on the occasion of Kumbh cuts the sins and gives salvation to the pilgrims. The most auspicious day for the holy dip in Kumbh Mela is on the day of new Moon (Amavasaya). On the new Moon day, the day begins at 3 A.M. when first lot of people line up to take the holy dip. Pilgrims take a dip shouting amidst the chants of mantras, slogans.

Religious discourses are held at various places in the mela. Pilgrims take the advantage of these discourses for their spiritual uplift.

The Kumbh lasts for nearly two months. Some pilgrims stay there for a number of days depending upon their spiritual quest.

Pushkar Fair at Ajmer (Rajasthan)

Pushkar Fair at Ajmer in Rajasthan state is a popular mela. It is held for five days in Pushkar lake complex in Ajmer starting from the Kartika Shukla Ekadashi and up to Pooranmasi.

Pushkar Fair

There is the temple of Lord Brahma at Pushkar. The idol of Lord Brahma is chaturmukhi—four faced--with Gayatri and Savitri on his side. The temple houses the image of Brahma's carrier, the 'Swan'. Mythological story of Brahma having only one temple in India at this site, we have already covered under Pushkar Lake in the chapter on Hindu Teerathsthanas.

Over the years, Pushkar Fair has also become an event for the trade of camels--the ship of desert. Other animals are also traded but the mela has become popular specially for camel trade. Camel races and acrobatics add to the charm of fair.

Suraj Kund Mela

"Suraj" means Sun and "Kund" means a pond. A kund, a Sun Temple and an amphitheatre was built by Raja Surajpal during 1000 AD at this place in Faridabad in Haryana; hence the place has been named after him. The site was initially developed as a tourist spot. However, seeing the flow of tourists, the site was converted for hosting a mela named as Suraj Kund Crafts Fair.

Suraj Kund Mela

The mela has become one of the biggest meeting ground of thousands of craftsmen of all categories from all over the country and that of the arts and craft lovers and tourists. Visitors get a chance to see live working of artisans and their products. The artisans in turn get benefitted by selling their products and exposure to elite customers

The mela is held every year for two weeks between Feb 1 to Feb 15. At this time winter is on the decline, and weather is fine. The crowd, the colourful dresses of women, artisans at work, smell of spicy and delicious food, the music and dance programmes and shopping make the visit to the mela very very refreshing. It is great occasion to buy original and genuine products like silk sarees from Mysore, Tamil Nadu, Varanasi; carpets and Pashmina shawls from Kashmir; handlooms from Panipat; Rajasthani bedsheets, bangles of lac; chinaware from Jaipur and Khurja; brass pots from Moradabad; cotton from Maharastra and Bengal, woollens from HP, Kashmir and Ludhiana; perfumes from Kanauj; cane furniture from Assam etc.

Gangasagar Mela

Gangasagar Mela is a very popular fair of West Bengal. Holy river Ganga joins Hugli river at Gangasagar and ultimately goes in to sea at Bay of Bengal. A fair is held at this site every year on the last day of Paush month of Hindu calendar. Lakhs of pilgrims take part in Gangasagar Mela. It is considered specially auspicious to take a dip in Ganga at this site on the occasion of Makar Sankranti. This place also has the temple of Kapil Muni.

Nauchandi Fair

Nauchandi Fair is held in Meerut (UP) every year on the second Sunday after Holi. It lasts for nearly a month. The mela attracts a huge crowd from Delhi and neighbourhood towns and villages. The mela is a great symbol of communal harmony having both Hindu and Muslim shrines—Nauchandi Temple and mausoleum of Bala Mian- a Muslim saint.

The mela offers everything which a tourist generally looks for i.e. fun and food and shopping. There are shops of all famous products from various parts of UP like Varanasi silk sarees, leather products from Kanpur, brass utensils from Moradabad, chickan work from Lucknow, footwear from Agra, bangles from Firojabad, china clay items from Khurja, etc. The mela also attracts products from other parts of India e.g., cane furniture from Assam, jewellary from Jaipur etc. The mela offers a variety of food items both modern and traditional. Traditional items include paratha, halwa, jalebi, sarson ka saag, makka ki roti, kulfi and faluda etc. There are items of fast food and also special items like south Indian dishes, pizza, Chinese noodles, etc. And finally music and dance. A variety of cultural programmes are held here throughout the night. Rich music and traditional folk dances intoxicates the environment. Nauntankis – the traditional theatre show – continues to attract the dance and music lovers.

The mela thus provides a value for money to the fun lovers.

Tarnetra Fair

Tarnetra Fair is held at Tarnetra village of Surendranagar district, 75 kms from Rajkot in the state of Guajrat. There is a Shiva temple at this site; the fair draws its name from Shiva. Shiva is also called Trineteshwar.

Tarnetra Fair

The mela is celebrated in the first week of Bhadrapada month of Hindu calendar. The mela is visited by the people around Tarnetra. The tribal people of Saurashtra throng in thousands wearing colourful dresses; they dance and make merry with the beating of drums. It is extremely fascinating to watch hundreds of women performing Rasada folk dance to the tune of beating of drums.

It is also said that at this site the Swaymvara of Draupadi was held and Arjun won her hand by shooting the revolving fish over head as per the condition of Swayamvra. Because of this legend, the fair has now become famous as the meeting place for the tribal youths and girls specially the local tribe – Kolis, for the purpose of marriage.

Nagaur Fair

It is held in Nagaur in Rajasthan. It is mainly for the trade of animals of all types. People come here from all over the state to buy and sell the animals.

Sonepur Fair

On Kartik Purnima, people come and pay obeisance to Vishnu at Harihar Nath temple at Sonepur in Bihar. At the same time, cattle fair is also held at Sonepur. The cattle of all types are traded here in large numbers. The mela lasts for nearly a month.

Sonepur is in Saran district of Bihar State and stands on the confluence of Ganga and Gandak Rivers.

Ambubasi Fair

It is held in Kamakhaya Temple in Guwahati in Assam. The fair is held in monsoon season. The Kamakhaya Temple is closed for three days. People are allowed to worship the goddess on fourth day. The temple is famous for worship following the 'tantric' cult. The fair attracts thousands of devotees from all over the country. Folk dance, food and trading of local products of cane and bamboos are additional attractions of the fair. The mythological background of construction of this temple is as follows.

It is said that demon Narakasura fell in love with Goddess Kamakhya and expressed his desire to marry her. To avoid the marriage, Goddess Kamakhya put a condition that she would marry him only if he could construct a temple for her overnight. Narakasura agreed to the condition. He started building the temple and it was sure to be completed before dawn. Kamakhya Goddess got worried. She played a trick. She arranged a cuckoo to announce the dawn a bit earlier, thereby telling Naraksura that he could not fulfil his promise of making the temple before dawn and hence marriage would not be solemnised. Narkasura was extremely angry; he could not do anything except that he killed the cock.

It is one of the 'Shaktipeethas'. The 'Yoni' of Sati fell here and is worshipped in the form of a stone. The mythological story behind these 'Shaktipeethas;' we have covered under Hindu Teerathsthanas.

✡✡✡

9 789357 942171

Printed by Libri Plureos GmbH in Hamburg,
Germany